The Sociology of Language and Religion

The Sociology of Language and Religion

Change, Conflict and Accommodation

Edited by

Tope Omoniyi
Roehampton University, UK

First published 2010 by
PALGRAVE MACMILLAN

Palgrave Macmillan in the UK is an imprint of Macmillan Publishers Limited,
registered in England, company number 785998, of Houndmills, Basingstoke,
Hampshire RG21 6XS.

Palgrave Macmillan in the US is a division of St Martin's Press LLC,
175 Fifth Avenue, New York, NY 10010.

Palgrave Macmillan is the global academic imprint of the above companies
and has companies and representatives throughout the world.

Palgrave® and Macmillan® are registered trademarks in the United States,
the United Kingdom, Europe and other countries.

ISBN: 978-0-230-51699-1 hardback

This book is printed on paper suitable for recycling and made from fully
managed and sustained forest sources. Logging, pulping and manufacturing
processes are expected to conform to the environmental regulations of the
country of origin.

A catalogue record for this book is available from the British Library.

A catalog record for this book is available from the Library of Congress.

10 9 8 7 6 5 4 3 2 1
19 18 17 16 15 14 13 12 11 10

Printed and bound in Great Britain by
CPI Antony Rowe, Chippenham and Eastbourne

For Shikl, Joshua A. Fishman

Only the staff and the strategy of a tested generalissimo will prevail on linguistic pharaohs and instil confidence that drives the troops to heed the battle cry to re-soul heritage languages and reverse their shift towards imminent demise. There'll always be conflict, but a fair measure of change and accommodation neutralizes its potential to destroy. Language and religion both require faith and faith is a function of institutions as well as of people. In the sociology of language and religion they have an opportunity to join forces for their mutual benefit. Eighty cheers and counting for our General!

Contents

List of Figures

List of Tables

Acknowledgements

The Sociology of Language and Religion continues to grow as a field of scholarship through the joint efforts of all those who not only identify the issues engaged with as worthy of exploration and thorough examination but also recognize the interventionist potential of this new field. The organizers of the Limerick Sociolinguistics Symposium 2006 are to be thanked for providing the platform on which some of the ideas in this volume were first opened up for public debate. I thank Jill Lake formerly at Palgrave Macmillan for her support, encouragement and belief in this field of scholarship and for commissioning this volume in particular. My thanks too to Melanie Blair for midwifing the volume to delivery after Jill retired. I am extremely grateful to colleagues in the Academy who kindly agreed to read portions of the volume and offer very insightful comments which have ensured that this is a work of the utmost quality. I thank John Joseph our independent reader for his professionalism. And to Philip Tye our copy editor I offer a special thank you for rising to the demands and queries by my contributors and for persevering when we came up against his deadlines. Finally, I want to especially thank Gella Fishman for various forms of support for the field including two trips to Europe within a five-year span (2002–6).

TOPE OMONIYI

Notes on the Contributors

Phyllis Ghim-Lian Chew is Associate Professor, English Language Methodology and Sociolinguistics, at the Nanyang Technological University, Japan. She is widely published and has been invited as a keynote or plenary speaker for many international conferences. She is the project advisor for the textbook series 'In Step' used in Singapore schools since 2001.

Nkonko M. Kamwangamalu is Professor of Linguistics at Howard University, USA. Some of his major publications include *The Language Planning Situation in South Africa* (2001), *Language and Ethnicity in the New South Africa* (2000) and *Language and Institutions in Africa* (2000).

Tope Omoniyi is Professor of Sociolinguistics at Roehampton University, London, UK. His books include *The Sociolinguistics of Borderlands: Two Nations, One Community* (2004), and the co-edited volumes *Explorations in the Sociology of Language and Religion* (2006) and *The Sociolinguistics of Identity* (2006).

Rajeshwari V. Pandharipande is Professor of Linguistics and Religious Studies at the University of Illinois at Urbana-Champaign, USA. Her publications include *The Eternal Self and the Cycle of Samsara* (1990), *A Grammar of the Marathi Language* (1997) and *Sociolinguistic Dimensions of Marathi* (2003).

Aaliya Rajah-Carrim is a sociolinguist with special interest in language and religious identity, standardization of creoles and language and computer-mediated communication. She is actively involved in disseminating her research on Mauritian Creole among lay people in Mauritius.

Dipo Salami is Professor of Linguistics in the Department of English, Obafemi Awolowo University, Ile-Ife, Nigeria. He teaches and researches in the areas of language variation, language use, language policy and language in/and education. He has published in *Language in Society, Language Policy, Anthropological Linguistics* and the *Journal of Language, Identity and Education*, among others.

Bernard Spolsky is Professor Emeritus at Bar-Ilan University, Israel. Post-retirement, he has published *Language Policy* (2004) and *Language*

Management (2009) and he is currently preparing a *Handbook of Language Policy*. He has also edited the 2009 volume of *Annual Review of Applied Linguistics*. He received an Honorary Doctor of Literature from Victoria University of Wellington in 2008.

James M. Wilce is Professor of Anthropology, Northern Arizona University, USA, and author of *Language and Emotion* (2009), 'Magical Laments and Anthropological Reflections' in *Current Anthropology*, and 'Scientizing Psychiatry' in *Language in Society*. He edits the book series Blackwell Studies in Discourse and Culture.

Azzan Yadin is Associate Professor of Rabbinic Literature at Rutgers University, USA. He has published *Scripture as Logos* (2004), a book on rabbinic legal hermeneutics, and a number of studies on Jewish encounters with surrounding culture – Homer and the Bible, Rabban Gamliel and the Greek philosopher in the Mishnah, H. N. Bialik and Nietzsche, and others.

Ghil'ad Zuckermann is Associate Professor and Australian Research Council (ARC) Discovery Fellow in Linguistics at the University of Queensland, Australia. His most recent book, *Israeli, a Beautiful Language* (2008), became a controversial bestseller. His website is www.zuckermann.org

1
Introduction: Change, Accommodation and Conflict

Tope Omoniyi

The concepts of change, accommodation and conflict that are our focus in this volume are not new to the older traditional disciplines of sociology, social psychology and religion where they are experiential social phenomena that both characterize and define the relationships between two states of being, contexts or persons/groups. While change frames discussions of the transition between and into states, contexts and selves, conflict and accommodation are probable responses to such changes, one resisting and diverging the other embracing and converging. As a hybrid discipline, sociolinguistics had inherited these concepts but confined the experiential to language behaviour as we find when accounting for variation in different fields of linguistic analysis – phonology, lexis, morphology, syntax, pragmatics and discourse. Giles and Powesland refer to the 'individual speaker's diversity of speech possibilities' which warrant choice-making and modification aimed at 'controlling the way in which he is perceived by the listener' (1975: vi). They say that we accommodate in speech through speed of delivery, pitch range, phonological variables and vocabulary. These are all micro-level linguistic measures. The underlying thought then is the pursuit and preservation of harmony in society by managing the potential impact of social demarcations and difference based on speech performance.

In the sociolinguistic literature, conflict has been theorized traditionally along social class lines, anchored as it were to Marxist thinking and especially the works of Marx, Lenin and Weber. Class and capitalism, technology, and division of labour-derived hierarchies have been central to articulations of conflict in the social sciences (Giddens and Held 1982). These demarcations and differences mostly served to identify

1

subgroups and the dynamics of coexistence within the same ethno-linguistic or racial groups. Once we move outside these groups and are confronted with mixed ethnicity, race and religious groups, demarca-tions and differences require a redefinition of change, accommodation and conflict. Let us take a closer look at each of our three concepts separately.

Change

Change is conceptualized in Labovian sociolinguistics as a property of the linguistic system. In other words, modification to forms is to be found at the various levels of analysis, i.e. phonological, lexical, syntac-tic, semantic and the pragmatic. This field of scholarship accounts for change by citing internal as well as external factors. Anderson ((2008: 13) opts for a description of change in terms of 'internal constraints' and 'external motivations'. This approach to discussing change is a micro-analytical one in which conditions were proffered for specific vowel changes in Detroit. This model does not serve the purpose of the new disciplinary field that the essays in this volume have made their focus. Anderson and Milroy note that 'variationist research seldom attempts to integrate socially motivated and intrasystemic factors in accounts of language change' (unpublished manuscript cited in Anderson 2008: 13). We may interpret this criticism in two ways based on our interpretation of 'intrasystemic': either as factors internal to systemic units of analy-sis such as phonology, morphology, syntax, for example, or a group as a social system. Such conceptualization of change is simply narrow and too discipline specific. I shall take their critique one step further by noting one further shortfall. The approach overlooks ideologically motivated extrasystemic factors which account for nuanced language behaviour that may persist and become part of the sociolinguistic rep-ertoire of a community. By extrasystemic factors I refer to variable struc-tural leverages or events in secondary or external social systems outside of the primary system which through processes such as globalization, transnationalism and cosmopolitanism wield observable influences. These include influences from media information flows, political con-flicts and economic crashes with wider ramifications beyond nation-state boundaries such as 9/11 and 7/7. Kerswill (2006) describes these as contact-driven and includes extralinguistic factors. Let us take an example each from both of these.

The Anglican reform in Britain led to debates about the admission of women to the priesthood during the 1990s, a move that the religious right opposed vehemently. In that conflict we find a whole body of discourse texts in which gender, culture and religion mediate the linguistic form. The fact that there are now women priests in churches across England represents social change which impacts on language use in the Christian community. At a micro-level, the safe assumption one generation earlier that pronominal choice was predetermined with reference to the priesthood has had to be reviewed.

The second example is more dramatic. In an ironic twist, the tragic events of September 11, 2001 and the subsequent Bush Administration-led global 'war on terror' fed the arsenal of humour around the world. For instance, the repertoire of Nigerian humour was expanded to include the ascription of 'Osama' as an aka (also known as) to anyone who sported a luxuriant beard. Similarly, President George Bush's infamous geo-political construction of Iran, Iraq and North Korea as the 'Axis of Evil' is narrowly construed in some quarters as a geo-religious representation of the Middle East which pitched two religious civilizations (Christianity and Islam) against each other and was then appropriated by the humour trade. These are obvious reflections of sociolinguistic change in language behaviour that may be directly linked to sociopolitical events in other parts of the world and therefore extrasystemic in relation to Nigeria. Eventually, the solidarity evoked by Al-Qaeda among Islamic faithfuls caused skirmishes in predominantly Muslim northern Nigeria but it did not degenerate into another Iraq. Thus the narrow conceptualization of change in variation research falls even more woefully short of the mark where contemporary developments such as I have alluded to here are concerned. The new discipline of sociology of language and religion needs a broader, more encompassing framework in order to effectively cope with such new notions of change.

Popular religion or what arguably may be seen as the consequence of a process of secularization that I shall refer to as the popculturization of religion displays similar attitudes and practices to those that we associate with popular culture. For instance, the serenity and conservatism that traditionally define religion have been traded for the 'cool' factor which in functional terms makes religion attractive to youth as a demographic that was observably increasingly uninterested or at least apathetic (see Omoniyi, Ch. 10 this volume). Talking the talk and walking the walk in a manner of speaking is vernacularization – social processing; this is evidence of socioreligious change which from the standpoint of Christianity or the Church as institutions signals a certain degree of accommodation of secular culture.

What my illustrations above also do is not only show that the sociology of language and religion by default takes a macroanalytical perspective on change but also that it does not completely rule out the consideration of modifications to certain micro-level linguistic elements or their usage as it were. The new discipline's interest and focus are on languages as systems and the purposes and rationale advanced for choices made in language behaviour and I shall expand on that a bit. It is an established fact in the sociolinguistic research on diglossia that the High and Low varieties of Arabic are used for religious and everyday communicative purposes respectively (see Ferguson 1959, Rosenhouse and Goral 2006: 842). With this in mind then sociology of language and religion (SLR) research is interested in departures from native practice such as the use of the L-variety of English in religious texts as a strategy of evangelization among non-educated groups who have limited literacy skills in second-language contexts. The use of pidgin in Bible translations in Cameroon is an instance of this. This argument is not foolproof nevertheless, as pidgin has developed and risen in status in some regions. Zuckermann's most controversial support of the Tanakh Ram translation of the Hebrew Bible into Israeli makes the same point (see *Jerusalem Post*, 18 May 2009). Now let us take a closer look at accommodation.

Accommodation

Accommodating in the sociology of language and religion has several dimensions to it. First, in multi-faith societies, on several levels of social organization and contexts, institutions and groups as well as individuals negotiate their coexistence in different ways. Such negotiations entail varying degrees of convergence and/or divergence as society attempts to develop suitable models of integration or assimilation. Borrowing from Ferguson's idea of diglossia, Omoniyi espoused the concepts of *bifaithism* and *difaithia* to define the structural asymmetry between different religious groups in a multi-faith society (see Omoniyi 2006). Second, accommodation may also be articulated within the framework of Rampton's notion of 'language crossing' (1995) and apply it here to how we perceive people or groups and how we desire to be perceived in return by such people or groups. I shall argue that the appropriation of language practices associated with a faith group other than one's own as a strategy of signalling friendship or solidarity is an instance of accommodation. For example, using religious tropes like 'In Sha Allah', 'be'ezrat hashem', 'Praise God' and 'Holy Mary', as interjections (God willing) and exclamations in interaction with Muslims, Jews, Pentecostals and Catholics respectively marks convergence ordinarily, but if these groups constituted a cultural minority within a larger group then such forms may exemplify acts of accommodation by the majority.

Furthermore, change in the era of globalization includes the possibility of adoption of language forms from new cultural repertoires resulting from the contact situation. For example, in a predominantly Christian community the arrival of Muslim immigrants may expose both the latter and their hosts to each other's sociocultural practices including of course language behaviour. The direction of flow is dependent upon whether multiculturalism is conceptualized institutionally within integrative or assimilative ideological frameworks. Purists or conservative types will experience culture conflict while liberals will embrace accommodationism in both groups. Accommodation may support diversity and syncretism while conflict courts exclusion, both of which generate different discourses.

Another perspective of accommodation is that which we observe in the social and cultural fabric as a consequence of change in the ethnolinguistic composition of communities through migration. In the postwar period, for instance, British cities such as Liverpool, Manchester, Bristol, London, Leicester and a number of others experienced an influx of immigrants which altered their ethnocultural configuration. A town such as Southall (a London suburb) is said to have experienced attrition of its white population with the inflow of Asian immigrants from different parts of the subcontinent. The outcome of that process today is that Southall is recognized as a major British Asian community in south-east England. Its material culture reflects a mix of traditional British culture (weather, architecture and language) and the different cultures of the Asian subcontinent from which the immigrants derived: Pakistan, Punjab, India, Bangladesh, Sri Lanka and so on. Talk about the weather as a topic in Southall is shared by other English towns in a way that is not shared by the homelands from which the immigrants derived. So that Southall cannot be a replica of any one Asian town or city in the subcontinent. The multi-faithism (Omoniyi 2006) that abounds there is a peculiar post-Empire social reality. The linguistic landscape depicts this in the multilingual and multireligious practices evident in the names of places beginning with Southall Station which is also written in Urdu. Public services also acknowledge that composition and produce leaflets in English, Urdu and Arabic.

Sharia was a knotty issue in Nigeria at the beginning of the Third Republic with some northern states seeking to introduce an alternative judicial system – based on the Islamic religion but one challenged by those who seek to uphold secularism. On *Inside Africa*, CNN August 23,

Aisha Sesay ran the story of hip-hop artists in Kano who are censored. The artist Nazir Hausawa told CNN correpondent Christian Parefoy that the music industry was an alternative source of livelihood in a period of growing unemployment. But the authorities saw hip-hop as an element of the West's corrupting influence. One major complaint was about the scanty nature of hip-hop's fashion. Other illustrations of this form of change in the perception and practice of religion may be drawn from emerging evidence of basement rock bands, couture and fashion runways in the Islamic Republic of Iran carried by CNN in August 2008 in the programme *Inside the Middle East.*

Conflict

Conflict may be conceptualized as the counterpositioning of social groups (identities) or their beliefs both of which are discernible from language behaviour (see essays in Part 2 of Pütz 1994). These oppositions are observable in a number of contexts and I shall provide brief but apt illustrations from research on identity and translation. The construction and protection of ethnoreligious identities have been at the core of conflict perhaps more noticeably since events of 9/11 (September 11, 2001). However, the troubles in Chechnya, Kosovo and Northern Ireland to mention a few provide proof that religion-fuelled ethnic conflict goes much farther back than 2001. Clayton (1998: 41) claims that the conflict in Northern Ireland had more to do with settler colonial history and ethnic difference which were not mutually exclusive. He cautions that 'the idea that the conflict is religious deserves careful consideration. It is, however, very much a minority view among sociologists, and indeed participants, that the religious divide is both the cause of the conflict and the fount from which Protestant fears spring.' I may therefore be playing safe here by not making the conflict per se the chosen focus of my illustration. Instead, I shall look briefly at the deployment of the Truth Commission as a mechanism in the healing process to spotlight a language interest that is evidently linked to ethnolinguistic and religious identities at a macroanalytical level.

In post-conflict Northern Ireland, the Truth Commission was set up as a strategy of healing the nation which was divided by religion. The Commission which was chaired by Bishop Desmond Tutu of South Africa led the two communities through a narrative-based process to purge them of endemic hatred that had built up over the better part of the twentieth century.

At a microanalytical level, the production of contemporary versions of religious literature is fraught with evidence of linguistic change, both intralanguage as well as between languages (cf. Zuckermann's discussion of *maxima in minimis* in relation to 'Othering' in Omoniyi and Fishman 2006). Hephzibah Israel remarks in a conference abstract proposed to the 2009 International Association for Translation and Intercultural Studies conference in Melbourne, Australia, on the theme 'Mediation and Conflict: Translation and Culture in a Global Context' that:

> In order to represent the religion as a culturally recognizable faith system, yet unique in character and structure, all levels of religious translation either modify or control target language use. As a result, a new religious vocabulary is often created. Since the language of the convert derives largely from this newly created religious vocabulary, the politics and aesthetics of translation practices and language use influence the way the self is articulated to construct new religious identities. For this very reason, religious translations have often been the site of conflict where the authority to control language use has meant the authority to define identity.

Israel (email communication) reports that in her doctoral research on Bible translations in South India and its impact on the formation of religious identity among the Protestant community she 'found that, interestingly, each time there was a split in the community the arguments over what it meant to be a Protestant and what best represented the Protestant faith was expressed in terms of the right translation of the Bible and the correct register of religious terminology to be used in the translation'. This view which she articulates in a number of articles (see Israel 2005, 2006, 2009) underlines the observed variations in the understandings of Christianity that derive from which version of the Bible people have access to. In other words, faith is neatly anchored to the language of the text in which it is accessed. Naturally, such differences of opinion are directly relevant to discussions of change, conflict and accommodation in the sociology of language and religion.

Four Kornerz, a UK gospel rap group, appeared on MTV Base UK on the *Download Chart* programme (8 December 2007) and remarked that their music 'is not just for the Church, it's for the culture'. They appeared alongside secular artists Alicia Keys, and Mark Ronsson FT (featuring) Amy Winehouse. This is a very strong indication of the group's sense of their secular global appeal, rather than restricted sacred themes and audience which is a departure from the traditional perception of religion. This is quintessential change acknowledged. This is an exploration of media globalization to move gospel music beyond the sacred space of a church and Christian congregation that it was traditionally associated with. This cannot be described as a one-off incident considering that in October 2007, G-Force, another UK gospel group, received the MOBO Award for the Best Gospel Album at the undoubtedly secular annual Music of Black Origin (MOBO) Award ceremony in London. Thus we must acknowledge this as an element of culture change (see Omoniyi, Ch. 10 this volume). And directly related to this is the issue of globalization, particularly of culture. Tomlinson (1999) presents cultural globalization as 'deterritorialisation' – decoupling of culture and space but which does not produce a 'homogeneous global culture'. Tomlinson did not have a discourse focus. Fairclough suggests that the hybridity that results from deterritorialization includes 'interdiscursive hybridity', that is 'the mixing of different discourses, different genres and different styles' (2006: 124).

Summary of chapters

In Chapter 2, Bernard Spolsky opens by posing three fundamental and probing questions based on a decision to engage with changes in both of the contributory fields to our new hybrid discipline. He queries if there is a cause and effect relationship between religion and the sociology of language, or that both are intertwined and mutually affecting each other. He also asks whether change results from conflict or from accommodation. One other dimension left out in these initial questions is the possibility of a reversal in which both conflict and accommodation result from change as I suggest in the earlier part of this introduction. In search of answers to these questions, Spolsky elects in his chapter to look at the development of language policy in Jewish religious life with specific focus on language choice for prayer. He attempts to explain changes in Jewish religious language practice by weighing up changing external circumstances, changes in belief and the results of identifiable management decisions. He draws on social change rather than linguistics for a model while acknowledging that at the micro-level, changes in pronunciation of Hebrew presumably changed like other linguistic changes, but at the macro-level, decisions about language and variety choice were more likely to be made abruptly even if diffusion was gradual.

In Chapter 3, Aaliya Rajah-Carrim analyses the changing linguistic practices of a minority religious group in a plurireligious secular society: Muslims in Mauritius. Although most Mauritian Muslims (MMs) are of Indian origin, they adhere to different theological groups. There are also ethnic differences within the community. These religious and ethnic identities are reflected in, and expressed by, linguistic practices.

In Chapter 4, Oladipo Salami argues that the Islamic religion, via its language of liturgy – Arabic – has impacted the Yoruba language. In doing this, he demonstrates that a number of lexical items covering aspects of material and intellectual cultures which were foreign to Yoruba before the contact with Arabic–Islamic culture have been borrowed. Invoking the Whorfian principle of linguistic determinism, he shows that Islam, via Arabic, has not only impacted Yoruba lexicon but also has caused changes in Yoruba world view, providing illustration from Yoruba naming practices where the influence of the Islamic religion on Yoruba personal identity is immense. A Yoruba person who converts to Islam drops their Yoruba indigenous names for Arabic–Islamic names. Although the history and narratives surrounding names are still very important to the Yoruba, with Islam some attempts at accommodation are evident in attempts to relate such histories to the lives of past prophets or important personalities in early Islam. He notes though that this element of change today makes it more difficult to preserve family histories and narratives in names. He also argues that the process of religious and language accommodation between Arabic and Yoruba has been largely unidirectional to the advantage of Arabic–Islamic culture. He conjectures that this pervasive presence of Arabic–Islamic culture in Yorubaland motivated Yoruba Muslims to demand the introduction of Islamic law (Sharia) to the south-west of Nigeria in the wake of the expansion of the Sharia legal system in Northern Nigeria at the dawn of the Fourth Republic.

In Chapter 5, Rajeshwari Pandharipande identifies a set of core research questions that the sociology of language and religion as a field of inquiry must engage with, and notes that those questions can only be answered by taking into account perspectives from both linguistics and religious studies. She notes that the extent and the nature of the impact of sociocultural change on languages and religions and the accommodation of the change crucially depend on the extent of the variability in the correlation between a particular language and the religion expressed by it. For example, the relationship between Islam (religious meaning) and the Arabic language (the linguistic code) is relatively invariable compared to Hinduism where there is a high degree of variability of languages (Sanskrit, Hindi, Bangla, Marathi, etc.) of the religion. Therefore, the impact of the change in the sociocultural setting on the languages of Islam and Hinduism will not be the same. She argues that for an adequate understanding of the concept of change in the language of religion, it is necessary for the framework of sociology of language and religion to take into account the perspectives of linguists as well as theologians. She addresses another important but hitherto ignored dimension of change and accommodation, that is, the issue of authentication of change in the language of religion within the new sociocultural context. In other words, we may ask, what is the authority which sanctions change, and what is the mechanism of this process of authentication?

In Chapter 6, Azzan Yadin and Ghil'ad Zuckermann claim that the main problem facing those attempting to revive Hebrew as the national language of Israel has been that of Hebrew lexical voids, which were not semantic voids but cases in which purists tried to supplant unwelcome guest words, foreignisms and loanwords. The 'revivalists' attempted to use mainly internal sources of lexical enrichment but were faced with a paucity of roots. They changed the meanings of obsolete Hebrew terms to fit the modern world. This infusion often entailed the secularization of religious terms. Thus their chapter explores the widespread phenomenon of semantic secularization, as in the ideologically neutral process visible in English *cell* 'monk's living place' > 'autonomous self-replicating unit from which tissues of the body are formed'. The main focus, however, is on secularizations involving *ideologically manipulative* 'lexical engineering', as exemplified by deliberate, subversive processes of extreme semantic shifting, pejoration, amelioration, trivialization and allusion.

In Chapter 7, James M. Wilce suggests that the sociology of language and religion explores the same terrain as linguistic anthropology, identifying for example the analysis of history (change), a major concern of SLR articulated in Principle 2 of Fishman's Decalogue (2006). Anthropology has for at least two decades discarded reifying approaches to 'culture' in favour of those approaches that focus on contestation as well as the situational production and 'dialogic emergence' of culture (Tedlock and Mannheim 1995), and the complex relationship of culture to discourse. Linguistic anthropologists have rejected simplistic equations of culture with text arising out of the humanities and cultural anthropology, preferring instead to explore *natural histories of discourse*. These explorations reveal processes by which discourse comes to appear, momentarily, as text-like (Silverstein and Urban 1996). This linguistic anthropological perspective on conflict, history, and everyday and macrosocial process, complements some of Joshua Fishman's principles (Decalogue).

In Chapter 8, Phyllis Ghim-Lian Chew takes the position that religion or more generally religiosity is increasingly playing a role in how adults potentially view the world, yet there is a paucity of literature on religious development in adolescence, a phase of contending with important questions of identity and meaning, characterized by many cognitive and social changes in the transition into adult life. She further argues that a study of change in adolescents' religious practice is important because their behaviour, attitudes and beliefs affect the political, economic and social future of the nation. To fill this gap, she examines oral and written texts produced by Singaporean adolescents for the use of English metaphors to describe switch of religion. The majority of adolescents in her study have switched from Taoism to Christianity and Buddhism. She notes that more specifically, the chapter focuses on adolescents' experience and articulation of change, conflict and accommodation in switching religion.

Nkonko Kamwangamalu suggests in Chapter 9 that a gap exists in African American Vernacular English (AAVE) scholarship around how African Americans use AAVE to construct or project their ethnic identity in both the secular and the sacred arenas such as the church (Smitherman 1994, 2002 [1973]). He explores this issue from the perspective of accommodation theory (Giles 1977, Giles and Smith 1979) and of ethnicity in the sociology of language and religion (Fishman 2002, 2006). Drawing on qualitative data from published literature, he argues that despite the diglossic relationship in which AAVE coexists with Standard American English and attempts to 'erase' it in a bid to enforce the myth of one true, invariant, uniform standard English, AAVE remains the key marker of ethnic identity for most African Americans. Depending on a speaker's linguistic repertoire, this identity is at times deliberately 'attenuated' especially in inter-group linguistic interactions to accommodate out-group members. In intra-group interactions and in not-made-for-TV African American church services, however, speakers tend to 'accentuate' the features of AAVE to project their ethnic identity. In these settings AAVE is unmarked and so it figures prominently in what Smitherman (2002 [1973]) calls sacred style characterized by call and response, rhythmic patterns, spontaneity, concreteness and signifying.

In Chapter 10, the last of the volume, Tope Omoniyi focuses on the appropriation of hip-hop for religious purposes, thus identifying sacralization and secularization as social processes of change and accommodation. He engages with the re-evaluation of both the source and direction of change in relation to the culture flow that globalization fuels. In other words, is the globalization of religious practice through transnational communities and institutions associated with Pentecostalism, televangelism, television and music ministries as cultural vehicles influenced by the spread of a variety of language or vice versa? The employment of hip-hop for the popularization of religious faiths becomes the site of the exploration of how sociolinguistic change may apply within the framework of the sociology of language and religion.

References

Anderson, Bridget (2008) *Migration, Accommodation and Language Change: Language at the Intersection of Regional and Ethnic Identity.* Basingstoke: Palgrave Macmillan.

Anderson, B. and Milroy, L. (no date) 'Internal and External Constraints on Change in the Detroit African American Vowel System: a Case Study and Some Further Implications'. Unpublished manuscript, The University of Michigan.

Clayton, P. (1998) 'Religion, Ethnicity and Colonialism as Explanations of the Northern Ireland Conflict', in D. Miller (ed.), *Rethinking Northern Ireland: Culture, Ideology and Colonialism,* London: Longman, pp. 40–54.

Fairclough, N. (2006) *Language and Globalization.* London: Routledge.

Ferguson, Charles (1959) 'Diglossia'. *Word,* 15, 325–40. Reprinted in P. P. Giglioli (ed.), *Language and Social Context,* London: 1972, pp. 232–51.

Fishman, Joshua A. (2002) '"Holy Languages" in the Context of Social Bilingualism', in Li Wei, Jean-Marc Dewaele and Alex Housen (eds), *Opportunities and Challenges of Bilingualism,* Berlin: Walter de Gruyter, pp. 15–24.

Fishman, J. (2006) 'A Decalogue of Basic Theoretical Perspectives for a Sociology of Language and Religion', in T. Omoniyi and J. A. Fishman (eds), *Explorations in the Sociology of Language and Religion,* Amsterdam: John Benjamins, pp. 13–25.

Giddens, Anthony and Held, David (eds) (1982) *Classes, Power and Conflict: Classical and Contemporary Debates.* Basingstoke: The Macmillan Press Ltd.

Giles, Howard (ed.) (1977) *Language, Ethnicity and Intergroup Relations.* London: Academic Press.

Giles, Howard and Powesland, Peter F. (1975) *Speech Style and Social Evaluation.* London: Academic Press.

Giles, Howard and Smith, P.M. (1979) 'Accommodation Theory: Optimal Levels of Convergence', in H. Giles and R. St Clair (eds), *Language and Social Psychology,* Oxford: Oxford University Press.

Israel, Hephzibah (2005) 'Contesting Language Use in the Early Nineteenth-Century Protestant Tamil Community,' in R.S. Sugirtharajah (ed.), *Postcolonialism and the Bible,* Blackwell, pp. 269–83.

Israel, H. (2006) 'Translating the Bible in Nineteenth-Century India: Protestant Missionary Translation and the Standard Tamil Version', in Theo Hermans (ed.), *Translating Others,* Manchester: St. Jerome, pp. 441–59.

Israel, H. (2009) 'Words…Borrow'd from Our Books: Translating Scripture, Language Use and Protestant Tamil Identity in Post/Colonial South India'. Published in *Postcolonialism and Religion,* a special issue of *Journal of Commonwealth and Postcolonial Studies,* Spring.

Kerswill, P. (2006) 'Migration and Language', in Klaus Mattheier, Ulrich Ammon and Peter Trudgill (eds), *Sociolinguistics/Soziolinguistik. An International Handbook of the Science of Language and Society*, vol. 3 (2nd edn), Berlin: De Gruyter.

Omoniyi, T. (2006) 'Societal Multilingualism and Multifaithism: a Sociology of Language and Religion Perspective', in T. Omoniyi and J.A. Fishman (eds), *Explorations in the Sociology of Language and Religion*, Amsterdam: John Benjamins, pp. 121–40.

Omoniyi, T. and Fishman, J. A. (eds) (2006) *Explorations in the Sociology of Language and Religion*. Amsterdam: John Benjamins.

Pütz, Martin (ed.) (1994) *Language Contact, Language Conflict*. Amsterdam: John Benjamins.

Rampton, B. (1995) *Crossing: Language and Ethnicity among Adolescents*. London: Longman.

Rosenhouse, Judith and Goral, Miral (2006) 'Bilingualism in the Middle East and North Africa: a Focus on the Arabic-Speaking World', in Tej K. Bhatia and William C. Ritchie (eds), *The Handbook of Bilingualism*, Oxford: Blackwell Publishers, pp. 835–68.

Silverstein, M. and Urban, G. (1996) *Natural Histories of Discourse*. Chicago: University of Chicago Press.

Smitherman, Geneva (1994) *Black Talk: Words and Phrases from the Hood to the Amen Corner*. Boston/New York: Houghton Mifflin Company.

Smitherman, Geneva (2002 [1973]) 'White English in Blackface, or Who Do I Be?' in T. Redd (ed.), *Revelations: an Anthology of Expository Essays by and about Blacks*, Boston, Mass.: Pearson Custom Publishing, pp. 313–18.

Tedlock, Dennis and Mannheim, Bruce (eds) (1995) *The Dialogic Emergence of Culture*. Chicago: University of Illinois Press.

Tomlinson, J. (1999) *Globalization and Culture*. Cambridge: Polity Press.

Zuckermann, G. (2006) 'Etymological Othering', in T. Omoniyi and J.A. Fishman (eds), *Explorations in the Sociology of Language and Religion*, Amsterdam: John Benjamins.

2
Jewish Religious Multilingualism

Bernard Spolsky

Introduction

The boundaries between sacred and profane language are not fixed. One of the most famous international language management actions of recent years was the decision of Vatican II to permit conducting the mass in the vernacular rather than in the traditional Latin, thus moving a large number of modern languages into the sacred category. Fishman (2002) demonstrates that even without adding specific religious functions, Yiddish in the twentieth century took on many of the attributes of holiness.[1] Some religions are less flexible: the fact that Arabic is so widely spoken today is partly accounted for by the insistence of Islam that all religious services be conducted only in it. Hebrew was kept alive for nearly 2000 years after people stopped speaking it by its continued use as language of prayer and religious learning. In much of Africa and in other parts of the world too, the current sociolinguistic situation owes a great deal to decisions by missionaries on which local dialects to standardize for Bible translation and prayer. All of these point to the central role that religion and religious institutions play in language policy. Thus, there is a fruitful mutual influence between religions and language policies – religions and their institutions have language policies, and these in turn have wider influences on the societies in which they exist.

Study of the interaction of language and religion is comparatively recent (Spolsky 2003). In much of the world today, religion remains an important social force.[2] For its members, the religious institution is often the first social structure outside the family that aims to influence language use. Western Europe may be moving out of a long period of secularization,[3] as it comes to grips with the fundamentalism of some of its new residents.[4] Religion is no longer banned in the former Soviet Union. Most Arab countries are by definition Islamic (the same clause in the Constitution commonly declares Islam the religion and Arabic the national language). Nation states which once separated Church and state are again struggling with new religious movements or efforts to assert the authority of religion in matters of morality and of ethical choice.[5] For many immigrants, church or mosque or synagogue remains the principal domain helping to preserve their heritage language and customs.

To understand the sociology of language and religion, one approach is to concentrate on changes in both of the contributory disciplines. Is one the cause and the other the effect? Or are the two intertwined, showing a kind of mutual construction? Does change result from conflict or accommodation? To contribute to a study of this complex set of questions, my approach in this chapter will be to look at the development of language policy in Jewish religious life, focusing in particular on the choice of language for prayer. Language policy is conveniently analysed under three related headings, practice, beliefs and management (Spolsky 2004). Looking at the changes in Jewish religious language practice (the introduction of Aramaic, the regular changes in the language for sermons, the modification of Hebrew pronunciation, the experiments in using secular languages), our concern will be to attempt to account for them by looking at changing external circumstances (as for instance migration leading to exposure to new co-territorial vernaculars and in some cases to changes in internal Jewish languages), or changes in belief (different attitudes to co-territorial vernaculars leading to their acceptance in previously restricted functions), or the results of identifiable management decisions (such as the papal decision replacing Latin with the vernacular at Vatican II). Our models, it will become clear, come from social change rather than linguistic. True, at the micro-level, changes in pronunciation of Hebrew presumably changed like other linguistic changes, but at the macro-level, decisions about language and variety choice were more likely to be made abruptly even if diffusion was gradual.

Jewish language policy

Language policy in Judaism has a long recorded history, even if much of the history (like most historical sociolinguistics) is still open to controversy. With all the changes in Jewish sociolinguistics over three millennia, the use of Hebrew as the language of sacred text and for prayer has remained consistent, in spite of occasional exceptions.

While the details continue to be in dispute,[6] the general picture of Jewish language use over the last 3000 years can be summed up like this. Up until the time of the Babylonian exile (seventh century BCE), the common language in Judah was Hebrew, although a few diplomats and courtiers had learned the Aramaic which was the major imperial language of the region.[7] During the period of exile, certainly in Babylon and also in occupied Judah, growing language contact led to the beginning of Jewish individual plurilingualism and social multilingualism. Dubnow (1967), for instance, believed that Aramaic spread with 'remarkable speed' after the return from Babylon, becoming the language of conversation not just in cases of intermarriage. While he agreed that this Aramaic was Hebraized, he believed that it was not just the language of legal acts (official documents are quoted in the Book of Ezra in Aramaic) and for intercourse with those Jews who remained in Babylon and those who went to Egypt, but was also needed for translating the Bible to the 'unlearned'; it was the learned alone who, he imagines, kept the working knowledge of Hebrew required to compose the Mishnah. But there is good reason to believe that this account anticipated the death of spoken Hebrew by 600 or 700 years. In the accounts of the return from exile in Nehemiah, we find complaints that some of the men who stayed behind had intermarried with non-Jews, with women of Ashdod, and that their children could not speak 'the language of Judah' (Hebrew), but spoke 'half in the speech of Ashdod' (Nehemiah 13: 24). This is hardly the picture of complete rapid loss of Hebrew that Dubnow and others assumed.

True, some time after the return, then, it became the custom to accompany the public reading of Hebrew sacred texts by an Aramaic translation or interpretation.[8] Over the next centuries, Aramaic became more and more not just a foreign imperial language and the customary language for legal contracts, but the vernacular especially for those living in those parts of Palestine where there was reasonably close association with Gentiles. But most still had varying degrees of proficiency in Hebrew.

To this bilingual repertoire was added Greek, the language first of settlers who established new cities in various parts of Palestine and then of the Greek and Roman governments, their puppets and their subjects. The evidence of widespread knowledge of Greek has been presented in particular by Lieberman (1942). By 150 BCE, knowledge of Greek could be expected of the Palestine Jewish aristocracy; one sees from 1 Maccabees 8: 17–23 that Judah and some of his supporters knew enough Greek to negotiate in Rome and Sparta. A young Jew who wanted to rise in the world would have to learn Greek; a good number of Jewish books were written in Greek at this time. Lieberman has demonstrated the extent of rabbinic knowledge of the Greek language. In a number of places in the Talmud (e.g. Babylonian Talmud *Shabbath* 31 band 63b, *Sanhedrin* 76b), points are made with Hebrew–Greek puns of the kind that only bilinguals would be able to follow. And not just knowledge, but also belief in its value and support for learning and using it:

> Rabbi said, why use the Syrian (= Aramaic; also, pun on *sursi*, clipped) language in Palestine? Either the Holy tongue or Greek. (Babylonian Talmud *Sotah* 49b)

> Four languages are of value: Greek for song (poetry), Latin for war, Aramaic for dirges, and Hebrew for speaking. (Jerusalem Talmud *Sotah* VII)

Greek was also the language of Greek colonies in Palestine such as Caesarea, Ashkelon, Acco, Jaffa, Gadara, Philadelphia and Beth Shean (Scythopolis), just as it was in the rest of Asia Minor; many Jews lived in these towns. Greek was the first (and in many cases only) language of the Jews of Egypt and of those who lived outside Palestine. By the time of Philo, Hebrew was virtually unknown in Egypt. It was presumably for the sake of Egyptian and other Diaspora Jews that permission was given to pray in Greek in the foreigners' synagogue in Jerusalem (*Tosefta Megillah* iv 3).

There is evidence confirming the continuity of spoken Hebrew. Rabin (1974) demonstrated that the language in which the Mishnah is composed is not an artificial language, but the normal development that one might expect if biblical Hebrew had continued to be a spoken language. Its grammatical and lexical changes are those of a living language, and not the attempts by scholars to reproduce an extinct language. Indeed, Rabin points out that there was still writing in biblical Hebrew until quite late, showing that the rabbis could have written in this archaic style had they chosen. Since the Mishnah was composed and transmitted orally and not in writing, there would have been no reason for writing it down later in Mishnaic Hebrew had it not been a record of a spoken version. There is no doubt, therefore, that the rabbis of the Talmud spoke Hebrew and did not use it only for prayer and writing. There is also evidence of the use of Hebrew by ordinary people. In one passage, the rabbis report learning the meaning of an archaic term from a Judaean villager working as a servant. Also, among the Bar Kokhba letters are several (42–52) written in this same living Hebrew. It does, however, seem that Hebrew was better maintained in Judaea than in Galilee, an area where a great number of peoples had been settled during the Babylonian exile:

> The Judaeans who had been careful about their language succeeded in preserving the Torah, while the people of Galilee, who did not care for their language, did not preserve the Torah. (Babylonian Talmud *Erubin* 53a)

We see then that Hebrew continued to be a fully spoken language well into the first century and beyond.

By the end of the millennium, at the time of Jesus and shortly before the destruction of the Second Temple, Palestine was multilingual and triglossic, with each of the three main languages spoken dominantly in different parts of the country. The functional division for Jews was between Aramaic as a vernacular, Greek for relations with government, and Hebrew for religious life (Spolsky 1983).[9]

These were not hard-and-fast rules, however, and the Talmud reports the existence of flexibility. First, it lists certain ritual passages and prayers that had to be recited in Hebrew. Second, it reports (admittedly as exceptions) certain uses of other languages for prayer (e.g. in one synagogue in Jerusalem for pilgrims from Egypt and other Greek colonies, or in Greek towns in the special prayers for rain in a drought year). Third, as mentioned, there was a tradition of permitting translation of the Bible, as shown by the Aramaic versions and the later translation into Greek in the Septuagint.[10] Thus, in contrast to Islam which emphasizes the need to read and learn the Qur'an only in the original Arabic, and to the Roman Catholic long-standing insistence on the Latin version of the Bible and of prayers, there was well-established tolerance for multilingualism, something shown by the comfortable Hebrew–Aramaic code-switching of the Babylonian Talmud.

Each of the languages had different literacy patterns. One of Bar Kokhba's letters to his captains was in Greek, so we can assume that there was some popular literacy in Greek. But essentially, Greek was not a Jewish language for literacy in Palestine, although of course it was at this time the primary Jewish language for literacy in most of the Diaspora, especially Egypt. In the opinion of some, Greek had a higher status than other languages in this respect, for whereas some authorities held that the Bible could be written in any language (Mishnah *Megillah* i 8), Rabbi Simeon said that it could be written only in Hebrew or Greek

(Jerusalem Talmud *Megillah* i 1). All legal documents seem to have been written in Aramaic. The documents of which we have most knowledge are marriage contracts and divorces: a tractate of the Talmud deals with each. The formulae to be used in each were clearly prescribed, but it is interesting to note that the written word of the contract was not the last word: if a marriage contract had by mistake omitted a required section, the rabbis held that the normal provision rather than the words written in the contract applied. Basically, this agreed with a general stipulation that testimony in writing was invalid, except as it functioned as a record of permanent contracts. One other kind of item was written in Aramaic, the *targum* or Aramaic translation or interpretation of the Bible. We have already mentioned the requirement that such an interpretation accompany the public reading of the Written Law, but the *targum* was considered part of the Oral Law and as such was not allowed to be read from a text but had to be delivered, one verse at a time, following the reading of the Hebrew (Babylonian Talmud *Soferim* 39b) from memory or extemporaneously. It was in fact not permitted to write down the *targum*.

> The Holy Scriptures may only be written down in the original Hebrew. If they were written in any other language, they may not be used for the reading in public worship. (Babylonian Talmud *Soferim* 35a)

But there is an account of one written *targum*, and others probably existed:

> Rabbi Halafta found Rabban Gamaliel reading a Targum of Job. He told him he had seen Rabbi Gamaliel the elder (his grandfather) order a Targum of Job buried in the foundations of building under construction on the Temple Mount. (Babylonian Talmud *Soferim* 37b)

While such documents could not be used in statutory services, they still had the sanctity of other sacred writings:

> The sages held that all holy writings, in any language, may be saved from fire (on the Sabbath) and must be stored away (when worn out, and not destroyed). (Babylonian Talmud *Soferim* 41a)

In the first century, sacred-text literacy in Hebrew was divided between two roles: that of the ordinary educated person and that of the *sofer* or scribe. The skill required of the ordinary person was to be able to read a portion of the Written Law aloud, with correct cantillation, when called up for that purpose as part of a public worship service. This scripture reading constituted divine worship. It could be done in public only with a congregation of ten present (Mishnah *Megillah* 4: 3), and took place on Sabbaths, holy days, and market days (Mondays and Thursdays). To participate in this reading required considerable training: because of the absence of written marks for vowels and cantillation, no adult or child could read a given passage correctly unless he had received the tradition for reading it from his teacher (cf. Babylonian Talmud *Kiddushin* 33a, *Pesachim* 117a).

The maintenance of the tradition depended on the *soferim* who had several tasks: first, they were responsible for copying and maintaining the accuracy and authenticity of the text; second, they were expected to teach the skill of reading aloud to young boys; and third, they were expected to be able to teach the *targum,* the most general level of interpretation of the text. At the time of Ezra, the term *sofer* was used for wise men in general, but by the Rabbinic period, although there were *soferim* who were also rabbis, the tasks and roles were clearly distinct: *soferim* taught reading and *targum; rabbis* taught a higher level of interpretation called *midrash.* The school in which a *sofer* taught was a *bet sefer,* an elementary school; the school in which a rabbi taught was a *bet midrash* or a *bet talmud.*

It was the *soferim* who took over from fathers the responsibility of teaching the Written Law to all boys. Originally, education was probably a task of the Temple and its officials, but it gradually became associated with the synagogue. The inhabitants of a town were responsible for providing a *bet sefer* (Babylonian *Sanhedrin* 17b); there were, by the time of the Second Temple, schools of that kind in every town and large village (Gerhardsson 1961: 59), attended, it is believed, by most boys or at least by the sons of the propertied class and of the pious. According to the Talmud,

> There were four hundred and eight synagogues in Jerusalem (before 70 CE), each of which had a *bet sefer* and a *bet talmud,* the 'house of reading' for the Written Law and the 'house of learning' for the Oral Law. (Jerusalem Talmud *Megillah* iii 73d)

The same pattern continued after the destruction of the Temple: 'There were five hundred schools in Betar and in the smallest of them there were no less than five hundred children' (Jerusalem Talmud *Taanith* iv 69a). Boys started elementary school between the ages of 5 and 7 and continued there until 12 or 13; they first learned to read the letters from a wax board; then read some passages in a small scroll; then learned from the *Sefer Torah* starting with the Book of Leviticus. The learning was by rote: the text had to be memorized, from the written text, and never from the teacher's mouth, although as mentioned the teacher would teach the *targum* orally. By the end of their study, the students (especially those who went on to study in a *Bet Talmud)* must have known the Scriptures by heart: the form of reference to the Scriptures in the Talmud assumes people who did know it very well.

After the Romans drove the Jews out of Palestine, the Jewish communities in their various exiles created a new multilingual pattern, developing in each a Jewish variety (Rabin 1981) based on a Gentile language for internal community functions (Judaeo-Greek, Judaeo-Aramaic, Judaeo-French, Yiddish, Ladino, Judaeo-Venetian, to name only a few); in addition, they learned the local language for dealing with non-Jews (how well they learned it depended on their acceptance in the local community), and maintained Hebrew to which had been conjoined Talmudic Aramaic as a language for religious activities (in particular, prayer and study) and as time went on for any literacy functions.

This triglossic pattern, with many minor variations and with regular changes of community and co-territorial languages as Jews were driven or chose to emigrate for economic or safety reasons from one country to another, continued more or less until the Enlightenment and emancipation that started in the eighteenth century in Western Europe. The removal of some external barriers to civil freedom was accompanied by language changes too. In Germany, for instance, the opening of ghetto gates led some Jews to replace their Yiddish with standard German.

At the same time, there were proposals to substitute German similarly for religious uses of Hebrew, one of the characteristics of the Reform movement. This tendency continued after Jewish immigration to the United States, where many Jews switched to English for all three functions. Similarly, the successful revival of Hebrew in Israel led to the loss of earlier Jewish plurilingualism as it replaced immigrant languages, including most traditional Jewish languages (Spolsky and Shohamy 1999).

Most of the changes we have been tracing can be attributed to accommodation to the changing sociolinguistic ecology in which Jews lived. It was accommodation to the Gentile co-territorial language that added a new variety and influenced the internal Jewish variety. But the stable element generally remained the use of Hebrew for prayer and Hebrew and Aramaic for study. To what extent, it seems reasonable to ask, was this a result of language management undertaken by and on behalf of Jewish religious institutions?

A first critical issue is to clarify as much as possible the notion and nature of Jewish religious authority. A pioneering study of the place of language choice in Jewish law by Glinert (1991) starts with an explanation of *Halakhah* or normative Jewish law. Like other religious legal systems, it covers not just relations between man and God but also civil and criminal matters, and claims its basis in 'absolute and incontrovertible principles not subject to rational challenge'. At the same time, it differs from other systems as a result of the loss of Jewish sovereignty and legal autonomy after the destruction of the Second Temple. For the most part, since the loss of enforceable authority,[11] Jewish law is 'a private matter between observant Jews and their conscience'. Throughout the ages, there has been continuing study and discussions among observant Jews, for whom the study of Jewish law is a religious duty, so that *Halakhah* has constantly been developing and growing. At any point in time, there are likely to be differences in detail within a broad canvas of consensus. In theory and practice, an observant Jew selects not just a congregation with whom to pray but also a rabbi whose rulings he or she will follow. There is no single central authority; while some rabbis may be more respected than others, each can only expect to bind his followers; and observant Jews are of course nowadays in a minority.

Glinert (1991) traces the varied opinions and changing rulings in *Halakhah* that deal with the choice of language for religious practice. The Talmud recorded the rulings of earlier periods. Generally, it preferred Hebrew for prayer, but allowed exceptions – during the period of Greek rule for example, it recognized the possibility of praying in Greek under certain circumstances. It was ambivalent about Aramaic, but agreed that certain prayers and certain documents (marriage and divorce contracts) could or should use Aramaic. It was ambivalent about learning Greek, at times banning it as a language of government and informers and at other times considering it an ornament for girls to learn.

Glinert (1991) notes first that in the Mishnah (the major first compilation of Jewish law edited in the second century CE) some specific details are given of what must be said in 'The Holy Tongue' (some ritual texts used in certain ceremonies) and what may be said in any language. Glinert next deals with rules concerning language choice in some specific situations. He traces the debate as to whether the formula required in the Jewish marriage ceremony must be in Hebrew or in a language that the participants understand (especially the woman who at certain periods was not expected to know Hebrew). Another matter for debate over the centuries was the use of "foreign formulas" serving as vows and oaths. In each case, the authorities that he cites are rabbis whose contribution to the debate are recorded either in edited texts such as the Talmud and the commentaries that accompany it or in collections of individual *responsa* in which individual named rabbis answer specific questions that had been put to them. These named rabbis, whose statements form part of *Halakhah*, are the language managers within Jewish religion. As these first cases suggest, though, there is no uniformity either at any one time or over time.

As a general rule, and with exceptions some of which will be discussed, the common pattern has been for Hebrew to be the normative choice for Jewish ritual and prayer. The regular weekly readings from the Five Books of Moses and other scriptural readings that form part of regular services are normally in Hebrew. As mentioned earlier, at one period, the practice developed to follow each sentence in Hebrew by a translation into Aramaic; in some communities, this practice continued long after the members of the community stopped speaking and perhaps even understanding Aramaic. Most of the prayers in public and private worship are also in Hebrew. One major exception is the *Kaddish* in Aramaic which marks certain divisions in the service and which in recent centuries has come to play a special role as the prayer for mourners (Wieselter 1998). In the Diaspora, the prayer for the king or local head of state was usually in the co-territorial Gentile language. A sermon (like most other religious teaching) was normally presented in the vernacular language of a congregation: during the classical East European period, rabbis taught in Yiddish (but published what they had taught in Hebrew).

At various periods, some communities applied an early Vatican II approach, switching to the local vernacular. Reif (1993) argues that the early Diaspora synagogues probably preferred Aramaic and Greek as languages of worship. This seems to have happened in Alexandria at the time of Philo. It was also the approach taken by the Reform movement in Germany and later in the United States, but more recently, since the establishment of the state of Israel, more Hebrew seems to have moved into Reform worship (Reif 1993: 322).

In spite of the strong preference for Hebrew for ritual and public worship, there has been a continual willingness to accept translation of sacred texts into the vernacular language of the community, and it has generally been assumed that the teaching of these texts, at whatever level, will be in a vernacular. The Aramaic translations were developed for pragmatic purposes, but are now regularly studied for the interpretations of the sacred texts that they preserve. When the Bible was translated into Greek, contemporary Jewish authorities rejoiced in the miracle of 70 scholars agreeing on a common version. Some centuries later,[12] authorities were less happy at the effects of the translation – the opening up of the text to people without teachers, and the single interpretation enshrined in translation – and proclaimed a fast day on the anniversary of the translation.[13] But generally, Judaism recognizes the value of translation in increasing access to the sacred texts, provided only that the original text be preserved and recognized (together with its traditional interpretations) as the authority.

The status granted to Hebrew as the language of sacred text and daily worship had one critical language outcome, the need to make sure that children develop proficiency in Hebrew as well as in their home language. The Talmud lays down the requirement that as soon as a boy[14] reaches the age of five, his father should start to teach him Hebrew. In practice, fathers joined together to set up schools in which their sons could be instructed, and at a later stage, the *Halakhah* stated that the Jews living in the town could require other Jews to support the school. The Leipzig *Mahzor* (prayer book) includes a picture of the ceremony at which young boys were introduced to reading by being given candy and letters coated with honey. In practice, the system seems to have been quite successful, leading to very high standards of Jewish literacy in the Middle Ages. There are tiny medieval Jewish communities in which each head of household is known to have been the author of a learned study.

The revival of Hebrew by the Zionists at the end of the nineteenth century raised a number of language questions for observant Jewish communities. Israeli Hebrew, like most revived languages, developed its own pronunciation that is different from the many different regional pronunciations of ritual Hebrew. Before the establishment of the state of Israel, most Western Jewish communities continued to use their traditional Ashkenazi pronunciation, but slowly many of them were persuaded to accept the modified Sephardic pronunciation that had become the norm in Israel. Ultra-orthodox communities resisted this change, continuing to use the various Yiddishized pronunciations that they brought with them from different parts of East Europe, just as Oriental communities used their Arabic-influenced pronunciation. One recent trend noticed in Israel has been for some younger observant Jews to attempt to recreate what they imagine to be their grandfathers' pronunciation for public worship.

One of the principal concerns of the *Haredi* (ultra-orthodox) Jewish communities, and in particular of the Hasidic sects among them, has been to maintain separation from the outside community. This is marked by living in more or less segregated neighbourhoods, by wearing distinctive black clothing, by strict interpretation and observance of dietary laws, and also by language practices. Fishman (1966) noted that the two groups in the United States most successful at preserving their heritage languages were the Amish and the Hasidim, each of whom attempted to avoid other aspects of the behaviour and practices of their neighbours. Hasidic groups in the United States, the United Kingdom and Belgium remain the most committed to the maintenance of Yiddish in the home. In Israel, while maintaining other aspects of communal separation, *Haredi* Jews have in the main moved to home use of Israeli Hebrew in place of Yiddish (Baumel 2002, 2003). Certain Hasidic sects, under the influence of their religious leaders, have been making an effort to reverse this trend (Isaacs 1998, 1999). One common technique has been to use Yiddish as language of instruction in the schools for boys, with the result that most yeshiva graduates in these communities are more fluent in Yiddish than in Hebrew. Women who are not allowed to learn the Talmud in *Haredi* communities however commonly continue to speak Hebrew, so that some of the sects have now started to teach Yiddish as a language in schools for girls (Bogoch 1999).

The spelling system for biblical Hebrew texts was set by Masoretic scholars in the tenth century CE. Their language management activities paralleled efforts of Sanskrit and Islamic linguists and grammarians to maintain sacred texts. The decision to maintain the ritual reading of Jewish sacred texts in Hebrew led to the development of a special kind of sacred literacy (Spolsky 1991). The reading of the Bible in the synagogue must be done, the *Halakhah* lays down, from a text written by hand on a parchment or vellum scroll. The texts are written in square Hebrew letters, without punctuation or vowels. A synagogue reader must have learned the correct punctuation, vocalization and cantillation of the text. He must also know when to replace a written word with another word laid down in the tradition. Thus, learning to read requires the moderation of a teacher. Traditionally, and this tradition is maintained in some Yemenite communities and in a few others, any congregant honored as a participant in the public reading of the Torah was expected to be able to read for himself, but in more recent times, the reading has devolved on a single person.

Rather than the rigidity of some other religions, there developed in Judaism an attitude to and method of managing the sacred language

(Hebrew) that served to preserve traditional texts, while providing a method of controlled access to them in changing secular languages, Jewish or non-Jewish. Jewish society was traditionally multilingual, accepting plurilingualism in many co-territorial vernaculars and developing Jewish varieties of them like Yiddish and Ladino which subsequently became major transmitters of culture, but establishing and supporting a popular education system (for boys at least) that kept knowledge of Hebrew alive and able to serve for the mobilization of modern Jewish nationalism. These developments were essentially accommodation to changing demographic and social conditions.

Notes

1. It might in fact be argued that when secular states proclaim languages as 'national', they are in effect sanctifying them.
2. For a discussion of this, see the special section in the *Economist*, 7 July 2007.
3. Just count the deserted churches in rural England!
4. As witness the riots and the headscarf dispute in France.
5. Abortion in Ireland and the USA, definitions of marriage in many Western countries.
6. Towards the end of 2004, arguments about the origin of Yiddish and about the relationships between pre-revival and revived Hebrew have burst into public view again. For a recent summary of the first question, see Jacobs (2005). For a presentation of one side of the second, see Zuckermann (2003).
7. In 2 Kings 18: 26, the courtiers of the King of Judah ask the visiting Assyrian emissaries to speak Aramaic rather than Hebrew ('the language of Judah') which they are afraid that the common people will understand.
8. In Nehemiah 8: 8, there is a passage attributing to Ezra the institution of the public reading of the Law after the return from exile in Babylon. The rabbis of the Talmud, writing much later, interpret the sentence as meaning that the Hebrew reading was accompanied by a translation into Aramaic, a view consistent with the belief that Jews had already lost the ability to understand Hebrew. This custom continued: Goitein (1967–93: 1751) describes the pride of medieval Jewish parents (at a time when Aramaic was no longer understood) that their children could recite by rote the *targum* accompanying the weekly Torah reading, and tells also of a Yemenite woman who criticized modern Israeli education for not keeping up this special training.
9. The position of Latin, probably used in the army, is less certain.
10. There are in fact two conflicting traditions concerning the Septuagint. One calls attention to the miracle of 70 scholars coming up with a single translation. The second establishes an annual fast day (no longer observed) for the tragedy of translation, with its limiting of interpretation on the one hand and its opening the text to the unlearned.
11. One issue regularly debated in Israel is the status of Jewish religious law in the civil law.

12. Peters (2003: Vol. II, Ch. 1) suggests that this was probably the result of 'an ever-increasing Christian use of this rather loose translation, with its elastic canon'.
13. It is no longer observed.
14. Organized religious education for girls started only at the beginning of the twentieth century.

References

Baumel, Simeon D. (2002) 'Language Policies of Ethnic Minorities as Influenced by Social, Economic, Religious and Political Concentrates: an Examination of Israeli Haredim'. Unpublished PhD, Bar-Ilan University, Ramat-Gan, Israel.

Baumel, Simeon D. (2003) 'Teaching English in Israeli Haredi Schools'. *Language Policy*, 2(2), 47–67.

Bogoch, Bryna (1999) 'Gender, Literacy and Religiosity: Dimensions of Yiddish Education in Israeli Government-Supported Schools'. *International Journal of the Sociology of Language*, 138, 123–60.

Dubnow, Simon (1967) *History of the Jews: From the Beginning to Early Christianity*, trans. M. Spiegel. New York: Yoseloff.

Fishman, Joshua A. (ed.) (1966) *Language Loyalty in the United States: the Maintenance and Perpetuation of Non-English Mother Tongues by American Ethnic and Religious Groups*. The Hague: Mouton.

Fishman, Joshua A. (2002) 'The Holiness of Yiddish: Who Says Yiddish is Holy and Why?' *Language Policy*, 1(2), 123–41.

Gerhardsson, Birger (1961) *Memory and Manuscript: Oral Tradition and Written Transmission in Rabbinic Judaism and Early Christianity: With Tradition and Transmission in Early Christianity*. Lund, Sweden and Copenhagen, Denmark: Gleerup and Munksgaard.

Glinert, Lewis (1991) 'Language Choice and the Halakhic Speech Act', in Robert L. Cooper and B. Spolsky (eds), *The Influence of Language on Culture and Thought: Essays in Honor of Joshua A. Fishman's Sixty-Fifth Birthday*, Berlin: Mouton de Gruyter, pp. 157–82.

Goitein, S.D. (1967–93) *A Mediterranean Society: the Jewish Communities of the Arab World as Portrayed in the Documents of the Cairo Geniza*. Berkeley: University of California Press.

Isaacs, Miriam (1998) 'Yiddish in the Orthodox Communities of Jerusalem', in Dov-Ber Kerler (ed.), *Politics of Yiddish: Studies in Language, Literature and Society*, vol. 4, Lanham, Md: Altamira Press, pp. 85–96.

Isaacs, Miriam (1999) 'Contentious Partners: Yiddish and Hebrew in Haredi Israel'. *International Journal of the Sociology of Language*, 138, 101–21.

Jacobs, Neil G. (2005). *Yiddish: a Linguistic Introduction*. Cambridge, UK: Cambridge University Press.

Lieberman, Saul (1942) *Greek in Jewish Palestine*. New York: JTS.

Peters, F.E. (2003) *The Monotheists: Jews, Christians and Muslims in Conflict and Competition*. Princeton, NJ: Princeton University Press.

Rabin, Chaim (1974) 'Hebrew and Aramaic in the First Century', in Shmuel Safrai and Menahem Stern (eds), *Compendia Rerum iudicarium ad Novum Testamentum*, Assen: Van Gorcum & Co., vol. 2, pp. 1007–39.

Rabin, Chaim (1981) 'What Constitutes a Jewish Language'? *International Journal of the Sociology of Language,* 30, 19–28.

Reif, Stefan C. (1993) *Judaism and Hebrew Prayer: New Perspectives on Jewish Liturgical History.* Cambridge: Cambridge University Press.

Spolsky, Bernard (1983) 'Triglossia and Literacy in Jewish Palestine of the First Century'. *International Journal of the Sociology of Language* (42), 95–110.

Spolsky, Bernard (1991) 'Control and Democratization of Sacred Literacy', in Samuel Rodin (ed.), *Encounters with Judaism: Jewish Studies in a Non-Jewish World*, Hamilton: Waikato University and Colcom Press, pp. 37–53.

Spolsky, Bernard (2003) 'Religion as a Site of Language Contact'. *Annual Review of Applied Linguistics,* 23, 81–94.

Spolsky, Bernard (2004) *Language Policy.* Cambridge: Cambridge University Press.

Spolsky, Bernard and Shohamy, Elana (1999) *The Languages of Israel: Policy, Ideology and Practice.* Clevedon: Multilingual Matters.

Wieselter, Leon (1998) *Kaddish.* New York: Alfred A. Knopf.

Zuckermann, Ghil'ad (2003) *Language Contact and Lexical Enrichment in Israeli Hebrew.* London: Palgrave Macmillan.

3
Mauritian Muslims: Negotiating Changing Identities through Language

Aaliya Rajah-Carrim

Introduction

This chapter analyses the changing linguistic practices of a minority religious group in a plurireligious secular society: Muslims in Mauritius. Although most Mauritian Muslims (MMs) are of Indian origin, they adhere to different theological groups. There are also ethnic differences within the community. These religious and ethnic identities are reflected in, and expressed by, linguistic practices.

MMs' language ideologies have evolved over time (Rajah-Carrim 2004). Some religious leaders have adapted their linguistic practices to meet the community's changing sociolinguistic situation and theological stances. This chapter aims to enhance our understanding of the dynamic linguistic practices and ideologies within the MM community and further our limited knowledge of how religious groups add social meaning to language. It specifically asks the following questions: (a) what are the language practices and ideologies in force in the MM community? (b) how and why have these evolved? (c) how important is language in the formation of a religious identity for MMs? (d) how has Kreol, the first language of most MMs, affected, and been affected by, Islamic practices?

The chapter is structured as follows. In the second section, I describe the demographic and sociolinguistic situation of Mauritius. I then look more closely at the MM community. The fourth section presents the wider theoretical issues relevant to the MM community. Using these issues as background, I discuss the linguistic practices and ideologies of the community in the fifth part. The next section deals exclusively with the role of Kreol in Muslim religious practices in Mauritius. In the seventh section, I briefly compare the situation between Indo-Mauritian Muslims and Hindus. I conclude with some final remarks.

Mauritius: people and languages

Mauritius, a post-colonial nation 600 kilometres east of Madagascar, has a multi-ethnic and multilingual population of 1.2 million. At the time of its first discovery in the twelfth century, Mauritius had no indigenous population. The island has been populated by successive waves of colonizers, slaves and indentured labourers – the most significant colonization and immigration periods being the eighteenth, nineteenth and twentieth centuries. During the French period (1715–1810), slaves were brought from Africa, Madagascar and India. Slavery was abolished under British rule which spanned from 1810 to 1968. Indentured labourers were then brought from India to work in the sugar-cane fields. By the middle of the twentieth century, immigration became relatively rare in Mauritius. In 1968, the country acquired independence and in 1992, it acceded to the status of republic.

The Mauritian population is usually divided along ethnic lines, where ethnicity is associated with 'family origins, language, religion, physical appearance (phenotype) and/or lifestyle' (Eriksen 1998: 49). For official purposes, the population of Mauritius is divided into four ethnic and/or religious groups: *Hindus, Muslims, general population* and *Sino-Mauritians*. Together the Hindus and Muslims make up the Indo-Mauritian group. While the terms 'Hindus' and 'Muslims' refer to religious groups, the term 'Indo-Mauritians' refers to a racial group. This Indo-Mauritian group makes up the largest segment of the population. There is a discrepancy between official and actual categorizations. The way in which identity is constructed in everyday life in Mauritius is more complex than suggested by the official records. For instance, in real life, the official Hindu group (52 per cent) is divided into Hindus (40 per cent) and also Tamils (7 per cent), Telugus (3 per cent) and Marathis (2 per cent).

Ethnicity and religion are two important criteria in Mauritian society. In some cases, ethnic identity coincides with religious identity. As mentioned above, most Hindus and Muslims are of Indian ethnicity. It is very unlikely to find a Franco-Mauritian or an Afro-Mauritian Hindu. Unlike the Hindu and Muslim communities, the Christian community forms an ethnically heterogeneous group. In fact, it comprises members from all the ethnic groups of the island, i.e. Afro-, Franco-, Indo- and Sino-Mauritians and also members of the coloured population.

Intra-faith and intra-ethnic marriages still appear to be the norm within the Mauritian community. These marriages ensure the maintenance of ethnic and religious boundaries on the island.

One of the means by which Mauritians can assert inter- and intra-ethnic/religious differences is through language. Languages act as important indices of ethnic and religious identity. Most ethnic groups have an 'ancestral language' with which they identify. Ancestral languages are the languages that the Asian migrants spoke at the time of their arrival in Mauritius and include Bhojpuri, Hindi, Gujarati, Mandarin, Marathi, Tamil, Telugu and Urdu (Baker 1972: 14–18). Today, most of these languages do not function as native languages but as important markers of religious and ethnic identity (Rajah-Carrim 2005). Bhojpuri is the only ancestral language that is still widely spoken in Mauritius.

Alongside these ancestral languages, we find Kreol and the colonial languages, English and French. English is the official language of the nation. For most Mauritians, English is the language acquired at school (Stein 1997). French is widely used by Mauritians. It is the native tongue of the Franco-Mauritians but has also become that of some Mauritians of African, Chinese or Indian origins (Baggioni and Robillard 1990).

Kreol, a French-lexified plantation creole which evolved in the eighteenth century at the time of French colonization, is unquestionably the language most often spoken in Mauritius. In the 2000 Population Census, 69 per cent of the population reported having Kreol as their native language (Rajah-Carrim 2005).

Kreol is valued as the language of national solidarity. Although it has been described as 'an "unofficial" national language' (Eriksen 1990: 14), it is not positively viewed by all users. There are two main reasons for this: a 'linguistic' one and an 'ethnic' one. Kreol, like other creoles (Sebba 1997), is sometimes viewed as a broken non-standard language which is only appropriate for use in informal domains. Another possible reason why Kreol is negatively perceived is because of its association with the Afro-Mauritians, locally known as the Creoles. Kreol is the native and also ancestral language of the Creoles who tend to be part of the lowest classes of Mauritian society (Eriksen 1998). This link between Kreol and the Creoles could serve to strengthen the idea that those who speak Kreol cannot perform well on the social and economic fronts. The 'ethnic' and 'linguistic' reasons therefore reinforce each other and serve to perpetuate negative attitudes towards the language.

Unlike the other languages present on the island, Kreol indexes three types of identities: ethnic (Creole), religious (Christian) and national (Mauritian). That most Mauritian Creoles are Christians and most Mauritian Christians are Creoles leads to the establishment of a link between the language and Christianity. The importance of Kreol at national level and its significance in creating a sense of Mauritian nationhood means that the language is also an index of national identity. Because of these indexical values, the use of Kreol in the religious practices of non-Christian groups (and even non-Creole Christian groups) can be seen as problematic.

The section below describes the demographic, theological and sociolinguistic situations of MMs and highlights the importance of Kreol and Arabic/Urdu for the community. It also points to the potentially problematic tension between Kreol and the 'MM' languages.

Muslims in Mauritius

Muslim presence in Mauritius dates back to the eighteenth century. The first Muslims, the Surtees and the Memans, arrived in Mauritius as free traders from India. They were mostly from Surat, Kutch and surrounding regions in Gujarat. The majority of Muslims, the Kalkattiyas, arrived in the nineteenth and twentieth centuries as Indian indentured labourers. Their main language was Bhojpuri. Through the Surtees and Memans, religious education was made accessible to the Kalkattiyas. The wealthy traders have had a crucial role to play in the building of religious schools across the island.

The division between these three so-called ethnic groups is made on the basis of place of origin, occupation at the time of arrival and ancestral language. Generally, the Kalkattiyas live in rural places or suburbs of towns and cities while the Memans and Surtees live in urban places. However, nowadays with equal access to education and urbanization, the socio-economic differences are gradually disappearing. For instance, many Kalkattiyas hold university degrees and have white-collar jobs, just like their Surtee and Meman counterparts. Socio-economically the Kalkittyas can be ranked with the Surtees and Memans even though culturally, certain differences persist.

Although most Mauritian Muslims are Sunnis and come from the Indian subcontinent, they belong to two main theological groups: the Ahle-Sunnah and the Deobandis, a group affiliated to the Tablighi Jamaat. While the former have retained some Indian cultural influences (e.g. building shrines for saints, performance of devotional hymns in praise of the Prophet Muhammad), the latter 'advocate a purified Islam which combines religious reform and the fight against social problems'

(Eisenlohr 2006: 403). The Deobandis endorse a version of Islam that is devoid of Indian cultural practices and see Saudi Arabia as the reference point for Muslims. Deobandi ideologies are shared by numerous Muslims across the world as the Tablighi Jamaat is 'probably the most popular and widespread Islamic movement in the world today' (Sikand 2002: 1–2). Ahle-Sunnah presence in Mauritius predates that of Deobandi by a couple of decades only – Ahle-Sunnah traditions have been practised in Mauritius since the 1920s and the Deobandi ones since the 1950s. Leaders and followers of each of these two groups claim to represent the authentic version of Islam.

The tension between these groups is heightened by ethnic differences. The Surtees tend to belong to the Deobandi theology while the Memans belong to the Ahle-Sunnah one. As for the Kalkattiyas, some endorse Deobandi ideologies while others endorse Ahle-Sunnah ones. The main mosque and official representative of Muslims in Mauritius, Jummah Masjid, is part of the Ahle-Sunnah tradition (Hollup 1996). The Markazi Masjid, the second most important mosque in Mauritius, endorses the Deobandi theology.

Language serves as a fundamental means of separating these theological groups (Eisenlohr 2006). The Ahle-Sunnah are associated with Urdu and the Deobandis with Arabic. Each group claims that their respective language is the language of MMs. The Ahle-Sunnah followers view the Indian subcontinent as 'a site of Muslim life and Islamic authenticity' and support the study of Urdu 'as the "Islamic culture" of Mauritians of Indian origin' (Eisenlohr 2006: 402). The Deobandis oppose the promotion of Urdu on the grounds that it is a cultural and not a religious language. They believe that Arabic is the language of Islam and should be promoted irrespective of Muslims' ethnic background. Deobandi leaders are responsible for the setting up of Arabic classes and awareness campaigns promoting the language. Their argument suggests that the ethnic language of the MM community is not as important as the religious language. They highlight the similarities between Muslims in Mauritius and Muslims around the world. They promote a transnational and pan-Islamic approach to defining the linguistic identity of MMs.

Therefore, although MMs are mainly of Indian origin, they do not form a monolithic religious group. However, there appears to be an increasing drive towards the adoption of Kreol for preaching in both Ahle-Sunnah and Deobandi mosques around the island (Rajah-Carrim 2004). Since Kreol is a socially charged language, any interaction between Kreol and the two traditional 'Muslim languages' will be significant at both a local and national level.

This chapter aims to shed light on the interaction between Kreol and Arabic/Urdu by discussing the linguistic practices and ideologies in the two main mosques. I assess these practices with respect to religious ideologies and changing social conditions, then discuss how the linguistic strategies employed by the imams and mosque leaders reveal different attitudes to languages and different degrees of accommodation to the national sociolinguistic landscape. The discussion is based on interviews conducted with leaders of the two main mosques in 2004. We focus specifically on language use in Friday sermons, *khutbahs*. Given the importance of sermons in Islamic practices, it is essential to study language in this context. In the section below, we shall examine those theoretical issues that will be relevant to our exploration of linguistic ideologies in the Jummah Masjid and the Markazi Masjid.

The larger context

Our next task in this chapter is to analyse the role of ideologies in influencing and changing macro-linguistic practices in the MM community. Language ideology research shows that individual patterns of language use and societal issues like language policies and groups' identification with a language, are intimately linked to users' 'sets of beliefs about language' (Silverstein 1979: 193). These ideologies are political in that they are 'part of the total set of social principles by which the community organizes itself institutionally' (Watts 1999: 68). They entail the existence of indexical relations at both individual and societal levels.

The notion of indexicality underlines the interdependence of social identities and language. Different societies construct local indexical models differently (Irvine 1998). While some indexical relations are constantly reproduced, others can be contested leading to the establishment of new indices. In Mauritius, languages have become indices of ethnic and/or religious identities (Eisenlohr 2004). Using this vital indexical link as background, we investigate the language ideologies in force in the MM community, a religious community that has received fairly limited attention (Eisenlohr 2006).

To understand some of the changes that have taken place in the MM community, we need to draw upon Giles and Powesland's Accommodation Theory (1975). Accommodation can take place both at intra- and inter-religious levels in the community. For example, by adopting Arabic and/or Kreol in their mosques, Deobandi leaders and followers diverge from their Ahle-Sunnah counterparts. Within the same community, therefore, divergence from one subgroup enables another subgroup to assert their identity. A change in linguistic practices thus highlights intragroup differences. At an interethnic level, adoption and promotion of Urdu and Arabic in *khutbahs* – instead of the ancestral language Bhojpuri and the mother tongue Kreol – can serve to distinguish Muslims from Hindus locally. Hence, language practices are ideologically loaded and any change in linguistic behaviour potentially has social significance. Language is one of the ways in which Muslims and Mauritians generally can define what counts as 'us' and what counts as 'them' in such a multi-ethnic and multilingual setting.

This research also draws on the larger and still embryonic discussions on the sociology of language and religion (Omoniyi and Fishman 2006). Sociologists of language and religion argue that language, which has been disregarded by religious studies scholars, is a vital 'explanatory variable' in religious identities (Fishman 2006: 13). Pandharipande (2006) suggests that language of religion can be divided into three components: linguistic form, religious content and use or function. What is particularly significant to our discussion is her claim that the combination of these components can vary within the same religion: 'the change in this equation is primarily caused by the change in the ideology of the religious community regarding the composition of religious language' (p. 142). It is clear that the two theological groups within the MM community are associated and promote different languages. But how does their understanding of what a religious language means differ or resemble? Has the presence of Deobandi theology altered the way Muslims perceive linguistic practices within the religious domain?

To answer these questions, we will also draw on Woods' (2006: 201) notion of 'language religion ideology' (LRI) which 'describes the nature of the link between language and religion [through] a continuum'. A strong link between language and religion would require the use of a 'special language' as 'God is so special'. A weak link implies a close relationship with God and requires the use of an intimate ("ordinary") language' (p. 202). According to Woods (2006), there might be different language–religion ideologies within the same religion. These 'subideologies' can correspond to different 'spiritual orientations' (p. 201).

Building on Woods' and Pandharipande's recent theories, we will establish whether an Islamic sermon conducted in Kreol, for instance, can be as Islamic as one conducted in Urdu or Arabic. Have the linguistic practices in sermons in the Jummah Masjid and Markazi Masjid evolved and will they reveal different LRIs? I address these questions in the sections below. I shall begin with a description of the linguistic practices in sermons in the Jummah Masjid and then move on to the Markazi Masjid.

Mauritian Muslims: language, religion and identity

The Jummah Masjid

In the main mosque of the island, Urdu is the main language used for the Friday sermon. This has been the practice since the creation of the mosque more than 150 years ago. It has been possible to maintain this tradition partly because the imams of the mosque have always come from India or Pakistan. Although the present imam has learnt some Kreol, he never uses the language for Friday sermons. The head of the administration of the mosque estimates that 60 per cent of the Friday audience understand Urdu. He argues that although youngsters do not speak Urdu, they understand it as there is wide exposure to the language (e.g. through Urdu films).

Although the head of the mosque supports the use of Kreol in other mosques on the island, he asserts that this language cannot be used in the Jummah Masjid. His claim is based on two interesting and non-religious arguments: (a) the Jummah Masjid is the stronghold of traditions and (b) the Friday sermon is broadcast on national radio every Friday afternoon as part of a weekly Urdu programme on Islam.

First, let us examine argument (b) which is articulated in seemingly practical terms. Every Friday afternoon, there is an Islamic programme on one of the national radio channels that includes the sermons of the Jummah Masjid. Because this programme is entirely in Urdu, the sermons have to be delivered in this language. It would be reasonable to argue that reason (b) has ethnoreligious undertones. The fact that a programme on Islam is totally in Urdu underlines the link between the language and the religion. The question remains whether a change in language use in the Jummah Masjid would lead to a change in the radio programme and consequently, a weakening of the association between Urdu and Islam in Mauritius.

However, a change in linguistic, religious and cultural practices in the Jummah Masjid seems unlikely, as pointed out by the head of the mosque in the first argument above. He claims that the Jummah Masjid has to adhere to the tradition of using Urdu and cannot simply switch to other languages. He adds that MMs have two languages: Arabic, which is their first religious language, and Urdu, which is their cultural and second religious language. Therefore, the use of Urdu for the Friday sermon celebrates both the cultural and the religious identities of Muslims.

The above paragraph suggests that Arabic and Urdu exist in competition in the Jummah Masjid. It is noteworthy that little mention is made of the most important spoken language in Mauritius, Kreol. Although Kreol carries no religious value to Mauritian Muslims, it is their first language. More Muslims speak Kreol than Urdu at home (Rajah-Carrim 2005). This situation, ignored by the decision-makers in the main mosque, is one of the main factors influencing language choice in the Markazi Masjid.

The Markazi Masjid

In the Markazi Masjid, Kreol is the preferred language for preaching. The imam of the mosque is originally from India but has been in Mauritius for over 20 years. He speaks Kreol fluently. According to him, preaching can be done in any language including Kreol and Urdu. The main aim of preaching is to ensure that the audience understand the message conveyed. It therefore logically follows that the language that is most accessible to the nation should be used.

Although Arabic is valued as the holy language of the Qur'an and prescribed prayers, it is not used for preaching. This is because very few people in the audience would understand him. Even the use of Urdu in the Markazi Masjid, the language that is most strongly associated with MMs, is steadily decreasing. The imam consciously accommodates to the linguistic needs of the Muslim population. In the matter of preaching, therefore, he sees languages purely as a utilitarian means of communication devoid of any symbolic meaning. Thus, through his language choice, the religious leader of an influential mosque of the island conveys the message that there are no strict rules when it comes to language use in sermons and other forms of preaching.

The imam makes no mention of culture when talking about language use in sermons. This is in line with Deobandi ideologies which advocate separation between culture and religion. Accordingly, the Markazi Masjid, unlike the Jummah Masjid, does not stand for an ethnoreligious icon. The section below discusses this point further and highlights the role of the Jummah Masjid as the ethnoreligious, rather than purely religious, representative of MMs.

Mauritian Muslim identities: Ahle-Sunnah versus Deobandi

Change has been noted at the level of ideological and linguistic representations. Linguistic practices in many mosques have undergone major changes. The differences in linguistic practices reflect different theological stances. Language in this context is a powerful tool for the two main theological groups to assert their differences from each other. While most, if not all, MMs started off as Ahle-Sunnah practitioners, half of the community have now turned to Deobandi or other schools of thought (Donath 2006). Each group claims that they represent the true or pure version of Islam as practised by the Prophet Muhammad, while the other theologies are corrupted versions of the religion.

Most Muslims therefore would have started off endorsing the use of Urdu in mosques. The ethnoreligious language was and still is used in the Jummah Masjid 'to bring Muslims closer to their religion' (Head of Jummah Masjid administration). When ancestral languages were still used in the community, Urdu enabled Muslims to understand their religion. According to the Head of the Jummah Masjid, preaching does not have to be done in Arabic because the Prophet Muhammad himself encouraged preachers to learn 'the language of the people'. In the Ahle-Sunnah context, 'language of the people' was and still is equated with Urdu. Not only is Urdu an ethnic language but it also has religious connotations. Many religious books and hymns (*naats*) have been written in Urdu. It is thought to be a better mirror of the realities of MMs than Arabic in that it encompasses both their religious and ethnic identities. This observation is reflected in language choices in the main Ahle-Sunnah mosque of the island where the use of Arabic is minimal – as opposed to that of Urdu.

However, as differences grew within the community, it was important to distinguish between the various theologies. Arabic thus acquired an additional dimension in the Muslim community – it already had a privileged position as the language of the Qur'an and prescribed prayers. It has now become a tool for the Deobandis to distance themselves from the Ahle-Sunnah. Language is thus embedded with double religious significance: the Islamic language, Arabic, becomes an index of a specific Muslim identity within the MM community. The mosque, therefore, is an important medium through which one can assert one's linguistic, religious and sometimes cultural identity. In the MM community, linguistic identity is tied with ideologies of religion and authenticity.

The increasing presence of Arabic can be understood in terms of its significance as a religious language and an index of specific religious ideologies. But how do we explain the increasing use of Kreol, a [+Christian] and [+Creole] language, in mosques? We address this question in the next section.

Kreol: the New Mauritian Muslim language?

A pilot study conducted in 2004 confirmed that most young Muslims speak Kreol at home instead of their ancestral language, Bhojpuri, and/ or ethnoreligious language, Urdu (Rajah-Carrim 2004). Kreol is also gradually replacing Urdu as the language of sermons and is the preferred language of social interactions in mosques.

Positive attitudes towards the use of Kreol in religious talks were observed. There was a general consensus among participants in the 2004 study that religious leaders have to accommodate to the linguistic preference and competence of their audience – even if such an accommodation means transgressing traditional linguistic customs and practices. These views show that the traditional division of labour between the 'Muslim languages' and Kreol in the religious practices of MMs is being renegotiated. This could suggest a wider acceptance of Deobandi theology or a relaxation of rules relating to linguistic practices among Ahle-Sunnah followers.

This incorporation of Kreol in linguistic practices raises a major question: can an Islamic sermon conducted in Kreol be as Islamic as one conducted in Urdu or Arabic? To answer this question, we need to draw in Pandharipande's (2006) and Woods' (2006) theories presented above.

If Kreol were to become the 'linguistic form' through which 'religious content' (Pandharipande 2006) was transmitted, we would expect it to be embedded with Islamic values. It would then acquire social significance as a religious language for Muslims, specifically in the mosque. In this case, it might develop an Arabicized variety. This would lead to elevated status for the language, and a change to its current association with local Christians and Creoles. However, the data from the pilot study suggest that Kreol is only used as a medium of communication, not a carrier of religious baggage in the Muslim context. In this case, it is not the language of religion but only the 'linguistic form' through which 'religious content' is transmitted (Pandharipande 2006). Paradoxically, it could retain a Creole and Christian index *in the mosque*.

Both scenarios involve sociolinguistic change: sacralization and creolization. Further research into the variety of Kreol used in mosques is needed to assess exactly which of the two scenarios is taking place in the MM community. An analysis of religious sermons, for instance, would establish (a) which languages are used in *khutbahs*, (b) whether and when an Arabicized variety of Kreol is used and (c) whether we find instances of code-switching, i.e. alternation between two or more language varieties within the same sermon. This would clarify the so far poorly understood interaction between Kreol and Urdu/Arabic.

The linguistic changes can also be explained in terms of Woods' LRI. The presence of Kreol in mosques suggests that the ideologies surrounding language use in religious domains are being renegotiated. We find a weakening link between language and religion. This observation seems to apply more strongly to the Deobandi theology. The change in linguistic practices could be a reflection of the infiltration and adoption of new theologies within the MM community. The language–religion sub-ideologies among Muslims index different schools of thought.

Interestingly, interviews with religious leaders and the study conducted in 2004 suggest that the use of Kreol in the mosque is devoid of any ethnic or religious connotations. Urdu and Arabic are strongly associated with MMs even though Kreol is widely used in mosques. Although the actual use of Urdu in mosques might be decreasing, this language is still an important marker of Islamic identity on the island. Participants in the 2004 study believed that the use of Kreol in sermons did not affect Islamic identity in any way.

The study also highlighted the importance of Urdu rather than Arabic as a marker of religious identity in Mauritius. From a purely religious perspective, we might think that Arabic, being the language of the Qur'an, should be claimed as the language of the Muslims. However, unlike Urdu, Arabic has no cultural or direct historical meaning for the MMs who largely originated from India. Therefore, a language that denotes the historical, cultural and religious identities of the Muslims takes precedence over a language that only symbolizes their religious identity. Also, it could be said that the use of Urdu in talks and sermons in the main mosque of the island can act as reinforcement for the association between Islam and Urdu. The fact that Urdu has institutional backing from the Jummah Masjid gives it added authority over Arabic (Pandharipande 2006). We can expect this situation to change in the coming years with the increasing adoption of Deobandi ideologies by Mauritians.

Indo-Mauritian identities: Muslims versus Hindus

In Mauritius, loyalties usually lie with specific ethnic and religious groups rather than the nation as a whole. In present-day Mauritius, ethnic groups constantly compete over limited resources and access to power. The competitive relationship that exists among ethnic and religious groups is reflected in local language behaviours.

Language is used by Muslims to differentiate themselves from Hindus. Many Kalkattiyas share their linguistic heritage with those Hindus who came to Mauritius as indentured labourers (Benedict 1961). The indentured labourers, as mentioned above, spoke Bhojpuri. However, Bhojpuri is not considered as a fully fledged language and does not have much prestige itself. Therefore, many Muslims and Hindus report having Urdu and Hindi, respectively, as their ancestral language (Moorghen and Domingue 1982, Stein 1986). It should be noted that although Hindi and Urdu are generally considered as two different languages, structurally, they are very similar. However, Hindi, written in the Devanagari script, is associated with Hinduism, while Urdu, written in the Arabic script, is associated with Islam (Stein 1982: 125). In the Mauritian context, therefore, Urdu has a unifying religious role which Bhojpuri, Gujarati and Kutchi – the ancestral languages of MMs – lack. In order to be distinguished from each other, Hindus and Muslims claim Hindi and Urdu respectively, instead of Bhojpuri, as their ancestral languages (Hollup 1996, Stein 1986). In other words, Urdu serves two important functions in the MM community: it cements differences among Muslims who have different ancestral languages and serves to distinguish MMs from their Hindu counterparts.

In the 2000 Population Census, we also find MMs reporting Arabic, instead of Bhojpuri or Urdu, as their ancestral language (Rajah-Carrim 2004). In his book *The Muslims of Mauritius*, Emrith (1967) makes no mention of Arabic. Yet, we find that 798 Mauritians claim that Arabic is their ancestral language. As a minority group, some Muslims feel threatened by the majority Hindus (Hollup 1996). Therefore, it is possible that by claiming that Arabic (instead of Bhojpuri) is their ancestral language, they are distancing themselves from the Indian subcontinent and redefining their identity in terms important to them. This is an example of changing linguistic affiliations within the MM community. These Muslims could be part of the Deobandi group which stresses the significance of Arabic over Urdu as the language of MMs. Ancestry here seems to be defined by religious rather than ethnic criteria.

Through language, therefore, Muslims can assert their identity and change their allegiances. In a nation where a group can claim 'more power the larger the number of members it can credibly claim' (Eriksen 1998: 79), the census becomes an important instrument for asserting one's identity. The presence of Arabic in the census should therefore be seen as an ideological statement that enables Muslims to distance themselves from other Indo-Mauritian groups and establish a new religious rather than ethnoreligious identity.

Conclusion

The diversity within the MM community is reflected in the diversity of their linguistic, religious and cultural practices and ideologies. In this minority community, religion is just one aspect of identity. On the one hand, there is the interaction between religious and ethnic identities and on the other, between religious and linguistic identities. MMs' social and ethnoreligious positioning influences their linguistic practices and ideologies.

The increasing influence of Deobandi ideologies has helped to promote Arabic as the religious language of Muslims on the island. However, Urdu still tends to be seen as *the* language of MMs. But it is no longer widely used in mosques.

In Mauritius, the transmission and dissemination of Islamic knowledge are being re-engineered linguistically. The above sections show that both the linguistic practices and ideologies of MMs are evolving. This is due to the changing sociolinguistic profile and theological affiliations of the community. It is clear that there is a drive among Muslims – leaders and followers – to use Kreol in the religious domain. It seems that the dwindling knowledge of ancestral languages has forced Muslim religious leaders to reconsider their language choices and adopt Kreol. Adaptation to the local sociolinguistic setting is one of the perduring strengths of the Muslim community in plurireligious Mauritius. The question remains whether the situation and position of Kreol can change to such an extent that it acquires meaning as a Muslim language in Mauritius – that is, can Kreol be islamized in the Mauritian context?

Acknowledgements

I am grateful to Miriam Meyerhoff for interesting discussions on language and religion in Mauritius. My thanks also go to Roummane Rajah for her support during fieldwork, Zia Carrim for challenging comments on an earlier version of this chapter and Jibraan Carrim for his good humour and enthusiasm for this work.

References

Baggioni, D. and de Robillard, D. (1990) *Ile Maurice: Une Francophonie Paradoxale.* Paris: L'Harmattan.
Baker, P. (1972) *Kreol: a Description of Mauritian Creole.* London: C. Hurst.
Benedict, B. (1961) *Mauritius: the Problems of a Plural Society.* London: Institute of Race Relations.

Donath, F. (2006) 'How to Carry Owls to Athens? Performing Scriptural Authenticity among *Wahhabi* Muslims in Mauritius', http://www.gzaa.uni-halle.de/eng/studyday/studyday.php?semid=03&tid=009&pid=037 (accessed on 31 March 2007).

Eisenlohr, P. (2004) 'Register Levels of Ethno-National Purity: the Ethnicization of Language and Community in Mauritius'. *Language in Society*, 33, 59–80.

Eisenlohr, P. (2006) 'The Politics of Diaspora and the Morality of Secularism: Muslim Identities and Islamic Authority in Mauritius'. *Journal of the Royal Anthropological Institute*, 12, 395–412.

Emrith, M. (1967) *The Muslims of Mauritius*. Port Louis: Editions Le Printemps.

Eriksen, T.H. (1990) 'Linguistic Diversity and the Quest for National Identity: the Case of Mauritius'. *Ethnic and Racial Studies*, 13, 1–24.

Eriksen, T.H. (1998) *Common Denominators: Ethnicity, Nation-Building and Compromise in Mauritius*. Oxford and New York: Berg.

Fishman, J.A. (2006) 'A Decalogue of Basic Theoretical Perspectives or a Sociology of Language and Religion', in T. Omoniyi and J.A. Fishman (eds), *Explorations in the Sociology of Language and Religion*, Amsterdam and Philadelphia: John Benjamins, pp. 13–25.

Giles, H. and Powesland, P.F. (1975) 'A Social Psychological Model of Speech Diversity', in H. Giles and P.F. Powesland (eds), *Speech Style and Social Evaluation*, London and New York: Harcourt Brace, published in cooperation with the European Association of Experimental Social Psychology by Academic Press, pp. 154–70.

Hollup, O. (1996) 'Islamic Revivalism and Political Opposition among Minority Muslims in Mauritius'. *Ethnology*, 354, 285–300.

Irvine, J.T. (1998) 'Ideologies of Honorific Language', in B.B. Schieffelin et al. (eds), *Language Ideologies: Practice and Theory*, New York and Oxford: Oxford University Press, pp. 51–67.

Moorghen, P.-M. and Domingue, N.Z. (1982) 'Multilingualism in Mauritius'. *International Journal of the Sociology of Language*, 34, 51–66.

Omoniyi, T. and Fishman, J.A. (eds) (2006) *Explorations in the Sociology of Language and Religion*, Amsterdam and Philadelphia: John Benjamins.

Pandharipande, R.V. (2006) 'Ideology, Authority and Language Choice: Language of Religion in South Asia', in T. Omoniyi and J.A. Fishman (eds), *Explorations in the Sociology of Language and Religion*, Amsterdam and Philadelphia: John Benjamins, pp. 140–63.

Rajah-Carrim, A. (2004) 'The Role of Mauritian Creole in the Religious Practices of Mauritian Muslims'. *Journal of Pidgin and Creole Languages*, 19, 363–75.

Rajah-Carrim, A. (2005) 'Language Use and Attitudes in Mauritius on the Basis of the 2000 Population Census'. *Journal of Multilingual and Multicultural Development*, 26, 317–32.

Sebba, M. (1997) *Contact Languages: Pidgins and Creoles*, Basingstoke: Macmillan.

Sikand, Y.S. (2002) *The Origins and Development of the Tablighi-Jama'at (1920–2000): a Cross-Country Comparative Study*. Hyderabad, A.P.: Orient Longman.

Silverstein, M. (1979) 'Language Structure and Linguistic Ideology', in P.R. Clyne et al. (eds), *The Elements: a Parasession on Linguistic Units and Levels,* Chicago: Chicago Linguistic Society, pp. 193–247.

Stein, P. (1982) *Connaissance et Emploi des Langues à l'Ile Maurice*. Hamburg: Helmut Busche Verlag.

Stein, P. (1986) 'The Value and Problems of Census Data on Languages: an Evaluation of the Language Tables from the 1983 Population Census of Mauritius', in J.A. Fishman et al. (eds), *The Fergusonian Impact: In Honor of Charles A. Ferguson,* Berlin: Mouton de Gruyter, vol. 2.

Stein, P. (1997) 'The English Language in Mauritius: Past and Present'. *English World-Wide,* 18, 65–89.

Watts, R. (1999) 'The Ideology of Dialect in Switzerland', in Jan Blommaert (ed.), *Language Ideological Debates,* New York: Mouton de Gruyter, pp. 67–103.

Woods, A. (2006) 'The Role of Language in some Ethnic Churches in Melbourne', in T. Omoniyi and J.A. Fishman (eds), *Explorations in the Sociology of Language and Religion,* Amsterdam and Philadelphia: John Benjamins, pp. 197–212.

4
Arabic and Sociocultural Change among the Yoruba

Oladipo Salami

Introduction

In an earlier study, I examined the sociolinguistic dimensions of language use in the mediation of religious experience with particular focus for Yoruba language and religious practices (Salami 2006). In that study, I tried not only to show that for the Yoruba people religion is a critical domain of experience but also that the use of the Yoruba language plays a pivotal role in this experience. In the present study, I intend to look at the impact of a foreign language – Arabic – as well as the religion of Islam on the religious life and world view of the Yoruba people as they are manifested in the Yoruba language. In doing this, I will attempt to investigate the process of change in Yoruba culture as it tries to accommodate the linguistic and religious influences from Arabic and Islam.

There is no gainsaying the fact that the Arabic language plays an active role in the mediation of the religious experience of Yoruba Muslims. It is a language they use to express their religious experience, the language of their religious education, and for them a potent tool for healing and magical practices. Furthermore, the Arabic language is used as a boundary marker, as it is the sacred language of all who profess Islam and, therefore, can also be used to reinforce Muslim identity. According to Malik (1995: 427), the relevance of Arabic to the Yoruba Muslim community cannot be overemphasized because whether they speak it or not, it is the religious language of Muslims all over the world as they must use it in their five daily prayers and in their confession of faith (*kalimat al-shahadah*). As noted by Samarin (1976: 5), it can be observed that groups adhering to a given set of beliefs and practices are also often set apart linguistically.

Studies in historical linguistics have demonstrated that changes taking place in language are not motivated solely by internal linguistic factors. The literature shows that language change is *caused* by both social and historical factors (Weinreich 1974, Labov 1972, Bynon 1977, Francis 1983, Milroy 1987). The contact between the Yoruba-speaking southwestern Nigeria, Islam as well as the Arab world has produced tremendous changes in the sociocultural life of the Yoruba people as reflected in their language. Studies have shown this impact on the phonetic, phonological as well as the lexical structures of the Yoruba language (see, for example, Abdul 1976, Ogunbiyi 1980, Abu Bakre 1984, Malik 1995).

This chapter focuses on lexical borrowing. It examines and analyses the interaction of Islamic religion and the Arabic language with specific focus on change and accommodation in Yoruba language and culture. In doing this, it discusses the nature of the contact of the two languages and examines the sociocultural motivations for the adaptation of the Arabic language. The chapter concludes that there is a pervasive influence of Arabic–Islamic culture on Yoruba and that this influence has motivated demand for change in the sociopolitical life of Yoruba Muslims as demonstrated, for example, in the demand for the Islamic legal system.

Culture contact, language change and accommodation

The literature shows that there exists a relationship between culture contact and language change. However, the progression from contact to change is not without its tension or conflict. As this happens to language, it is also the case with other aspects of culture, including religion. As noted by Silva-Corvan (1994, cited in Chiung 2006), intensive language contact is a powerful external promoter of language change. Borrowing, which is one consequence of language contact, is influenced greatly by the politico-social position of the speakers of a borrowing language. Thus it is the sociolinguistic history of the speakers, and not the structure of their language, that is the primary determinant of the linguistic outcome(s) of language contact. In other words, the social structure and the behaviour of members of the language-using community are the critical ingredients in the character and outcome(s) of language contact phenomena.

Hansell (1989, cited in Chiung 2006) thinks that cultural contact is language contact that results from cultural diffusion but does not require widespread bilingualism, while intimate contact is characterized by widespread societal bilingualism and by the wide variety of functions that both languages are used for. The literature shows that religion is noted to be a major force acting on language change as religious factors may bring about not only cultural–linguistic change but may also account for language spread. For example, Kaplan and Baldauf (1997: 230, cited in Chiung 2006) hold that Christianity in Taiwan, as well as in Rwanda, has not only changed language structure but also changed the nature of familial relationships, the social hierarchy and the economic structure. Kaplan and Baldauf (1997: 230, cited in Chiung 2006) also note that widespread missionary efforts have had most insidious effects on language ecology, on language and their speakers, as well as on the well-being of those speakers.

As noted by Crystal (1976: 19), the field of language contact is an important area to study the interaction between religion and linguistics as languages do tend to influence one another via religion. This can take place, for example, if one of the languages in contact is a medium of prayer, liturgy or some rituals of the religion or belief system. The influence from the language will not only be manifest in loanwords but will also constitute a site for looking at the sociolinguistic experience of the peoples in contact. Crystal (1976) observes that classical Arabic, for example, is both a religious language as it is the language of the Qur'an and a language that is used in many Islamic practices – prayers, sermons, *tafsir* (exegesis), etc. What then follows is that the language pervades the religious life of adherents of Islam. Thus Islam is expected to provide the framework which not only gives meaning to Yoruba Muslims' social life but also acts as the compass to chart their life's course and shape their hopes. However, as noted in our earlier study, the Yoruba are very pragmatic about religion and thus it is not unusual to find a Yoruba Muslim who also takes part in some traditional religious practices (Salami 2006). In other words, for the Yoruba Muslim, there is hardly a conflict as the two cultures try to accommodate each other in his/her social and religious life. According to Falola (2005: 13), religious converts in Africa were not docile recipients of new religious ideas as they often refined them in a way that either Islam or Christianity was blended with local traditions.

Yoruba vocabulary and Arabic origin

Abdul (1976) and Malik (1995) observe the existence of many words of Arabic origin in Yoruba. Studies have shown that languages do tend to share vocabulary items, very often through borrowing, and that it happens in almost all world languages (see for example, Weinreich 1974,

Bynon 1977). Furthermore, such borrowings or loanwords could also be a result of the level of accommodation between the two languages and cultures in contact. With contact, new potentialities tend to result and changes take place in one or both of the languages and cultures. These changes may take the form of selection from among the elements of either of the languages and cultures that are found useful. The changes may also involve modifying the borrowed or selected elements to conform to the demands of the selecting culture. The selected or borrowed elements become integrated into the culture of the borrowing society. In the case of Arabic, what the Yoruba people have taken from Arabic–Islamic culture, for example, they have tried to redefine and sometimes subordinated to Yoruba world view and attitudes. According to Malik (1995: 429), the encounter between Yoruba and Arabic was not intensive enough to enable Arabic to supersede Yoruba but it was effective enough to lend a great deal of Arabic vocabulary.

Sociolinguistic studies of language contact show that the vocabulary of a language is the best domain of borrowing and that is why the first elements to enter the borrowing language are lexical items. According to Weinreich (1974: 56), prominent reasons for lexical borrowing are: attitudinal factors (such as social value or prestige of the source or recipient language), linguistic innovation (need to designate new things, persons, places, etc.), to show acculturation, need for identity (see also Higa 1979).

Odhiambo (2002) makes three observations about culture contact and change in Africa. The first is that the appropriation of foreign cultural forms depends on the adaptive capacity of the indigenous tradition, and that the exercise of this adaptive capacity will make the adopted elements of the alien tradition meaningful and understandable to the practitioners of the indigenous tradition. Such practitioners are also able to build on and contribute to the advancement of the alien culture. The second thing is that if the alien tradition is imposed, it may have a damaging effect on the self-perceptions and understandings of the recipients of that tradition. Thus the circumstances of the imposition may affect the endurance of the alien tradition in its new cultural environment as the people upon whom it is imposed may not easily appreciate it and may therefore have little, if any, commitment to it. Thirdly, an imposed tradition will find recipients absorbed merely in the outward frills or confused in the pursuit of the practices and institutions of the imposed tradition.

Islam was a major stimulus for economic, social and cultural change in Yorubaland at the beginning of the nineteenth century especially following the Fulani jihad. The contact with Islam generated both conflict and interest in the Yoruba community. For example, while the Yoruba resisted the territorial ambition of the Fulani jihadists on one hand, they patronized Hausa Muslim cleric-medicine men and traders on the other. According to Lloyd (1969: 255, cited in Barret 1991: 16), Islam had sympathy towards traditional beliefs in magic and witch-craft, while Loiello (1982: 52, cited in Barret 1991) also points to Islam's approval of polygamy and sale of charms. Following the Yoruba civil wars, many displaced Yoruba were attracted to Islam by the perceived dignity and spiritual power of the Muslim clerics and by the business opportunities associated with Muslim traders (Barret 1991: 17).

From the foregoing, we can see that the Islamic religion in Yorubaland provides a veritable site for looking at accommodation of cultural and linguistic changes resulting from culture contact. This is particularly so as it was possible that a large number of material and conceptual borrowings from the Arabic language and culture could have diffused into Yoruba through such agents as clerics and traders. Although the contact between Yoruba and Arabic has not led to the evolution of a Yoruba–Arabic bilingualism at a societal level, we observe in the speech practices of the Yoruba, generally, Yoruba–Arabic code-mixing. In other words, the Yoruba situation of contact-induced language change shows that borrowing of individual words can take place from any language, even if the learner's knowledge of that language is very superficial.

Arabic–Islamic culture and the spheres of influence

In this section, we describe the specific domains of loans from Arabic into Yoruba. These include, among others, religion, personal and social relations and social life (naming, marriage, expressions relating to time, days and months and so on). Specifically, it might be pertinent to mention here that the genres in which some form of Arabic is used among the Yoruba include prayers, stock phrases/sayings in public speech, songs (*were* and *fuji*), oath-taking, promising, faith, fate, penitence and so on. These Arabic loanwords, which are not written in any special characters to indicate their foreignness, have become full 'citizens' of Yoruba.

Yoruba religious lexical stock

In this category, we will find words transferred into Yoruba from Arabic which cannot be used for concepts other than their original representa-tion in Arabic. They are religious ideas or concepts that were new to the Yoruba world at the time of contact. They are also words that show accul-turation or accommodation to Arabic–Islamic culture as they have not only become part of Yoruba world view but have also been phonologically modified to conform to the structure of the Yoruba language. Examples of these religious loanwords can be classified into (a) new concepts and new names and (b) new names for pre-existing concepts as given below.

New concepts, new names

These are scriptural items from the Holy Qur'an or connected specifically with the religion of Islam (Table 4.1).

New names for pre-existing concepts

This group contains words that are used for pre-existing concepts in the Yoruba world view. Today, the Arabic words are used most often in place of the original Yoruba forms in conversation. Examples are given in Table 4.2.

Table 4.1   Concepts new to the Yoruba world

Yoruba form	Arabic form	Gloss
alukuraani	al-qur'an	The Holy Qur'an
asetaani	al-shaitan	Satan
sura	surah	chapter
mosalasi	masjid	mosque
alujanna	aljannah	paradise
alujannu	al-jin	jinn
bilisi	iblis	devil
alukiyamo	al-qiyawm	resurrection day
aluwala	al-wudhu	ablution
alaaji	al-hajj	a pilgrim
waasi	wa'z	sermon
adura	ad-du'a	prayer
woli	wali	saint, holy man
lamulana	al-ramadan	Muslim fast

Table 4.2   New names for pre-existing concepts

Yoruba form	Arabic form	Pre-existing concept	Gloss
adura	al-du'a	iwure/ire	invocation
aniyan	anniyah	ipero	intention
saa	sa'ah	asiko	time
sanmoni	zaman	igba	period
sina	zina	agbere	adultery

It is observed that a large number of Arabic words used in the domain of religion have not only become culturally and linguistically integrated into Yoruba, they have become so well established that they are no longer perceived by speakers as borrowed. Today, for example, the following words in italics are not often recognized to be of Arabic origin or code-mixing between Yoruba and Arabic:

1. Nwon da *seria* fun < Nwon se idajo fun (S/he was punished)
   seria < shari'a: Islamic law
2. Mo *fitina* okunrin naa < Mo daamu okunrin naa (I caused the man a lot of trouble)
   fitina < fatana: to rouse to rebellion/to incite/to trouble
3. Okunrin naa onije *haramu* < Okunrin onije wobia (The man engages in illegal act/cheating)
   haramu < haram: forbidden, illegal
4. enikan ko le we *duniyan* lai farapa< enikan ko le we ile aye ja lai farapa
   (It is difficult to sail through the world/life without some accident)
   duniyan < duniya(h): world, life
5. *alubarika* lo ju oun gbogbo lo: God's blessing is the best
   alubarika < albarakah: blessing
6. Ki Olorun oba fun wa ni *arisiki* < Ki Olorun oba fun wa ni: May God give us sustenance/fortune
   arisiki < ar-rizq: fortune, sustenance
7. *Sababi* Olorun ni < Amuwa Olorun ni: It is God's doing
   sababi < sababun: cause, reason
8. *alukawani* emi ati re < ipinu emi ati ire: the agreement between you and I
   alukawani < al-kawanin: agreement
9. *aniyan* mi niwipe ki nlo < ipinun mi ni wipe ki nlo (My intention was/is to go)
   aniyan < an-niyya(h): intention, purpose
10. *alujonun* eniyan ni o nse < abami eniyan ni o nse (S/he is a spirit)
    alujonun < al-jin: 'spirit', 'superhuman being'

Stock phrases

In conversation, certain expressions occur in the speech of Yoruba Muslims and, at times, non-Muslims, regularly in social and religious contexts often to facilitate some actions such as oath-taking, promising, affirmation of faith and so on. Examples include the following:

bisimillahi	in the name of Allah	uttered to commence a thing/ an idea/a job, a journey and so on
ausubillahi		uttered to seek protection from God
astagafurullahi		uttered to seek forgiveness from God but has become a common expression to mitigate a misdemeanour even by non-Muslims
wallahi	by God	uttered as an oath to back a promise
Insha Allah	God willing	uttered to show optimism
Qadarallahi	God's will	uttered to acknowledge God's control over human destiny

These stock expressions could, otherwise, have been uttered or rendered in Yoruba but it seems they either have no equivalent expressions in Yoruba or where they do, such expressions have receded to be replaced by the Arabic expressions. For example, it would be strange to say 'In the name of Sango' or 'I seek forgiveness from Ogun'. The Yoruba never had a world view of 'sins' as found in Islam and Christianity wherein they needed to seek forgiveness from the various Yoruba traditional deities as Sango and Ogun. Furthermore, Yoruba people are more wary of taking oaths using the names of traditional deities rather than God, Allah or Olorun as it seems that they have psychologically conditioned themselves to believe in the potency of these deities.

Cultural items

Apart from ideas and concepts, material and cultural items have also been borrowed into Yoruba and are reflected in its vocabulary stock as shown in the examples in Table 4.3. These items show that Islam also impacted on the material and cultural lives of the Yoruba to the extent that its language needed to incorporate these changes. The examples given above seem also to index some cultural and material gaps in Yoruba culture at the time of contact with Arabic–Islamic culture.

Table 4.3 Material loans from Arabic

Yoruba loan	Arabic form	Gloss
alumogaji	almiqass	scissors
gaasi	kas	wine glass
abere	ibra	needle
alikamo	al-qamh	wheat
alubosa	al-basal	onion, leak
buka	bukka	tent
fitila	fatila	a lamp

Table 4.4 Arabic loanwords for days of the week

Yoruba form	Arabic form	Gloss	Yoruba names
atinii	al-ithnaini	Monday	Aje
atalata	althulaatha	Tuesday	Isegun
alaruba	al-arba'	Wednesday	Ojoru
alamisi	al-khamis	Thursday	Ojobo
jimoo	jum'ah	Friday	Eti
		Saturday	abameta
		Sunday	Aiku

Days of the week

It is not common to hear the Yoruba names for the days of the week being used today as they seem to have been replaced by loans from English and Arabic in regular conversation or interactions among the Yoruba. These Yoruba forms are provided in textbooks and taught in school, but using them in conversation, other than the borrowed forms from Arabic or English, sounds rather pedantic. Examples are given in Table 4.4.

Naming practice and names: the Arabization of names

Hallgren (1988: 158) observes two important functions of Yoruba names. The first is that Yoruba proper names are bearers of both symbolic and precise information useful for the study of religious culture. Secondly, Yoruba names reflect certain attitudes and values. For Hallgren (1988), therefore, studies of Yoruba (traditional) names are of great importance for the understanding of Yoruba socioreligious attitudes and thought. This is because the traditional name of a Yoruba person might say a great deal about occupation, family traditions, which deity was worshipped

Table 4.5   Examples of personal (Islamic) names

Yoruba form	Arabic form
Abudu	'abd
Abudu Lasisi	'abd'laziz
Buraimo	Ibrahim
Adamu	Adam
Yesufu	Yusuf
Momodu	Muhammad
Amodu	Ahmad

and so on (Hallgren 1988: 159). In other words, naming among the Yoruba carries a lot of sociocultural load as it reflects thoughts, beliefs, attitudes and values.

Although as a result of conversion to Islam the Yoruba people also took up new identification labels by assuming Arabic names found in the Qur'an and the Sunna or the names of personages recorded in the early history of the religion, the basic principle of giving children names on the grounds of history/circumstance of birth, attitudes and values is still hidden in the new Arabized Yoruba names. For the Yoruba, it is believed that the name has a psychological effect on the behaviour and character of the bearer. Thus conversion to Islam behoves on the adherents to drop those names that reflect some attachment to Orisas (Yoruba traditional deities) and take on what Oseni (1980) calls names which are devoid of polytheism. Oseni (1980) notes that Muslim names can now be classified into three categories: (a) names connoting submission to God (e.g. Abdu'l Rahman, Abdu'lMalik, Abdu'l-Jalil), (b) names of the Prophet (e.g. Muhammad, Ahmad, Mahmud, Bashir) and (c) names of Islamic heroes and heroines. The last group is subdivided into three: (i) names of other Prophets of God (e.g. Adam, Nuh, Ibrahim, Yusuf, Yahya, Isa), (ii) names of angels (e.g. Jibril, Mikail, Ridwan) and (iii) prominent heroes and heroines (e.g. Abu Bakr, Umar, Ali, Uthman, Khadijah, Aisha, Maryam). Our observation is that Yoruba Muslims have tried to create Islamic names on the model of Yoruba as found in naming by circumstance. For example, children are named Jimo or Jamiu (male) and Anjimo (female) on the ground that they were born on a Friday which is the day of the Juma'h prayer. Examples of personal (Islamic) names are given in Table 4.5.

It is important to mention that the Yoruba have traditional titles to mark particular political roles certain individuals play in the governance of Yoruba traditional communities. The coming of Islam has, however,

Table 4.6 Arabic titles in Yoruba

Yoruba form	Arabic form	Gloss
Lemomu	imam	leader at congregational prayer
Ladani	al'adhan	caller to prayer
Seriki adiini	(sarki-) al-din	a hybrid of Hausa and Arabic words, meaning a leader of the *ummah*/Islam
Balogun adiini		captain of the *ummah*/Islam
Iyalode adiini		woman leader/madam of the *ummah*
Alaaji	al-hajj	someone who has performed the pilgrimage to Mecca

also brought new titles to reflect the new status that emerged with the development of the Muslim *ummah* or community in Yorubaland. Such titles relate most especially to religious roles and commitment to the *ummah*. Examples of such titles are given in Table 4.6.

Medicine and healing

In Salami (2006), I mentioned earlier that the Yoruba people are pragmatic as far as religious practice is concerned. It must be noted also that as observed by Horton (1971, cited in Barret 1991), the Yoruba religion itself is very dynamic as it tends to respond to the problem of meaning generated by rampant social change or as a result of social circumstances. Thus the Yoruba consider that problems of existence to be solved are of this world, this life and its continuity (Hallgren 1988: 9). For the Yoruba, religious and social lives are not often perceived to be in conflict. Therefore, we can readily find traditional thinking, attitudes and behaviour among Yoruba Muslims. As noted by Hallgren (1988: 172), Yoruba religious attitudes are life supporting and this is why the wishes of (traditional) Yoruba people concern the best possible existence on earth – health, wealth and children. Thus they were, among other things, endeared to Islam ostensibly by their belief that the Arabic teachers and *alfa*s (Muslim clerics) possessed some occult powers transmitted to them through their knowledge of the language. In other words, they thought that the Arabic language must be imbued with some magical powers. Divination, preparation and application of medicines and charms and amulets as found in *yepe tite, hantu, tira* and *yaasin kike* among Yoruba Muslims bear some testimony to the cultural impact of Arabic–Islamic culture on Yoruba. According to Mitchell (1970, cited in Barret 1991: 23), for the Yoruba, Islam contains within it a functional alternative to the cultural emphases of traditional Yoruba religion such as the *alfa* who provides divination and healing services much like the Yoruba *babalawo*. For Mitchell, this is saying that Islam already provides the explanation–prediction–control function that Yoruba wanted.

Conclusion

I have attempted, in this chapter, to show that the Islamic religion, via its language of liturgy – Arabic – has impacted the Yoruba language. In doing this, I have tried to demonstrate that a number of lexical items covering aspects of material and intellectual cultures which were foreign to Yoruba before the contact with Arabic–Islamic culture have been borrowed.

I have also shown that Islam, via Arabic, has not only impacted the Yoruba lexicon but also has caused changes in the Yoruba world view. This can be seen particularly in the aspect of naming where the influence of the religion on Yoruba personal identity is immense. Yoruba converts to Islam dropped their Yoruba indigenous names for Arabic–Islamic names. Although the history and narratives surrounding names are still very important to the Yoruba, with Islam some attempts are made to relate such histories to the lives of past prophets or important personalities in early Islam. This change will, however, make it today more difficult to keep family histories and narratives in names.

Finally, the study shows, however, that the process of religious and language accommodation between Arabic and Yoruba has been largely unidirectional to the advantage of Arabic–Islamic culture. It was probably as a result of this pervasive presence of Arabic–Islamic culture in Yorubaland that some Yoruba Muslims were motivated to demand the introduction of Islamic law (sharia) to the south-west of Nigeria in the wake of the expansion of the sharia legal system in Northern Nigeria.

References

Abdul, M. A. (1976) 'Arabic Loan Words in Yoruba'. *YORUBA: Journal of the Yoruba Studies Association of Nigeria*, 2, 37–42.

AbuBakre, R. D. (1984) 'The Learning of Arabic by Yoruba Speakers.' *JOLAN: Journal of the Linguistics Association of Nigeria*, 2, 143–52.

Barret, S. R. (1991) 'Issues and Perspectives on Religion and Society', in J. K. Olupona and T. Falola (eds), *Religion and Society in Nigeria*, Ibadan: Spectrum Books Limited.

Bynon, T. (1977) *Historical Linguistics*. Cambridge: Cambridge University Press.

Chiung, Wi-vun, T. (2006) *Lexical Change and Variation in Taiwanese Literary Texts, 1916–1998*. supercrawler.com/science/social sciences/.../Sino-Tibetan/ Taiwanese. Recovered 25/5/06.

Crystal, D. (1976) 'Nonsegmental Phonology in Religious Modalities', in William J. Samarin (ed.), *Language in Religious Practice*, Rowley, Mass.: Newbury House Publishers Inc., pp. 17–25.

Falola, T. (ed.) (2005) 'Introduction', in *Christianity and Social Change in Africa: Essays in Honour of J. D. Y. Peel*. Durham, NC: Carolina Academic Press, pp. 3–25.

Francis, W. N. (1983) *Dialectology: an Introduction*. London: Longman.

Hakan, R. (1983) 'Borrowing and Lexical Transfer'. *Applied Linguistics*, 4(3), 208–12.

Hallgren, R. (1988) *The Good Things in Life: a Study of the Traditional Religious Culture of the Yoruba People*. Loberod: Bokforlaget plus Ultra.

Heath, J. (1984) 'Language Contact and Language Change'. *Annual Review of Anthropology*, 13, 367–84.

Higa, M. (1979) 'Sociolinguistic Aspects of Word-Borrowing', in W.F. Mackey and J. Orstein (eds), *Sociolinguistic Studies in Language Contact: Methods and Cases*, The Hague: Mouton, pp. 277–91.

Labov, W. (ed.) (1972) *Sociolinguistic Patterns*. Philadelphia: University of Pennsylvania Press.

Malik, S. H. A. (1995) 'The Impact of Arabic on the Linguistic and Cultural Life of the Yoruba People', in Kola Owolabi (ed.), *Language in Nigeria: Essays in Honour of Ayo Bamgbose*, Ibadan: Book Publishers, pp. 424–39.

Milroy, L. (1987) *Language and Social Networks*. Oxford: Basil Blackwell.

Odhiambo, E. (2002) 'The Cultural Dimensions of Development in Africa'. *African Studies Review*, 45(3), 1–16.

Ogunbiyi, Z. I. (1980) 'Phonological Problems Faced by the Yoruba-Speaking Learners of Arabic Language'. *NATAIS: a Journal of the Nigerian Teachers of Arabic and Islamic Studies*, 2(1), 109–27.

Olaniyan, R. (1982) 'Islamic Penetration of Africa', in R. Olaniyan (ed.), *African History and Culture*, Lagos, Nigeria: Longman Nigeria Limited, pp. 38–55.

Oseni, Z. I. (1980) 'Islamic Names in Nigeria'. *NATAIS: a Journal of the Nigerian Teachers of Arabic and Islamic Studies*, 2(1), 37–50.

Salami, L. Oladipo (2006) 'Creating God in our Image: the Attributes of God in Yoruba Socio-Cultural Environment', in Tope Omoniyi and Joshua A. Fishman (eds), *Explorations in the Sociology of Language and Religion*, Amsterdam: John Benjamins, pp. 97–118.

Samarin. W. J. (ed.) (1976) *Language in Religious Practice*. Rowley, Mass.: Newbury House.

Weinreich, U. (1974) *Languages in Contact*. The Hague: Mouton.

5
Authenticating a Tradition in Transition: Language of Hinduism in the US

Rajeshwari V. Pandharipande

1 Introduction

'Language of religion' is as illusive a concept (if not more) as 'religion' and it is understood differently within different disciplines. For example, sociolinguists treat language of religion as a register of a natural language, which they perceive as a system or a resource from which utterances are composed (Samarin 1976). In linguists' view, what separates language of religion from its non-religious counterpart is the selection of linguistic material at different levels (lexical, syntactic, phonological, semantic, stylistic, etc.) in the religious register. A theologian, on the other hand, may treat language of religion as a construct of thoughts which is different from its non-religious counterpart, and which is expressed through various linguistic structures. This difference in the perspectives on the language of religion is relevant for the discussion on the change, conflict and accommodation within the framework of the sociology of language of religion. For the sociolinguists, the change and conflict would imply the change and conflict in the choice of the linguistic code (and its function), linguistic repertoire of the speech community, and the linguistic structure as well as the function of the language of religion. Similarly, accommodation would mean the structural and/or functional changes within the new system to resolve conflict. In particular, sociolinguists' inquiry focuses on the following questions: (a) which sociocultural change affects the linguistic repertoire of the speech community? (b) how does the change in the repertoire change the choice of the language of religion (functional distribution of languages)?, and (c) what is the impact of the change on the structure/function of the language of religion? In contrast to this, theologians' inquiry would focus more on the impact of the sociocultural change and/or the change in the linguistic code (at the structural and/or at the functional level(s)) on the thought patterns (or the deep structure) of the system of religion. I argue that in order to adequately answer the above questions, we must take into account perspectives of both disciplines – linguistics and religious studies.

It is important to note here that the extent and nature of the impact of the sociocultural change on languages and religions and the accommodation of the change crucially depend on the extent of the variability in the correlation between a particular language and the religion expressed by it. For example, the relationship between Islam (religious meaning) and the Arabic language (the linguistic code) is relatively invariable compared to Hinduism where there is a high degree of variability of languages (Sanskrit, Hindi, Bangla, Marathi, etc.) of the religion. Therefore, the impact of the change in the sociocultural setting on the languages of Islam and Hinduism will not be the same. I argue that for an adequate understanding of the change in the language of religion, it is necessary for the framework of sociology of religion to take into account the perspectives of linguists as well as theologians. Another important but hitherto ignored dimension of change and accommodation is the issue of authentication of the change in the language of religion within the new sociocultural context. In other words, we may ask, what is the authority which sanctions the change, and what is the mechanism of this process of authentication?

In his monumental work on the multifaceted relationship between language and ethnicity, Fishman (1999: 4) points out,

> The last third of the twentieth century – often referred to as a time of ethnic revival – has often been witness to a renewed stress on language in various mobilizations of ethnicity throughout the world. How and when the link between language and ethnicity comes about, its salience and potency, its waxing and waning, its inevitability and the possibility of its sundering, all need to be examined. And, as with ethnicity and ethnic identity, so too in the case of language and its manifold links with ethnicity: varied regional and disciplinary perspectives overtime would be highly desirable and is undoubtedly overdue.

Additionally, Fishman (2006: 18) correctly claims, 'All sources of sociolinguistic change are also sources of change in sociolinguistic repertoire vis-à-vis religion, including religious change per se.'

This chapter is based on two major points in the above quotes: one, the need for regional and disciplinary perspectives to examine the link between language and ethnicity, and second, sociocultural change (source of sociolinguistic change) affects the language of religion (sociolinguistic repertoire). The chapter examines the language of transplanted Hindu tradition, which is currently undergoing tremendous transformation in the United States (US hereafter), and argues for the need to answer the following hitherto ignored major questions for an adequate understanding of change (transformation) and its conventionalization in the new sociocultural context: (a) when a tradition, Hinduism in this case, and the language, which expresses it, undergo change in a new sociocultural context, who authenticates these changes? (the question of authority), (b) which strategies are used to promote, crystallize and conventionalize those changes? (the question of the mechanism of its conventionalization), and (c) how do these changes affect the language structure and function on the one hand, and the religious system on the other?

It will be demonstrated with evidence that these changes (among others) conflict with the traditional 'authority' of scriptures, religious practices, and most importantly, the internal logic of the religious system (which justifies the choice of a language, religious content, and practices). It will be further argued that the Hindu mystics and saints (who function as a link between India and the US), who are traditionally viewed as 'authority' by the Hindu community and who conventionalize those changes by incorporating them in their religious practices in the US, are instrumental in resolving the conflict. The chapter will discuss the strategies used by the mystics and the saints to accommodate the 'global' influences (the use of English for example) by redefining and reconstructing the 'local' (Hindu) identity in the US. Finally, the chapter will raise some important questions for understanding the new ethnicities in the world, where the micro- and macro-identities are intertwined and continuously reconstructed and expressed through a complex network of linguistic codes, and more than one system of logic. For example, the discussion raises the question, namely, when English is used for Hinduism, does its semantics change? Does the theology of Hinduism change? The discussion in this chapter will present a framework for cross-cultural and cross-linguistic analysis of language of religion in diaspora, and the role of the 'authority' in determining its structure and function.

2   Sociocultural change: the Hindu diaspora in the US

In this section, I will focus on the change in the sociocultural context of the Hindu community in the US. One of the major impacts of globalization in the last few decades is the large-scale migration of people from their native to the new homeland, which is perceived as the land of opportunities. Although migration from India to the US dates back to the eighteenth century, a large number of Indian immigrants arrived after the 1965 Immigration Act signed by Lyndon Johnson. While the Indian immigrant population is religiously, linguistically and regionally diverse, recent (2001) record[1] shows that 766,000 Hindus currently reside in the US. Religion has become a major marker of their sociocultural identity in the US (Fenton 1998, Pettys 1994, Rangasamy 2001, Saran and Eams 1988, Williams 1996, among others). Thus for a large fraction of the Hindu diaspora, maintenance of Indian sociocultural identity equals maintenance of their Hindu identity. The Hindu immigrants in the US have come from different nations (India, UK, Uganda, Kenya, South Africa, Fiji, etc.) and their castes, languages, sects and regional affiliations (in India) are varied. However, they share the common motivation of maintaining their Hindu identity in the US. Regardless of their mutual differences, the axis at which they converge is the Hindu religious rituals (specifically related to the life cycle). The religious rituals have become an important space for the Hindus to articulate and transfer their Hindu heritage to their children in the US.

Some of the factors which differentiate the Hindu community in the US from its counterpart in India, are:

(a) Hinduism is a majority religion in India while it is not in the US, where the Indian/Hindu community is surrounded by the two dominant religions (Christianity and Judaism). As much as the Hindus in the US would like to maintain their Hindu identity separately from the dominant religions, the mode of presentation, expression and communication of religions through well-established churches, the Sunday services/schools, and most importantly, through the English language have significantly impacted the Hindu religious practices in the US. Whether it is the Hindu temple in Hawaii, the Aurora Balaji temple in Chicago, Vedanta Center in Los Angeles, or the Hindu-Jain temple in Pittsburgh, the Sunday school has become a prominent institution for the Hindu religious practices. Unlike in India, in most temples in the US the announcements are in English, and in many temples, the priests explain the rituals in English even when the performance of the rituals is in Sanskrit or other Indian languages. Additionally, a number of temples and Hindu groups use English as the language of rituals as well;

(b) in India, there is no emphasis on consolidating the Hindu community at the cost of compromising differences among various sects of

Hinduism. In contrast to this, in the US the diasporic Hindu community generally strives to be inclusive of Hindus' various nationalities (Indian, Kenyan, South African, British among others) with diverse Hindu sects in order to consolidate the community;

(c) one of the most important differences is that the sociocultural context in India (which naturally provides the experiential dimension of religion within which to sustain religious identity, is absent in the US. Therefore, the Hindu community tries very hard to compensate for it by 'recreating' the Indian/Hindu ambiance through rituals, as well as through the cultural events so that the young generation can directly experience the culture and religion;

(d) unlike in India, the identity of the Hindu community in the US is hyphenated, 'Hindu-Indian-American'. Thus the Hindu identity is intertwined with the Hindu identity in India (which they see as their 'roots') as well as with their new American identity. In particular, the younger generation, born and brought up in the US, uses English in practically all walks of life. Their exposure to Indian languages is relatively limited. Therefore, similar to the Jewish, Buddhist, Muslim and other religions in the US, the religious instruction (with the exception of the Qur'an) is imparted in English. The history of these religions shows that there has been a gradual switch to English to a large extent from the original languages of the respective religions; and finally

(e) it is important to note that the US is one of the largest democracies which allows freedom of speech and freedom of religion. Moreover, the US is constitutionally a multi-religious nation where religious communities coexist and influence one another.

As Eck (2001: 384) points out,

> ...our religious traditions are constantly influencing one another. Christians encounter the faith of new Sikh or Hindu neighbors and rethink what it means to speak of God's universal providence. ...Jews in Sacramento find new allies in Christian and Muslim neighbors in the wake of synagogue burnings. Christians in Roslindale find themselves moved by the spirit of forgiveness they find in their Vietnamese Buddhist neighbors.

In this context it is important to understand that the Hindu religious community is constantly influencing and being influenced by the other religious communities. Therefore, the language of religion (as understood by the linguists and theologians) would not escape this mutual influence. The nature of change, conflict, accommodation and authority vis-à-vis the language of Hinduism needs to be analysed and understood against the backdrop of the above sociocultural context.

3 Change in the language of Hinduism in the US

In this section, I will discuss the change in the structure as well as the function of the language of Hinduism in the US: (a) one of the major changes in the form of the language of Hinduism is the introduction of English in the Hindu practices. English, which is viewed as a 'foreign' and 'spiritually polluted language' by the Hindu community (and therefore excluded from the Hindu rituals) in India, is readily used in some Hindu temples and the rituals of some of the sects of Hinduism in the US; (b) Sanskrit–English code-mixing is used in many worship rituals in both domestic and public religious practices; (c) English translations of the Hindu scriptures (the Vedas, the Bhagavadgita) are treated as legitimate Hindu scriptures and their recitation as religious ritual and; (d) composition and recitation of Hindu prayers in English, the use of the Sanskrit meters for the English compositions, and their recitation in the traditional Hindu style are acceptable practices in the domain of Hindu rituals.

It is important to note here that the use of Sanskrit and modern Indian languages in the religious practices also continues. The difference between India and the US is that English is not used in the religious rituals in India but it is in the US. Consider the following examples: the following devotional prayers and chants are taken from the book (*Saaii Devotional Songs*) put together and used by the devotees of the mystic/saint named Satya Saaii Baabaa (a contemporary Hindu saint in India, who is worshipped as an *avataara* [incarnation of God]) during their ritual worship offered to the saint. The text is a mixture of prayers (a) composed in English, (b) taken from the ancient Hindu scriptures in Sanskrit, (c) composed in or taken from the scriptures originally composed in modern Indian languages. Those are recited alternatively in the same ritual. The devotees code-switch between these languages within the same worship ritual. Although code-switching between Sanskrit and other modern Indian languages is not uncommon in India, the inclusion of English is certainly unique to this ritual in the US. Consider the following examples.

The use of English in Hindu rituals

I. Prayers in English[2]

(From the booklet *Saaii Devotional Songs* (devotional songs dedicated to the mystic/saint Saaii Baabaa).)

(1) Song 847 (page 208)

> O *Lord,* Take my Love, Let it Flow in Full devotion to thee (yes, it is)
> O Lord, Take my hands, Let Them work Unceasingly for Thee
> O Lord, Take my Soul, Let it merge in perfect oneness with thee
> O Lord, take my Everything, and Let Me Be an Instrument for Thee

(2) Song 691 (page 18)

> Love in My Heart, Love in My Home
> Love in My Life, Saaii is love
> Saaii is my heart, Saaii is My Home
> Saaii is My Life, Saaii is My Own
> Love, Love, love Is *God*
> Live, Live, Live In Love
> Love, Love, Love, In God
> Live, Live, Live In Love
> Halleluijah, Halleluijah, Halleluijah

(3) Song 1 (page 19)

> A Temple in My Heart, A Prayer in my Soul, a Song on my
> – Lips And I Sing to You.

> *Chorus:*
> Baabaa Saaii Baabaa Satya Saaii Baabaa Baabaa Saaii Baabaa I sing to you
> Satya Saaii Baabaa Baabaa Saaii Baabaa Satya Saaii Baabaa I call to You
> – Lips and I call to You.
> (Chorus: Baabaa Saaii Baabaa ...

II. Code-mixing: English with Sanskrit

(4) Devotional chants (page 17)

> I am God, I am God, I am No different From God, I am The Infinite Supreme, The one Reality, I am *Sat-Chit-Aananda-Svaruupa*, I am *Om, Tat Sat Om*

(Sanskrit: sat 'truth', chit 'consciousness', aananda 'joy', svaruupa 'embodiment', 'I am the embodiment of truth, consciousness, and joy')

(5) Code-switching from English to Hindi within the same ritual of chanting God's name (page 19)
(This Hindi song is written in English/Georgian script.)

Abhinandan He Saaii hamaaraa
Shubha Janam Din Aaj Tumhaaraa
Dhanya Dhanya he Sat Guru Deva
Sikhaa rahe Jo Gyaan Dhyaan Sevaa
Kripa Karo Ab Sab Bhakton par
Aas Liye KhaDe hai Darbaar
Abhinandana –

'O Saaii (please accept) our best wishes today is your auspicious birthday, *O Guru!* The blissful one! The blissful one, Who gives (us) the knowledge, concentration and service. Have mercy on your devotees, who are waiting at your door full of hope. Our best wishes –'

(6) Switch to Sanskrit prayers: Song 748 (page 186)

Maataa Maheshvarii Tribhvana Jananii
Premamayii Satya Saaii jananii
Shivamana mohinii Paapa Vinaashinii
Veda Kalaamayiikalyana Daayinii
Jagadoddhaari~ii Parti Naraaya~ii
Premamyii Satya Saii jananii.

'Mother of three worlds, Mother Satya Saaii Baabaa, whose form is love, destroys sins and is lord Shiva's delight. The resident of Parti, mother of the Vedas and arts, bestows good fortune and sustains the universe.'

(7) Switch to Telugu: Song 21 (page 24)

Allah Yeshu Buddha Deva Andar Niivee
Maulå Saaii Mahaaviir Naanak Niivee
Raama Krishna Shiva Ruupa Dhaariyu Niive
Matmulanni Puujinchu Deevudu Niivee
Sarva Dharma Priya Satya Saaiivi Nivee
Saaii Raam Saaii Raam Saaii Raam Satya Saaii Raam

'O Saaii, You are Allah, Jesus, Buddha, Mahavir, Nanak, Krishna, and Shiva. You are the essence of all religions. Followers of all religions pray to you.'

(8) Switch to Tamil

Allåh Yesu Niiyanro
Anaittumee Saayii Un Uruvamanro
Makkaa Madinaa Vaazh Deivamanro
Nabigal Naayagam Niiyallavo
Buddha Mahaaviir Zoaastranumi
Y'suvai Avataaram Seidavanee
Ellayillaa Karunai kadalallavo
Nambinaarkkaruibvam Niiyallvo

'Lord Saaii, you are Allah and Jesus. Everything visible is Your own form. You are the Lord Nabi of Mecca and Median. Incarnated previously as Buddha, Mahavir, Zoaraster and Jesus. You are the boundless ocean of compassion and the lord who blesses the faithful.'

It is interesting to note that the above prayers are in many different Indian languages (English, Hindi, Sanskrit, Telugu and Tamil). Examples (1)–(4) are of the prayers in English while example (5) is in Hindi, (6) in Sanskrit, (7) in Telugu and (8) in Tamil. Example (4) shows English–Sanskrit code-mixing. This pattern of using English is not restricted only to the sect of Saaii Baabaa. In many other Hindu temples/shrines English is indeed used for the prayers. For example, in the Vedanta Center of Chicago, which is a monastery of the Ramakrishna order, the morning prayer is in English (mixed with a few Sanskrit phrases in italic).

(9) 'Song of the Sanyaasin' Strike off thy fetters!

Bonds that bind you down,
Of shining gold or darker baser ore;
Love, hate, good, bad – and the dual
Throng,
Know, slave is slave, caressed or whipped,
Not free;
For fetters, though of gold are not less to bind,
Then off with them Sanyaasii bold!
Say, '*om tat sat om!*'

This prayer is not a translation; rather, it is originally composed in Sanskrit by Swami Vivekananda (see Swami Nikhilananda 1953: 863), the most well-known disciple of Ramakrishna. The last sentence in Sanskrit means 'that (divine) is indeed the eternal truth/reality'.

(10) English translations of the original scriptures (in Sanskrit)
In some Hindu temples (in the Hare Krishna temple In Honolulu, among others), English translations of the ancient Hindu scriptures (originally in Sanskrit) are treated as scriptures and read/recited as part of the ritual practices by the devotees. For example, the following couplet is taken from the Hindu scripture, the Bhagawadgita (3: 30)

mayi sarvaaNi karmaaNi samnyasyaadhyaatmacetasaa |
niraashiinirmamo bhuutvaa yudhyasva vigatajvra ||

'Therefore, O Arjuna, surrendering all your works unto Me with mind intent on Me, and without desire for gain and free from egoism and lethargy, fight.'

(11) Hindu concepts presented in the prayer in English (*Saaii Devotional Songs: Song 1248* (page 296))
In all of the above English prayers, the code/medium is English and the content is Hindu. In the following prayer, the Hindu theological concept of the Divine is expressed, i.e. the Divine is the only all-pervasive, eternal reality, and the perception of the separate forms is not real:

There is no Birth, There is no Death, There is no You or I.
There is Only Satya Saaii beloved Satya Saaii
Satya Saaii Satya Saaii, beloved Satya Saaii
There Is No Sun, There IS No Moon, There Is No You or I
There is Only Satya Saaii, beloved Satya Saaii
Satya Saaii Satya Saaii, beloved Satya Saaii

4 Change and accommodation: diglossia of a different kind

The above discussion shows that the inclusion of English has changed the linguistic repertoire of the Hindu community. The question may be asked, how is the choice of the languages determined? Or is the choice random? The answer is: the choice is not random. Different groups use different languages for the same functions. The priests use Sanskrit or modern Indian languages for performing rituals. The use of English as the language of rituals by the priests is not common. The priests generally use English for explanations of the rituals for the linguistically diverse congregation. Similarly, the priests give sermons in English, and all of the announcements in the temples/shrines are generally in English.

Those devotees who know Sanskrit recite prayers and perform rituals in Sanskrit. If they do not know Sanskrit, or do not know it well enough to use it, they use English or other Indian languages for rituals. This group generally performs domestic rituals in modern Indian languages, and almost always communicates with the second generation in English. This group may use Sanskrit vocabulary in the religious discourse.

The non-Indian (American) Hindus, and the second-generation young Hindus of Indian descent, who do not know Sanskrit or other Indian languages, mostly use English for rituals, discussions and other communication in the private or public domains.

This diglossia is presented in Figures 5.1–5.4.

In order to fully understand the change and accommodation in the language of Hinduism, it is necessary to analyse Figures 5.1–5.4 together. Figure 5.4 shows that English, which is absent in the religious rituals in India, is readily included within all domains of religion (actual ritual performance, explanations of rituals, philosophical discussions, religious sermons, etc.) However, Figure 5.3 shows that everybody does not use English in all of these domains of religion. The diglossia illustrated in Figures 5.1–5.3 clearly shows the distribution of languages according to the users as well. The inclusion of English in the linguistic repertoire of the Hindu community has changed the repertoire as well as the structure of the language of Hinduism. English took over the function of other modern Indian languages in the religious domain of sermons, explanations of the rituals, and philosophical discussions since it is the dominant language spoken by everyone in the community in the US. In the other domains (see Figure 5.4), English provides an alternative to other Indian languages. While the

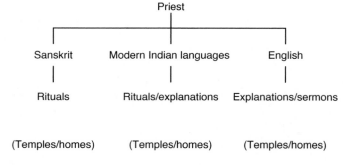

Figure 5.1   Diglossia: priests' languages

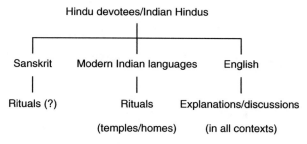

Figure 5.2   Diglossia: languages of Hindu devotees/Indian Hindus

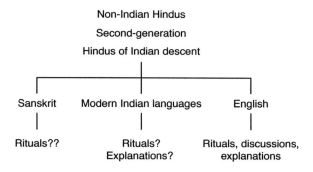

Figure 5.3   Expanding use of English in religious domains

change in the function of English (i.e. its use for expressing Hinduism) has changed the structure of English (code-mixing with Indian languages, borrowing vocabulary, and the Hindu concepts), it has also created a new correlation between English form/linguistic structure and the Hindu content. This new function has significantly affected the semantics of English. The words such as 'God', 'divine love', 'life', 'death', 'soul', 'incarnation', etc. have taken new Hindu meanings. In my earlier work (Pandharipande 1992, 2006) I discussed exactly the opposite situation in India where Indian languages are used to express many religions such as Hinduism, Christianity, Sikhism, Buddhism, etc. I argued there that in India, where Hindi is used as a language of Hinduism as well as Christianity (Buddhism and other religions), the 'clash' of semantics (Hindu and Christian) is resolved by using two sets of semantic structures, i.e. the word 'God' is contextually determined. The Hindi/Sanskrit word *Iishwar* 'God' when used in the context of

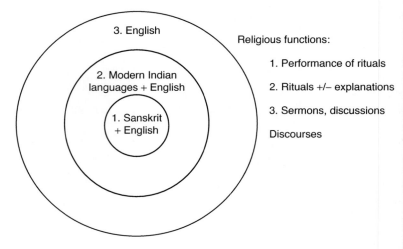

Figure 5.4   The functional distribution of the languages (independent of the users)

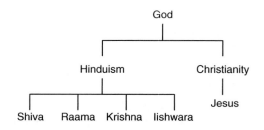

Figure 5.5   Semantic diglossia

Christianity would mean 'Christian God', in the context of Buddhism, it would mean 'the Buddha', etc. In the US, the situation is reverse. The English word 'God' in the US would convey the Hindu meaning in the context of Hinduism, while it would refer to the Christian God when used in Christianity. I would like to call this semantic diglossia. Figure 5.5 illustrates this point.

Current research on Hinduism in the US has not addressed the issues of accommodation of the newly introduced English in the repertoire of the languages of Hinduism.

5 Language as a system of thought: a religious studies perspective on the change and accommodation

The question which has received the least attention in the current literature on language of religion is: when a new language/code is introduced
to perform the function previously held by (ano)other language(s), does
the system of thought, that is, the system of religious belief in this case,
change as well? If it does, how is the change accommodated in the old
system? Before these questions are answered, it is necessary to know
the extent to which the relationship between the particular linguistic
structure (the medium of expression of the religious content) and the
system of thought (religious/content/beliefs) is perceived or believed to
be variable within a particular system. The more variable the perceived
connection, the easier it is to substitute one code for another.

As mentioned earlier, some theologians/scholars take the approach
that the language of religion is basically a system of thought (religious
beliefs), and therefore, the change of the linguistic code does not affect
the internal system of thought. As Barr (1979: 435) points out,

> Thus we may suspect that the 'language of religion' in Finnish
> Lutheranism is very similar to the structure of the 'language of reli-
> gion' in Swedish Lutheranism, although the two natural languages
> are of different structure and type. Conversely, an English Buddhist
> and an English conservative evangelical Christian may have diffi-
> culty in finding a common 'language of religion', though the natural
> language of both is identical.

Within this view then, the substitution of English for the Indian languages should not create any problem as long as English shares the same
religious content/function (Hinduism) with other Indian languages.

In this context, the challenging question related to accommodation
of English is: how would English, the language of Christianity and
Judaism, express Hinduism? Earlier in Section 3 it is shown within the
linguists' perspective, namely that English is mixed with the Sanskrit
vocabulary and style, and the Hindu scriptural content, when it is used
as a language of Hinduism. At the functional level, it is 'semantic diglossia' (see Section 3 above). That is, the meaning of the English vocabulary is contextually determined. Within the theologians' perspective,
the accommodation of the new code is at the 'deeper' level of religious
thought. That is, the vocabulary, meters and other structures (beyond

their) surface meanings, convey the religious meanings. For example, the term *'om'* (Sanskrit) or *'Iishwara'*, the term for God in Hinduism, when mixed with English, not only convey their respective surface meanings/connotation, but they also function as 'triggers' to reconstitute the entire discourse as Hindu. This is what Barr (1979) calls the 'radiation' effect. According to this perspective, the material from the Indian languages mixed with English has a performative function, i.e. it 'radiates' the Hindu meanings throughout the English discourse, thus changing the signification of other English vocabulary, syntax and semantics according to the Hindu system of thought.

Previously I pointed out (Pandharipadne 2001a) how the translators of the Sanskrit scripture, the Bhagavadgita, mix Sanskrit (the language of the original text) with English (the language of the translation) to transfer the Hindu meaning of the original Sanskrit scripture (for further discussion, see Pandharipande 2001a: 301–16). This discussion, though it appears persuasive, faces the following problems: one, it raises an important question, namely, when the typically Judaeo-Christian religious expression, Hallelujah, is used in a Hindu ritual, what happens to its semantics? Does it refer to the Hindu god, and means 'praise the lord Ganesha, Vishnu'? If *Om*, the Hindu expression in Sanskrit, functions as a 'trigger ' for reconstituting the discourse (in English) as Hindu, then is it not justified to assume that the Judaeo-Christian expression 'Hallelujah' (Hallelujah, in the text of the songs) will act as a 'trigger' for reconstituting the discourse as Judaeo-Christian? How can 'Hallelujah' (example 1) convey the Hindu meaning 'praise the Hindu god'? Second, with the prayers in English, where there are no 'triggers' (Hindu expressions) to radiate the Hindu meaning throughout the discourse (example 4), what makes the prayer a Hindu discourse?

A close examination of the linguistic structure and its religious function shows that the answers to the above questions cannot be sought within the boundaries and parameters of language structure/meaning. I argue that the relationship between the language structure and its religious meaning is established by the power which lies beyond linguistic structures. It is the 'authority' which determines this correlation. In the case of Hinduism, it is the authority of the Hindu mystics and saints who, by using expressions which are apparently semantically 'deviant', first establish and then conventionalize the new meaning. In this case, the use of 'Hallelujah' in the Hindu ritual devoted to Saaii Baabaa establishes a new correlation between the typically Judaeo-Christian expression 'Hallelujah' and the Hindu meaning. This role of the Hindu saints in changing the structure and function of religious language has a clear precedence in the history of Hinduism. When Jnaneshwar, the thirteenth-century Hindu saint, argued for the legitimacy of the regional language, Marathi, and its use for expressing Hinduism, he deviated from then established norm/tradition which prohibited use of any language other than Sanskrit. His commentary on the Bhagavadgita, the Bhaawaarthadiipika, not only replaces the Sanskrit (linguistic structure) but also introduces native Marathi (and not the classical Sanskrit) metaphors for conveying the Hindu religious meaning. In the following section, I will discuss the role of the 'authority' in particular, and of the mystics and saints in general, in introducing and conventionalizing changes in the language of Hinduism.

6 Authority

In order to understand how the changes and the accommodations are authenticated and conventionalized within the Hindu system in the US, it is necessary to understand (a) the authority which has the power to sanction changes, and (b) the processes or mechanisms through which the change is authenticated and conventionalized. For example, the Vatican/Church is perceived as the authority to sanction changes in Catholicism. In this section, I will discuss the (Hindu) 'system-internal' authority of the scriptures and mystics and saints within the Hindu tradition. Additionally, I will point out that the global media acts as the 'system-external' mechanism through which the change is sanctioned.

'Authority' has been defined as 'legitimate power to require and receive submission and obedience' (Waida 1987: 1). Waida (1987: 1) further points out that different religions invest authority in different sources at different points in time. He lists the following five sources of authorities accepted by different religions: (1) persons, (2) sacred writings, (3) traditions, oral and/or written, constituting doctrinal truths and ethical precepts, (4) religious communities with priesthood and sacramental rites, (5) personal experience. Although the Vedas are the most ancient Hindu scriptures that are composed in Sanskrit, a large number of scriptures which were composed/written after the Vedas are also accepted as valid Hindu scriptures over a long period of 2000 years. These scriptures vary in their languages (ranging from Sanskrit to modern Indian languages), styles and their religious content. Therefore, the use of a new language (English in this case) to express Hinduism is not unique to Hinduism.

In the new sociocultural and religious context of the US, the Hindu mystics and saints reinterpret and redefine the tradition, authenticate it and practise it because they are perceived as the link between the roots of the Hindu tradition (in India), and its new residence in the US. The Hindu mystics and saints function as the 'scriptures' – the authority and mechanism of the changes in the Hindu tradition in the US. For example, the Hindu mystics and saints readily use English (or English translation) in their religious practices in the US, and thereby authenticate its use in the religious rituals. Also, they use a variety of patterns of language of Hinduism in their religious practices, and thereby authenticate all of them (Pandharipande 2001b).

It is important to note here that this role of the mystics and saints as the authority is not new; rather, the history of Hinduism shows that (unlike Christianity, Judaism and Islam) the mystics and saints have always been viewed as the authority to authenticate the Hindu tradition, as well as its transformation, because they are viewed as the 'gurus' or the incarnations of the divine whose role is expected to be of the guide in the Hindu tradition (for further discussion on the role of a guru, see Gold 1987). Hinduism lacks a counterpart structure to that of the Christian Church that has authority to introduce or dismiss changes in the tradition, and in contrast has always invested such authority exclusively in the mystics and saints. Some of the noted examples are Jnaneshwar, a thirteenth-century saint who, for the first time, interpreted the Bhagavadgita (the third-century CE Sanskrit scripture) in Marathi (a regional/vernacular language), thereby authenticating the use of a regional language (instead of Sanskrit) as a legitimate code of religion; Tulsidas, a fifteenth-century saint who interpreted the Ramayana (the fourth-century religious BCE text) in Awadhi; and the Vairashrawa mystic saints (twelfth and thirteenth-centuries CE) who rewrote the Hindu tradition in the medium and idiom of the Kannada language in south India. In each case, the mystics transformed and contextualized the tradition according to the language, culture and the demands of the contemporary context and integrated the change into the tradition by reinterpreting it. I argue that the Hindu mystics and saints in contemporary times are performing their age-old function of transforming and authenticating the Hindu tradition in the US. The history of Hinduism documents the role of mystics and saints in contextualizing the religious system in the changing society at various points in time. The most striking feature of those changes has been the change in the religious language. The saints mentioned above (Jnaneshwar and Tulsidas, among others) authenticated the language of the *bahujanasamaaj* 'common people' for the religious practices, thereby making the religion accessible to the masses (for further discussion see Raghavan 1966, Ranade 1933 [1982]).

There are two types of Hindu mystics and saints: some, who arrived from India and made the US their permanent home (e.g. Prabhupada (late twentieth century), and Maharshi Mahesha Yogi, and monks in the Ramakrishna Mission (late nineteenth century) among others), and those who live in India but regularly visit the US (e.g. Amritanandamayi, Karunamayi, Dayananda Saraswati, Jaggi Vasudeva, among others). Both have adopted English as one of the languages of Hinduism in their religious practices. This is not to say that the extent of the use of English is the same across the saints. While all of them use English (themselves or through a translator) for sermons, discussions, teaching and conversations with their devotees, not all of them use English as a substitute for Sanskrit or modern Indian languages in the Hindu rituals. Amritananadamayi, a contemporary woman saint of India, sings *bhajans* 'devotional songs' in English (in addition to Hindi, Malayalam, Telugu, Kannada and Tamil), and many monasteries of the Ramakrishna order use English prayers as well as prayers in other languages (Sanskrit, Bangla and Hindi). In contrast to this, Dayananda Saraswati does not himself use English in the rituals, but allows his disciples to use it. In my own research, and in interviews of mystics and saints, I found that there is variation in the opinions of the saints regarding the extent to which English should be used in Hindu religious practices. One of the saints said,

> I believe it is absolutely alright to use English if that is the language through which the devotees feel connected to the Divine. However, for myself, I believe, the use of English translations of the Vedas as a substitute for its Sanskrit counterpart is not acceptable. It is the sound of the Vedas in the rituals, which has the transformative effect on the consciousness of the devotees. The use of English will not be effective in this context.

Since the mystics and saints are viewed as the authority, their use of English as well as their sanction for the use of English by devotees, and the scriptural sanction for the use of different languages, have contributed to the acceptance of English as one of the languages of Hinduism in the US. What is different about the present role of these Hindu mystics is that they not only serve as the communicators of the Hindu tradition in the new context, but they also serve as the link among the Hindus (in India, and the US), as well as the non-Hindu Americans in the US.

7   Media as the medium/mechanism

In the contemporary world, media (both audio and visual) plays an important role in constructing and authenticating ideologies and identities. The media is the 'magic' which (re)constructs the phenomenal 'now' in language, pictures, music, dance, etc. It is a powerful mechanism to 'fix' the temporal moment as 'real'. English is used in over 100 websites of/for the Hindu mystics and saints in the US (or English mixed with Sanskrit and other Indian languages) to inform the Hindu (and non-Hindu) global communities (including American) about the background, activities, sermons and teachings of the Hindu saints. There are CDs of the devotional songs, journals and magazines, videotapes, and cassettes of the songs, sermons and other rituals performed by the saints. In fact, there are websites (praarthnaa.com for example) of Hindu rituals of *puujaa* 'worship' which allow Hindus to experience the worship ritual online. Almost all of the magazines, books, CDs, tapes and flyers use English or a Sanskrit-code-mixed language for Hinduism. An unprecedented connection between English and Hinduism is being established in the US. Additionally, the grand promoter of the Hindu ideology, doctor Deepak Chopra, a cardiologist in California, uses English to treat his patients using Hindu spirituality-based holistic medicine, and with his tremendous success in the field, he has inadvertently placed a stamp on the use of the Sanskrit–English code-mixed language.

The increased popularity of Ayurvedic medicine and yoga has certainly promoted the use of English in practising their systems. In the advertisements of yoga ('the Yoga Bolly workout', for example), Sanskrit couplets are played to Indian music and the commentary on good health is in English. On the one hand, this process marks the secularization of Hinduism, and authentication of the use of English for the process on the other.

In fact, the websites are equipped for the audience to offer *puujaa* (the worship ritual) to the deities in India, sitting at the computer in the US; the instructions for performing the ritual are given in English. However, the language of the most of the rituals can be Sanskrit, Hindi or English. Example (12) below is an excerpt in English, which explains the meaning of worship (*puujaa*) [from website: www.eprathana.com/virtual/vpooja.asp dedicated to a woman saint, Amritanandamayi] and the ritual of *puujaa,* which the devotees are expected to perform online! In South Indian Hindu tradition, devotees 'order' in the temple the worship ritual to be performed for a particular deity (of their choice) by the priest on their behalf. In the virtual worship, the names of the deities are given and the devotees are asked to choose the deities and the temples in India. The following text is taken from the website. The audience is guided by the instructions to perform the *pooja* (online). As is clear from the excerpt, the worship ritual is practically performed in English, thereby authenticating its use in the Hindu ritual.

(12) Puja[3]
'Your heart is like the real temple. It is there that you must install God. Good thoughts are the flowers to be offered to Him. Good actions are worship. Good words are hymns. Love is divine offering.' *Puja* or worship is an offering made to the divine and can take several forms. Mental worship is when one meditates on one's chosen deity. Whereas ritualistic worship takes the form of *puja* in which a sacred offering such as flowers, fruits, rice or vermilion powder are tendered to the divine on auspicious days amidst Vedic chants.

Image gallery. About gods and goddesses
This virtual *pooja* section was created purely for your viewing pleasure. This is in no way connected to the orders you place. Your orders/Archnas will be performed at the temple of your choice and temple's Prasadam (the food blessed by the divine) will be shipped to you.

Virtual *poojas* (names of deities)

Amman	Ayypam
Balaji	Ganesha
Hanuman	Krishna
Lakshni	Murugan
Rama	Sai
Baba	Shiva

Please make sure your speakers are switched on to listen to mantras.
    Click on the different artefacts like the bell, flowers, *aarti* and coconut to perform the virtual *pooja*.
    All virtual *poojas* require flash shockwave plug-in installed.

In addition to websites, CDs of the devotional songs are available online as well as in the shops. They show quite an interesting mix of the English language, Christian gospel music and Hindu religious lyrics. The CDs are played at the religious congregation of the saints who authenticate this mixture!

There are websites which provide original Sanskrit (or other Indian language) texts accompanied by their English translations. The devotees are expected to choose from the two. While the recitation of the scriptures is a very well-established Hindu ritual, the recitation of the text in its English translation is becoming common in the US, and is being accepted as a legitimate Hindu ritual. The following text is taken from a CD which is a collection of devotional songs offered as prayers to the woman saint, Amritanandamayi, who, though permanently based in Amritapuri in southern India, visits the US very frequently. The CD contains lyrics which were originally composed in English. The music is a mixture of Indian classical and gospel (Christian) music. The devotees of the saint Amritanandamayi arrange the lyrics and the music.

(13) Sweetness of devotion

> The sweetness of Devotion, like a gentle
> morning rain, will cleanse the heart of
> selfishness and wash away the pain.

1. the fear of separation, like shadows in
   the night, will vanish as the dawn of truth
   reveals its golden light.

2. The tears that come from longing, are
   like rivers made of fire. They burn into my
   aching heart like embers of desire.

3. The secret of surrender lives in children
   everywhere. They love the world with
   innocence, and laughter that they share.

4. To all who wish for happiness,
   remember what is true, the love you give
   with every breath will soon return to you.

The write-up on the CD says, 'The songs presented here range from those that gently blend East Indian and Western influences, to those in which the two styles are woven intricately together.' 'The instruments heard are: harmonium, *tabla* (drums), bells, tambourine, violin, flute, guitar, synthesizer, electric sitar, and bass. The music has been arranged and presented by followers of Mata Amritanandmayi (Ammachi).' The CDs are played and sold at the religious congregations of the saint.

This is an example of how the use of English as well as the blend of the Hindu and non-Hindu music is being authenticated by the saints, and is promoted by using the media.

Here, the accommodation of English, and the non-Hindu music serves many functions: consolidating the linguistically diverse Hindu community, the Hindu youth who typically lacks knowledge of Sanskrit and/or other Indian languages, but who is fluent in English, and most importantly, to let the devotees know that this process of connecting with the divine through listening to the mantras on the website is sanctioned by the saint. As the ancient Hindu saints contextualized Hinduism in general and the language of Hinduism in particular in the changing Indian society where Hinduism was located, the saints are contextualizing the religion as well as the language in the new American socio-cultural context.

The important but hitherto totally ignored question we may ask here is: does this mixing of the languages, music and thought remain at the theologically 'peripheral' level of Hinduism, or has it penetrated into the theology and the theological meaning is changing as well. I argue that it has. For example, in the US, the priests use the modern 'logic' or rationale to explain the use of offering coconut to the deities in the ritual. The rationale for offering a coconut in the ritual is explained as follows: a coconut is covered with a coarse shell like the mind with the ego. Removing the shell and breaking the coconut signifies removing the ego (which covers up the pure mind) and breaking it so that we can get to the pure 'mind', which is offered to the deity. Moreover, as Narayanan (1996) points out, in the Tamil Srinivaasa tradition, *Garuda* 'eagle' and *SheSa* 'the serpent' are shown as Vishnu's servants (serpent as an umbrella to protect him, and the eagle as his vehicle).

However, Narayanan claims that in an article published by the Shiva-Vishnu Hindu temple in Pittsburgh, the serpent and the eagle are interpreted as symbols of animal instincts of anger and ego respectively, and the lord as the tamer of these animal instincts. According to Narayanan (1996: 168), 'this interpretation certainly seems to owe more to some western mode analysis than to traditional Hindu exegesis'. While Narayanan's reading may be right in the sense that the new interpretation marks a departure from the Hindu tradition in India, it certainly provides evidence for an important change in the theological interpretation of the religious phenomenon. The discussion here shows that the change in the language of religion influences the religious meaning. There are plenty of examples in the websites of Hinduism, as well as in the religious discourses, where a similar logic is used to explain the ancient Hindu traditions/customs. The phenomenon indicates a change in the Hindu system where a logic different from the tradition is introduced.

8   Contesting identities and the revival of Sanskrit

The discussion on transformation of language use will not be complete without mentioning the role of Sanskrit in the Hindu practices in the US. Sanskrit, which is only marginally understood by the Hindu community, is being revived in the US with great enthusiasm. Hindu temples are 'importing' priests trained in Sanskrit from India. Almost all of the public practices (as opposed to the rituals at home) are being performed in Sanskrit, and there is a pronounced emphasis on identifying Sanskrit as the marker of Hindu identity. While in India the local Indian languages are commonly used in rituals (both private and public), and the scriptures in those languages (Jnaneshwar, Ramcharitmanas, Hanuman Chalisa, etc.) are recited as legitimate scriptures.

The following example prayer recited in a Hindu temple (Venkateshwara Balaji temple) in Pittsburgh, Pennsylvania, succinctly elaborates the transformation and authentication of the system:

> *americaa Vaasa jaya govindaa*
> *Pennhill nilaya Raadhe govinda*
> *Sri guru jaya guru, vitthala govindaa!*
> (from the tape of the devotional songs sung at the temple)
>
> 'Victory to Govindaa¬ (the divine), whose home is the Penn Hills in America. Victory to Raadhaa (the consort of Govindaa¬) Govindaa¬! Victory to our revered Guru, to Vitthala, to Govindaa¬!'

Note that the prayer contextualizes the deity, Venkateshwara/Govinda, by naming Penn Hills as his residence in America, while maintaining the link with the original Hindu tradition by using Sanskrit (the language of highest efficacy), and the discourse pattern (of glorifying the deity) of traditional Hinduism. Moreover, the priest authenticates the prayer by using it in the ritual for consecration of the temple. The proposed project will discuss similar examples of the change in the language of Hinduism in the US.

Another example, which clearly shows the use of Sanskrit and Sanskrit scriptures as the markers of Hindu identity, is seen in almost all of the websites on Hinduism:

> A large number of websites mention *Shruti* (the ancient 'revealed' scriptures, the Vedas) and *Smriti* literature (the scriptures 'recalled' reinterpreted/created in the later period, and which contextualized

the earlier scriptures in the new social contexts). Most of those include exclusively the scriptures in Sanskrit and exclude those composed in the regional languages.

The discussion brings up an interesting issue of the conflicting relationship of the Hindus with English and Sanskrit. While English is the expression of their American identity and is essential for the communication of Hindu beliefs, Sanskrit is seen as the essential marker/differentia of their Hindu identity. I have argued earlier (Pandharipande 2001b) that the choice of Sanskrit as the identity marker of the culturally and linguistically diversified Hindu community is justified because Sanskrit is 'transparent' to the function of expressing Hinduism. It has never been used for any other religion. In contrast, other Indian languages such as Hindi, Marathi, Tamil, etc. are opaque to Hinduism, that is, they do not exclusively express Hindu identity since they are used for communicating other religions as well. This shows how a diasporic community struggles between two counteracting forces of assimilation with the majority culture (accommodation) and the need to maintain a distinctive identity in the context of cultural religious diversity in the US.

9 Conclusion

The major points in the above discussion can be summarized as follows:

(a) in the process of the accommodation of a new language (English) to perform the function of other languages, the structure of the language undergoes change, and in the process the 'meaning' (Hinduism, in this case) also undergoes change;

(b) in order to fully understand the process of accommodation of the change in religious language, it is necessary to take into account linguists' as well as theologians' views of language of religion;

(c) it is important to examine the authority which authenticates changes. The discussion points out that in the diasporic religious communities, the process of authentication of the changes is complex, i.e. it refers to two authorities, internal (saints and mystics) as well as the external, secular authority (of the media in this case);

(d) the discussion clearly shows that the macro-level social phenomenon of globalization, i.e. migration of religion communities, has micro-level implications for the structure and function of religious language on the one hand, and for the religious system on the other; finally,

(e) the discussion points out that it is essential to take into account the interdependence of linguistic as well as extra-linguistic (societal) factors for a cohesive analysis of the language of religion.

Notes

1. For further discussion, see the American Religious Identification Survey (2001) Egon Mayer and Barry Kosmin (City University of New York).
2. The English prayers are taken from the booklet used in the worship ritual offered to the contemporary Hindu saint Satya Saaii Baabaa in the congregation of his devotees in the US. The group recites/sings the Saaii *bhajans* (devotional prayers) together. The booklet is an unpublished manuscript. I have not changed the spelling and punctuation used in the booklet, rather, I have kept the text as it is in the booklet. Capitalization of the first letters of the words is not necessarily systematic nor it is consistent.
3. The spelling conventions of the Sanskrit words (for example, *puja/pooja* for the Sanskrit *puujaa* 'worship') are kept as they appear in the website referred above. Archana is the special type of offering. (Flowers, fruit, rice and other ritual objects are offered to the deity. The offering is made directly by the priest on behalf of the devotee.) The devotees are supposed to order the kind of Archana they would like to be offered.

References

Barr, James (1979) 'The Language of Religion', in *Science of Religion*, Proceedings of the Study of the Conference of the International Association for the History of Religions, held in Turku, Finland, 27–31 August 1973. Mouton.

Eck, Diana L. (2001) *A New Religious America: How a 'Christian Country' has now Become the World's Most Religiously Diverse Nation.* San Francisco: Harper.

Fenton, John Y. (1998) *Transplanting Religious Traditions: Asian Indians in America.* New York: Praeger.

Fishman, Joshua, A. (ed.) (1999) *Handbook of Language and Ethnic Identity.* New York: Oxford University Press.

Fishman, Joshua, A. (2006) 'A Decalogue of Basic Theoretical Perspectives for a Sociology of Language and Religion', in T. Omoniyi and J.A. Fishman (eds), *Explorations in the Sociology of Language and Religion,* Amsterdam: John Benjamins Publishing Company, pp. 14–41.

Gold, Daniel (1987) *The Lord as Guru: Hindi Saints in the Northern Indian Tradition.* New York: Oxford University Press.

Narayanan, V. (1996) 'Creating South Indian Experience in the United States', in R.B. Williams (ed.), *A Sacred Thread: Modern Transmission of Hindu Traditions in India and Abroad.* New York: Columbia University Press, pp. 147–76.

Pandharipande , Rajeshwari, V. (1992) 'Language of Religion in South Asia: the Case of Hindi', in Edward C. Dimock, B.B. Kachru and Bh. Frishnamurti (eds),

Dimensions of Sociolinguistics in South Asia: Papers in Memory of Gerald Kelly, New Delhi: Oxford and IBH Publications Co., pp. 271–84.

Pandharipande, Rajeshwari, V. (2001a) 'Mixing as Method: the English Translation of the Sanskrit Text', in Edwin Thumbo (ed.), *The Three Circles of English: Language Specialists Talk about the English Language*, Singapore: The Center for Arts, The National University of Singapore, pp. 301–16.

Pandharipande, Rajeshwari, V. (2001b) 'Constructing Religious Discourse in Diaspora: American Hinduism', in B.B. Kachru and C.L. Nelson (eds), *Diaspora, Identity, and Language Communities. Studies in Linguistics Sciences*, 31(1), 231–52.

Pandharipande, Rajeshwari, V. (2006) 'Language of Religion in South Asia', in T. Omoniyi and J.A. Fishman (eds), *Explorations in the Sociology of Language and Religion*, Amsterdam: John Benjamins Publishing Company, pp. 141–64.

Pettys, Gregory (1994) 'Asian Indians in the United States: an Analysis of Identity Formation and Retention'. PhD dissertation, University of Illinois at Urbana-Champaign.

Raghavan, V. (1966) *The Great Integrators: the Singer Saints of India*. New Delhi: Publications Division, Government of India.

Ranade, Ramchandra, D. 1933 [1982] *Mysticism in Maharashtra*. New Delhi: Motilal Banasidass.

Rangasamy, Padma (2001) *Namaste America: Indian Americans in an American Metropolis*. University Park: The Pennsylvania State University Press.

Saran, P. and Eams, E. (eds) (1988) *The New Ethnics: Asian Indians in the United States*. New York: Praeger.

Samarin, William J. (1976) 'Language of Religion', in W.J. Samarin (ed.), *Language in Religious Practice*, Series in Sociolinguistics, Rowley: Newbury House Publishers, Inc.

Swami Nikhilananda (ed.) (1953) *Vivekananda: the Yogas and Other Works*. New York: Ramakrishna-Vivekananda Center.

Waida, Manabu (1987) 'Authority', in Mircea Eliade (ed.), *The Encyclopedia of Religion*, vol. 2, New York: Macmillan Publishing Company, pp. 1–6.

Williams, Raymond Brady (1996) 'Sacred Threads of Several Textures: Strategies of Adaptation in the United States', in R.B. Williams (ed.), *A Sacred Thread: Modern Transmission of Hindu Traditions in India and Abroad*, New York: Columbia University Press, pp. 228–57.

6

Blorít – Pagans' Mohawk or Sabras' Forelock? Ideological Secularization of Hebrew Terms in Socialist Zionist Israeli

Azzan Yadin and Ghil'ad Zuckermann

Introduction

> The greatest virtue of a new word is that it is not new.
> (Yechiel Michal Pínes, 1893)

versus

> It is absolutely impossible to empty out words filled to bursting, unless one does so at the expense of language itself.
> (Gershom Scholem, 26 December 1926)

One of the problems facing those attempting to revive Hebrew as the national language of the emerging state of Israel was that of Hebrew lexical voids. The 'revivalists' attempted to use mainly internal sources of lexical enrichment but were faced with a paucity of roots. They changed the meanings of obsolete Hebrew terms to fit the modern world. This infusion often entailed the secularization of religious terms.

This chapter explores the widespread phenomenon of semantic secularization, as in the politically neutral process visible in English *cell* 'monk's living place' > 'autonomous self-replicating unit from which tissues of the body are formed'. The main focus, however, is on secularizations involving *ideological* 'lexical engineering', as often exemplified by – *either conscious or unintentional, either top-down or bottom-up* – manipulative, subversive processes of extreme semantic shifting, pejoration, amelioration, trivialization, allusion and echoing.

An example of *defying religion* is בלורית. Mishnaic Hebrew [bəlo'rit] is 'Mohawk, an upright strip of hair that runs across the crown of the head from the forehead to the nape of the neck', characteristic of the pagan and not to be touched by the Jewish barber. But defying religious values, secular Socialist Zionists use *blorít* with the meaning 'forelock, hair above the forehead', which becomes one of the defining character-istics of the Sabra ('prickly pear', a nickname for native Israelis, allegedly thorny on the outside and sweet inside). *Is the 'new Jew' ultimately a pagan?*

This negation of religion fascinatingly adds to the phenomenon of negation of the Diaspora (*shlilát hagolá*), exemplified in the *blorít* itself by Zionists expecting the Sabra to have dishevelled hair, as opposed to the orderly diasporic Jew, who was considered by Zionists to be weak and persecuted.

An example of the complementary phenomenon, *deifying Zionism*, is משכן. Biblical Hebrew משכן [miʃ'kån] means 'dwelling-place' and 'Tabernacle of the Congregation' (where Moses kept the Ark in the wilderness), 'inner sanctum' (known as אהל מועד [ʔohɛl mo'ʕed]). Israeli משכן הכנסת *mishkán aknéset*, however, refers to 'the Knesset (Israeli Parliament) building'. Translating *mishkán aknéset* as 'The Knesset Building' (as in the official Knesset website) is inadequate. *The word mishkán is loaded with holiness and evokes sanctity, as if MKs (Members of Knesset, i.e. MPs) were at the very least angels or seraphs.*

In line with the prediction made by the Kabbalah scholar Gershom Scholem in a letter to Franz Rosenzweig (*Bekenntnis über unsere Sprache,* 1926), some ultra-orthodox Jews have tried to launch a 'lexical ven-detta': using secularized terms like 'dormant agents', as a short cut to religious concepts, thus trying to convince secular Jews to return to their religious roots.

The study of Israeli cultural linguistics and sociophilology casts light on the dynamics between language, religion and identity in a land where fierce military battles with external enemies are accompanied by internal *Kulturkämpfe*.

6.1 Background

This chapter explores semantic *change* which manifests the *conflict* between the religious and the secular in Israel. It also uncovers means of *accommodation* and negotiation, for example using vagueness or ambigu-ity resulting from semantic secularization to get out of a legal or political quagmire (see *bitakhón* 'faith in God'/'security' in Section 6.7).[1]

6.1.1   The Israeli language

Hebrew belongs to the Canaanite division of the north-western branch of Semitic languages. Following a gradual decline, it ceased to be spoken by the second century AD. The failed Bar-Kokhba Revolt against the Romans in Judea in AD 132–5, in which thousands of Jews were killed, marks the symbolic end of the period of spoken Hebrew. But the actual end of spoken Hebrew might have been earlier. Jesus, for example, was a native speaker of Aramaic rather than Hebrew. For more than 1700 years thereafter, Hebrew was not spoken. A most important liturgical and literary language, it occasionally served as a lingua franca for Jews of the Diaspora, but not as a mother tongue. (Please see proposed periodization of Hebrew and Israeli in the Appendix of this chapter.)

The genetic classification of 'Israeli' (Zuckermann 1999, 2006a, 2007), the language which emerged in Palestine at the end of the nineteenth century, has preoccupied linguists since its genesis. The still prevalent, traditional view suggests that Israeli is Semitic: (biblical/Mishnaic) Hebrew *revived*. The revisionist position defines Israeli as Indo-European: Yiddish *relexified*, i.e. Yiddish, the revivalists' mother tongue, is the 'substratum', whilst Hebrew is only a 'superstratum' providing the vocabulary (cf. Horvath and Wexler 1997). Zuckermann's m*o*saic (rather than M*o*saic) hypothesis is that 'genetically modified' Israeli is a 'semi-engineered' multi-layered language, which is a Semito-European, or Eurasian, hybrid, i.e. both Semitic (Afro-Asiatic) and (Indo-)European. It is based simultaneously on 'sleeping beauty'/'walking dead' Hebrew, *máme lóshn* ('mother tongue') Yiddish (both being *primary contributors*) and other languages (Zuckermann 2006c, 2008a, b, 2009). Therefore, the term 'Israeli' is far more appropriate than 'Israeli Hebrew', let alone 'Modern Hebrew' or 'Hebrew' *tout court*.

Almost all Hebrew revivalists – e.g. Eliezer Ben-Yehuda (born Perelman) – were native Yiddish speakers. Not only were they European but their revivalist campaign was, in fact, inspired by European – e.g. Bulgarian – nationalism. Although territory and language were at the heart of European nationalism, Jews possessed neither a *land* nor a unifying *langue*. Zionism could thus be considered a fascinating and multifaceted manifestation of European discourses channelled into the Holy Land – cf. George Eliot's *Daniel Deronda* (1876).

Nevertheless, the revivalists wished to speak Hebrew, with Semitic grammar and pronunciation, like Arabs. But, clearly, they could not avoid their European mindset. Their attempts (1) to deny their (more recent) roots in search of biblical ancientness, (2) negate diasporism and disowning the 'weak, persecuted' exilic Jew from public memory, and (3) avoid hybridity (as reflected in Slavonized, Romance/Semitic-influenced, Germanic Yiddish itself, which they regarded as *zhargón*) failed.

6.1.2   Lexical enrichment in Israeli

The main problem the revivalists faced was that of Hebrew *lexical voids*, which were not semantic voids but cases in which purists tried to supplant unwelcome guest words, foreignisms and loanwords. The purists tried to use mainly internal sources of lexical enrichment but were hampered by a paucity of roots.

* The number of attested biblical Hebrew words is roughly 8000, of which some 2000 are hapax legomena (the number of biblical Hebrew roots, on which many of these words are based, is roughly 2000).
* The number of attested Mishnaic Hebrew words is less than 20,000, of which (i) less than 8000 are Mishnaic par excellence, i.e. they did not appear in the Old Testament (the number of new Mishnaic Hebrew roots is roughly 800); (ii) around 6000 are a subset of biblical Hebrew; and (iii) several thousand are Aramaic words which can have a Hebrew form.
* Medieval Hebrew(s) added more than 6000 words to Hebrew.
* The approximate number of new lexical items in Israeli is 17,000 (cf. 14,762 in Even-Shoshan 1970: vii: 3062).

With the inclusion of foreign and technical terms we estimate that the total number of Israeli words, including words of biblical, Mishnaic, medieval and Maskilic descent, is more than 60,000. Even-Shoshan (1970) lists 37,260 words. Even-Shoshan (1997), the most comprehensive dictionary of Israeli, lists slightly more.

6.1.3   Sources of lexical enrichment

Figure 6.1 summarizes the main methods of lexical enrichment.

6.2   *Ex interno* lexical enrichment in Israeli

The following are some of the *ex interno* lexical enrichment methods applied by revivalists.

6.2.1   Creating secondary (and tertiary) roots from nouns

Consider Israeli מיקום *mikúm* 'locating', from מקם √*mqm* 'locate', which derives from biblical Hebrew מקום [må‿qom] 'place', whose root is קום √*qwm* 'stand':

> קום √₁ *qwm* 'stand' → מקום [maˈqom] 'place' →
> מקם √₂ *mqm* 'locate' → מיקום *mikúm* 'locating'

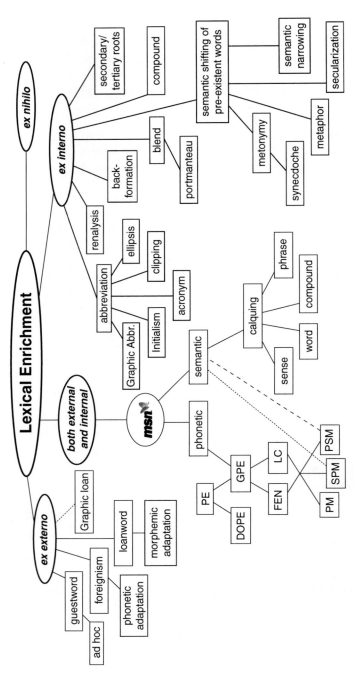

Figure 6.1 Sources of lexical enrichment

Abbreviations: CONSTR = construct-state; DEF = definite; DOPE = derivational-only popular etymology; FEN = folk-etymological nativization; GPE = generative popular etymology; LC = lexical conflation; m = masculine; MSN = multi-sourced neologization; PE = popular etymology; PM = phonetic matching; PSM = phono-semantic matching; sg = singular; SPM = semanticized phonetic matching

A recent example introduced by the Academy of the Hebrew Language in *Akadém* 8 (March 1996, p. 1) is מידרוג *midrúg* 'rating', from מדרג *midrág*, whose root is דרג √*drg* 'grade'.

This process is morphologically similar to the production of frequentative (iterative) verbs in Latin:

- *iactito* 'to toss about' derives from *iacto* 'to boast of, keep bringing up, harass, disturb, throw, cast, fling away', which in turn derives from *iacio* 'to throw, cast' (whose past participle is *iactus*)
- *scriptito* 'to write often, compose' is based on *scribo* 'to write' (< 'to draw lines, engrave with a sharp-pointed instrument')
- *dicto* 'to say often, repeat' is from *dico* 'to indicate, say, speak, tell'
- *clamito* 'to cry loudly/often, shout violently' derives from *clamo* 'call, shout'

Similar cases occur in Arabic:

- مركز √*mrkz*, cf. ['markaza] 'centralized (m, sg)', from ['markaz] 'centre', from ['rakaza] 'plant into the earth, stick up (a lance)' (< ركز √*rkz*)
- ارجح √*ʔrdʒ͡ħ*, cf. [taʔardʒ͡aħa] 'oscillated (m, sg)', from [ʔurˈdʒ͡uːħa] 'swing (n)', from ['radʒ͡aħa] 'weighed down, preponderated (m, sg)' (< رجح √*rdʒ͡ħ*)
- محور √*mħwr*, cf. [taˈmaħwara] 'centred, focused (m, sg)', from ['miħwar] 'axis', from ['ħaːra] 'turned (m, sg)' (< حور √*ħwr*)
- مسخر √*msχr*, cf. تمسخر [taˈmasχara] 'mocked, made fun (m, sg)', from مسخرة ['masχara] 'mockery', from سخر ['saχira] 'mocked (m, sg)' (< سخر √*sχr*)

The following is a tertiary root case in Israeli:

> מור √₁*mwr* 'change' → Hebrew תמורה [təmuˈrå] 'change (n)' →
> → תמר √₂*tmr* 'change, transform, substitute' → (phono-semantic matching) → Israeli מותמר *mutmár* 'transformed, metamorphic' →
> → מתמר √₃*mtmr* 'metamorphose' → Israeli מתמור *mitmúr* 'metamorphosis'

6.2.2 Blending two distinct roots

- Israeli דחפור *dakhpór* 'bulldozer' hybridizes (Mishnaic Hebrew>>) Israeli דחף √*dḥp* 'push' and (biblical Hebrew>>)Israeli חפר √*ḥpr* 'dig'.
- Israeli שלטוט *shiltút* 'zapping, surfing the channels, flipping through the channels' derives from (i) (Hebrew>)Israeli שלט *shalát* 'remote

control', an ellipsis – like *remote* (but using the noun instead) – of the (widely known) compound שלט רחוק *shalát rakhók* (cf. Even-Shoshan 1997: 1837b) – cf. the Academy of the Hebrew Language's שלט רחק *shalát rákhak* (*Laméd Leshonkhá* 19, October–November 1996); (ii) (Hebrew>)Israeli שטוט *shitút* 'wandering, vagrancy'. Israeli שלטוט *shiltút* was introduced by the Academy of the Hebrew Language in *Laméd Leshonkhá* 19 (October–November 1996) – cf. *Akadém* 11 (May 1997). Synchronically, it might appear to result from reduplication of the final consonant of *shalát* 'remote control'.

- Israeli גחלילית *gakhlilít* 'fire-fly, glow-fly, *Lampyris*' is another example of blending which has also been explained as mere reduplication. This coinage by Bialik blends (Hebrew>)Israeli גחלת *gakhélet* 'burning coal' with (Hebrew>)Israeli לילה *láyla* 'night'. Compare this with the unblended חכלילית *khakhlilít* '(black) redstart, *Phœnicurus*' (<<biblical Hebrew חכליל 'dull red, reddish'). Synchronically speaking though, most native Israeli speakers feel that *gakhlilít* includes a reduplication of the third radical of גחל √*ghl*. This is incidentally how Klein (1987: 97a) explains *gakhlilít*. Since he is attempting to provide etymology, his description might be misleading if one agrees that Bialik had blending in mind.

6.2.3   Semantic shifting of pre-existent words

Consider Israeli אקדח *ekdákh* 'handgun, revolver' (initially 'firing machine', cf. Ben-Yehuda 1909: i: 373a, 1978: 249–50), from biblical Hebrew אקדח [ʔeq'dåħ] 'carbuncle, carbuncle-stone' (red precious stone used for decoration) – see Isaiah 54: 12. The coiner, Eliezer Ben-Yehuda, points out that he was affected by Hebrew/Israeli קדח √*qdh* 'drill' (cf. Ben-Yehuda 1909: i: 373a: fn3). Note that the original אקדח [ʔeq'dåħ] 'carbuncle' can be traced back to קדח √*qdh* as well (see Ben-Yehuda 1909: i: 373a: fn1). If Ben-Yehuda had in mind English *drill full of bullets* or the like, אקדח *ekdákh* 'firing machine', which gained currency with the specific meaning 'handgun, revolver', would constitute an etymological calque, or a sense-calque introducing a new sense.

Bar-Asher (1995: 8) calls the process of recycling obsolete lexical items עקרון השאיבה מבפנים *ekrón hasheivá mibifním* 'The Principle of Drawing from Within' (also mentioned in *Akadém* 8, March 1996, p. 3), corresponding to the view expressed by Pínes (1893: 61) and Klausner (1940: 289):

הגדולה שבמעלות למלה חדשה – אם איננה חדשה

The greatest virtue of a new word is that it is not new. (Pínes 1893: 61)

כדי לחדש צריך למצוא מלה ישנה, שיש לה שורש עברי, שיש לה צורה עברית, שיש לה טעם עברי

In order to neologize one should find an old word, which has a Hebrew root, a Hebrew form and Hebrew stress. (Klausner 1940: 289)

In response to Ben-Yehuda's rebuke of not having neologized enough, Aaron Meyer Mazia said:

> Not only am I unashamed of it but I am in fact satisfied that the [Hebrew Language] Council decided on numerous words for athletics, arithmetic, dresses and the like, but that the majority of these words were nothing but old words [...] we would not want to create new words as long as we are able to satisfy our needs with what is available from our ancient literature. (cf. *Zikhronot Vaad Halashon* 4, 1914: 42; a similar view by Mazia can be found in *Zikhronot Vaad Halashon* 6, 1928: 85)

Very often, this infusion of new meaning includes the secularization of religious terms.

6.2.4 Semantic secularization

Secularization, in which an originally religious term is used with a non-religious meaning, is not unique to Israeli. Examples from English include the following:

- *cell* 'monk's living place' > 'autonomous self replicating unit from which tissues of the body are formed'
- *sanction* 'imposition of penance' > 'legal/political penalty'
- *office* 'church service' > 'commercial bureau'
- *hierarchy* 'medieval classification of angels into ranks (including cherubim, seraphim, powers and dominions)' > in the seventeenth century: ranking of clergymen > system of grading

See also *mercy, novice* and *sanctuary*. The reverse process to secularization is demonstrated in English *bishop* and French *éveque*, which come from Greek *epískopos* 'overseer', the modern religious meaning resulting from the use of 'overseer' within the Christian community (cf. McMahon 1994: 180).

However, lexical secularization is particularly widespread in Israeli, which is a non-genetic, hybridic Jewish language, 120 years old.[2]

Semantic secularization can occur for many reasons, and only sometimes does it reflect ideological tension. A term may be secularized as a result of phono-semantic matching (Section 6.3.1), calquing (Section 6.3.2), semantic shifting (Sections 6.3.3 and 6.3.4) and survival of the best fit (Section 6.3.5). Particularly interesting are subversive secularizations involving *ideologically manipulative* 'lexical engineering' (to employ a term used in Zuckermann 2006b) – see survival of the best fit (Section 6.4.1), mild and extreme semantic shifting (Sections 6.4.2 and 6.4.3), pejoration (Section 6.4.4), mild and extreme amelioration (Sections 6.4.5 and 6.4.6), ameliorative recycling of biblical first names (Section 6.4.7), trivialization (Section 6.4.8) and allusion (Section 6.4.9). The degree of manipulation is on a continuum and – *inter alia* since we are dealing with a new emerging language with numerous revivalists – it is sometimes hard to draw the line between *neutral* and *manipulative* secularization.

6.3   Ideologically neutral secularization in Israeli

Shift happens.

6.3.1   Phono-semantic matching (PSM)

PSM is defined as a *multi-sourced neologism* that preserves both the meaning and the approximate sound of the parallel expression in the source language, using *pre-existent* target-language words or roots (cf. Zuckermann 2003, 2004, 2008c, Sapir and Zuckermann 2008). Consider the following secularizing PSMs:

(1)   יובל [joˈbʰel] → *yovél*
Israeli יובל *yovél* is an 'incestuous PSM' introducing a new sense:

Biblical Hebrew (perhaps from יבל √*jbl* '(to) lead' >)
יובל [joˈbʰel] 'ram' > whole-for-part synecdoche (a type of metonymy) > 'ram's horn, *shofar*' > 'fiftieth anniversary (after seven cycles of years of *shemittah*)' >

Greek *iō bēlos* > *iōbēlaîos* >
PSM₁ (with **Latin** *iubilare* 'shout for joy' or **Latin** *iubilum* 'wild cry') >

Latin *iubilæus* (and not *iobelæus) > > >

French *jubilé*, **Spanish** *jubileo*, **Italian** *giubileo*, **Russian** юбилей *yubiléĭ*, **Polish** *jubileusz*, **German** *Jubiläum*, **Yiddish** יובילי *yubiléy*, **English** *jubilee* >
PSM₂ (with biblical Hebrew יובל [joˈbʰel] 'fiftieth anniversary (after seven cycles of years of *shemittah*)') >

Israeli יובל *yovél* '(happy) anniversary, celebration'

(2) אבוב [ʔabˈbubʰ] → *abúv*

Consider the following 'specificizing PSM', a special sub-category of *PSM that introduces a new sense*, consisting of the specification of the initially *vague* meaning of a *pre-existent* target-language word, so it becomes limited to the *specific* meaning of the matched source-language word:

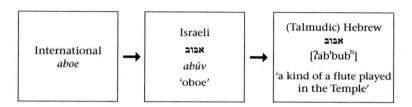

(3) סמל [ˈsɛmɛl] → *sémel*

Biblical Hebrew סמל [ˈsɛmɛl] is 'an object of idolatrous worship', perhaps originally a reference to a foreign deity – see Deuteronomy 4: 16, Ezekiel 8: 3 and 2 Chronicles 33: 7, 15. In Israeli, however, it simply means 'symbol' – due, at least in part, to the phonetic similarity with the internationalism *symbol*.

(4) תורה [toˈrå] → *torá*

Hebrew תורה [toˈrå] usually refers to 'the totality of the religious teachings that God has bestowed upon Israel' or to 'the book containing these teachings' (see Psalms 19: 8 and Nehemiah 8: 1), although the original sense of the word in the Old Testament is 'instruction' (see Leviticus 6: 2 and 6: 18). Israeli *torá*, however, means 'theory' as in תורת היחסות של איינשטיין *torát hayakhasút shel áynshteyn* 'Einstein's Theory of Relativity', cf. Israeli תורת לחימה *torát lekhimá* 'military strategy'. The phonetic similarity with the internationalism *theory* – cf. Israeli תאוריה *teórya* – might have facilitated this secularization.

6.3.2 Calquing

(5) קורבן [qorˈbån] → *korbán*

The European word for 'sacrifice' was transformed over time from a cultic term to a word designating the forfeiture of something highly valued for the sake of a still greater – though not necessarily religious – cause. Paralleling the semantic shift in European languages, the same dynamic is evident in קורבן [qorˈbån]: biblical Hebrew [qorˈbån] 'sacrifice' takes on in Israeli the non-cultic meaning of today's 'sacrifice'.

(6) פדי √*pdj*

Biblical Hebrew פדי √*pdj* 'redeem' occurs primarily in cultic and religious contexts, referring either to (a) the redemption of human firstborn from Temple sacrifice: 'The first issue of the womb of every being, man or beast, that is offered to the Lord, shall be yours; but you shall have the first-born of man redeemed' (Numbers 18: 15), or to (b) God's salvation of Israel: 'For the Lord will ransom Jacob, redeem him from one too strong for him' (Jeremiah 31: 11).

In Israeli, however, the primary meaning is financial: לפדות *lifdót* is 'to cash (a cheque)' and פדיונות גדולים *pidyonót gdolím*, lit. 'big redeems', refers to 'the trading volume on the stock market'. This shift mirrors the semantic expansion of *redeem* in English and other European languages into the financial sphere, so that one speaks of *redeeming stocks*, *redeeming coupons* and the like. The semantic expansion of the Hebrew root, then, may well be the result of calquing rather than of internal dynamics.

6.3.3 Semantic shifting: Temple utensils

There is a large group of words that have undergone semantic secularization, but their new meaning is so closely associated with the old that the shift does not reflect cultural tensions beyond secularization as such. Consider the Temple utensils, many of which mean kitchen utensils in Israeli:

(7) Biblical Hebrew כיור [kij'jor] is 'a pot used for cooking in Temple contexts' (see 1 Kings 7: 30, 38, 42) or 'the Temple/Tabernacle laver' (Exodus 30: 18, 28). In Israeli, these meanings are for all practical purposes abolished: *kyor* means 'a sink'.

(8) Biblical Hebrew קערה [qəʕå'rå] 'a dish found regularly in Temple context (Exodus 25: 29, Numbers 7: 13, 19, 25, 31, 37) → Israeli *keará* 'a kitchen bowl'.

(9) Biblical Hebrew כף [kapʰ] 'ritual pan vessel' (Exodus 25: 29, 37: 16; Numbers 4: 7, 15) → Israeli *kaf* 'tablespoon'.

(10) Biblical Hebrew מחבת [maħǎ'bʰat] 'pan used in baking the priestly grain offerings' (Leviticus 2: 5, 6: 14, 7: 9) → Israeli *makhvát* '(frying) pan, griddle'.

(11) Biblical Hebrew מזלג [maz'leg] 'a sacrificial implement for picking up meat' (1 Samuel 2: 13) → Israeli *mazlég* 'fork'.

6.3.4 Other semantic shifts

(12) משחה [miʃˈħå] → mishkhá

Biblical Hebrew משחה [miʃˈħå] 'the ointment of sanctified oil used in a variety of sacrificial contexts by the priests' (Exodus 25: 6, 29: 7,21, 31: 11) → Israeli mishkhá 'cream'.

(13) משנה [miʃˈnå] → mishná

Mishnaic Hebrew משנה [miʃˈnå] referred only to the religious–legal teachings of the rabbinic sages. Israeli mishná can refer to non-religious teachings as well, as in משנתו הפוליטית של בוש mishnató apolítit shel bush 'Bush's political doctrine'.

(14) פרקן [purˈqån] → פורקן purkán

Medieval Hebrew פרקן [purˈqån] means 'redemption, salvation'. In Israeli it usually means 'orgasm, relief'. Both meanings can be traced to the same semantic sense of 'release'.

6.3.5 Survival of the best fit

Often one meaning of a pre-existent word is superseded by another pre-existent sense either because the latter fits Zionist discourse (Section 6.4.1) or because it is more modern, as in the following:

(15) יריד [jåˈrid] → yaríd

Mishnaic Hebrew יריד [jåˈrid] is 'a meeting place' or 'an annual fair', often – though not always – dedicated to a pagan deity and thus a site of idolatry.

In Israeli it is a secular 'fair', for example an arts fair, with no negative connotation.

(16) תקון [tiqˈqun] → תיקון tikún

Mishnaic Hebrew תקון [tiqˈqun] means 'preparation, especially making fruits available by separating the tithes, the priest's share etc.', as well as 'establishment, institution, amendment, making right'.

In Israeli, תיקון tikún is simply 'fixing', as in 'fixing a car'.

The journey from the Temple to the kitchen (Section 6.3.3) is interesting, but the shift is secular and nothing more: cooking utensils in a sacred context now appear in a secular one, a sanctified ointment (12) is now a cream. Nothing here suggests a deeper ideological engagement with the earlier strata of Hebrew. Nothing reflects the structural tension inherent in the secular–nationalist return to a language containing religious-exilic strata. That is not the case in most of the following examples.

6.4   Ideologically manipulative secularization in Israeli

6.4.1   Survival of the best fit

(17) עבודה [ʕăbʰoˈdå] → *avodá*

Biblical Hebrew [ʕăbʰoˈdå] has both a religious and a secular sense, referring to 'work' or 'labour', as well as to 'ritual and cultic worship'. Examples of the former are the activity of the Hebrew slaves in Egypt (Exodus 2: 23) and the labour imposed by the Persian satrap on the Jews (Nehemiah 5: 18). Examples of the latter are the phrases עבודת המשכן [ʕăbʰoˈdåt hammiˈʃkån] 'the cultic service of the Tabernacle' (Numbers 3: 7, cf. Exodus 39: 32), עבודת הקודש [ʕăbʰoˈdåt haqˈqodeʃ] 'cultic worship' (Exodus 36: 3) and עבודת יהוה [ʕăbʰoˈdåt JHWH] 'the worship of the Lord' (Numbers 8: 11). The same two meanings carry into Mishnaic Hebrew, but the second becomes the more dominant, as evidenced, for example, by the tractate עבודה זרה [ʕăbʰoˈdå zåˈrå], lit. 'foreign worship', i.e. 'idolatry'.

In Israeli, the cultic meaning is replaced by 'labour' in the positive sense that this term carried in the labour movement. Consequently, one finds the decidedly non-cultic מפלגת העבודה *mifléget aavodá* 'the Labour Party' and תנועת העבודה *tnuát aavodá* 'the Labour Movement'.

6.4.2   Mild semantic shifting

(18) קלפי [qalpej] → *kálfi / kálpi*

Mishnaic Hebrew קלפי [qalpe] (from Greek, cf. *kálpis* 'a vessel for drawing water') refers to 'a Temple urn used for drawing lots – an ancient divination technique – by which various matters were decided':

> [The high priest] came to the east, to the north of the altar ... and there was a casket [qalpe] with two lots ... he shook the casket and took up the two lots. On one was written 'For the Lord' and on the other was written 'For Azazel'. (Mishnah Yoma 3.9 and 4.1)

The word undergoes an interesting resemanticization: Israeli *kálfi / kálpi* is not a tool for determining *vox dei* but *vox populi*: it comes to mean 'ballot box, voting/polling booth, polling station'.

(19) כנסת [kəˈnɛsɛt] → *knéset*

Mishnaic Hebrew כנסת ישראל [kəˈnɛsɛt jiɕråˈʔel] refers to 'the Jewish people as a collective', 'the community of Israel' – see Song of Songs Rabba 1: 4. In Kabbalah literature, [kəˈnɛsɛt jiɕråˈʔel] is one of the standard appellations of the tenth divine emanation, also known as שכינה [ʃəkʰiˈnå].

In Israeli, however, the phrase takes on a national, political meaning: 'Israeli Parliament, the Knesset' (Figure 6.2).

(20) משכן [miʃkån] → *mishkán*

Biblical Hebrew משכן [miʃkån] means 'dwelling-place' and 'Tabernacle of the Congregation' (where Moses kept the Ark in the wilderness), 'inner sanctum' (known as אהל מועד ['ʔohɛl mo'ʕed]).

Israeli *mishkán* is 'a building for a specific purpose', e.g. האומנויות משכן *mishkán aomanuyót* 'the Art Centre', משכן הכנסת *mishkán aknéset* 'the Knesset building'.

(21) קבע ['qɛbʰaʕ] → *kéva*

Mishnaic Hebrew קבע ['qɛbʰaʕ] refers to 'a fixed or permanent implementation of a practice', particularly prayer or Torah study. Rabbi Eliezer speaks of one who 'makes his prayer fixed ['qɛbʰaʕ]' (Mishna Berakhot 4.4).

In Israeli, however, the fixed and ongoing commitment is not to prayer or to Torah study but to military service: שרות קבע *sherút kéva* refers to 'military service that extends beyond the duty required by the draft'. Similarly, the standing army – as opposed to the reserves – is צבא קבע *tsva kéva*.

(22) מלואים [millu'ʔim] → מילואים *miluím*

Biblical Hebrew מלואים [millu'ʔim] refers to 'the days following the dedication of the Tabernacle but prior to the priests' inauguration' – see Leviticus 8: 33:

ומפתח אהל מועד לא תצאו שבעת ימים עד יום מלאת ימי מִלֻּאֵיכֶם

You shall not go outside the entrance of the Tent of Meeting for seven days, until the day that your period of ordination [millu'ʔim] is completed.

Figure 6.2 Israeli Parliament, the Knesset

The term also appears as modifying the sacrifices offered as part of the inauguration ritual: 'the ram of ordination [millu'ʔim]' (Leviticus 8: 22) and 'the bread that is in the basket of ordination' (Leviticus 8: 31).

The precise meaning of [millu'ʔim] in this context is a matter of controversy among Bible scholars, but the root מלא √*ml?* means 'fill' and it is this meaning that generates the Israeli appropriation of the word to refer to 'supplemental/reserve military service'. Thus, one's days of *miluím* are no longer served at the Tabernacle but in reserve duty.

Note that the [millu'ʔim] section in Leviticus is at the meeting of two portions:

(a) צו [sˤaw] (named after its opening verse: 'The Lord spoke to Moses, saying, 'Command [sˤaw] Aaron and his sons...' (Leviticus 6: 1–2)

(b) שמיני [ʃəmi'ni] (named after its opening verse: 'On the eighth [ʃəmi'ni] day Moses summoned Aaron and his sons...' (Leviticus 9: 1)

In Israeli, צו שמונה *tsav shmóne* 'Ordinance 8' is the document informing one of upcoming (often emergency) reserve service, i.e. of *miluím*. But this is mere serendipity!

In these examples, secularization is presented as superseding/supersession. For example, priestly service gives way to reserve duty (*miluím*). Though the modern concepts replace the ancient, they do so as heirs that are still somehow anchored in the Old Testament or the Mishnah, or at least as 'natural' or 'organic' outgrowths of earlier Jewish strata. This sense of a natural – almost inevitable – development is itself an expression of the ideological hegemony of Zionism. It is certainly true that the ultra-orthodox community has waged a fierce polemic against these semantic innovations (cf. Be'er 1992 and Scholem in Section 6.5). But for Israeli speakers the radical nature of the semantic change is no longer visible. The new meanings do not represent an antagonistic or revolutionary break with their ancient predecessors. The potentially problematic return to the religious strata of Hebrew is overcome by assimilating the premodern meanings into Israeli, subsuming the earlier under the later.

6.4.3   Extreme semantic shifting

A widespread strategy for overcoming the potential dangers inherent in the 'return to Hebrew' involves the 'transvaluation' of an earlier meaning, usually through an axiological reversal (e.g. a word with a positive connotation takes on a negative one, and vice versa), or a radical shift in the register (e.g. an elevated word is debased). It is worth noting that Eliezer Ben-Yehuda, the symbolic father of Israeli, was vehemently opposed to traditional, rabbinic Judaism (cf. Kuzar 2001).

The following words exemplify the transfer from a sacred to an unrelated profane realm. Whereas the Temple cooking utensils are resemanticized as secular cooking utensils (see examples (7)–(11)), here the transformation of the word is a marked, conscious act of transvaluation.

(23) מוסף [mu'åp^h] → *musáf*

Mishnaic Hebrew מוסף [mu'såp^h] refers to 'the additional sacrifices offered in the Temple on the Sabbath and the festivals' (Mishna Berakhot 3.10). With the destruction of the Temple and the institutionalization of prayer, מוסף השבת [mu'såp^h haʃʃab'båt] comes to mean 'the additional Sabbath prayer service'.

Israeli *musáf* refers to 'the weekend supplement included with the Friday edition of daily newspapers'. Though not denigrating the classical meaning, this undoubtedly constitutes a shift in register – from the exalted to the mundane.

(24) מעריב [maʕă'rib^h] → *maarív*

The path from prayer to newspaper is also evident in *Maarív*, the name of an (originally evening) Israeli daily newspaper that draws its name from medieval Hebrew [maʕă'rib^h] 'the evening prayer'.

(25) שחרית [ʃaħă'rit] → *shakharít*

Mishnaic Hebrew [ʃaħă'rit] means 'morning' and 'the morning prayer'. In Israeli, however, *shakharít* is 'matinée (in the original sense), theatrical/musical/cinematic performance before noon', e.g. מוזיקלית לנוער שחרית *shakharít muzikalít* (or *muzikálit*) *lanóar* 'a musical matinée for the youth'.

(26) קבלה [qabbå'lå] → *kabalá*

Mishnaic Hebrew קבלה [qabbå'lå], lit. 'that which is received, tradition', refers to 'the doctrines a disciple receives from his master', 'oral teachings not recorded in Scripture'. Later, the term becomes associated with a particular type of received tradition, the mystical doctrines known as the Kabbalah.

The 'Kabbalah' meaning is still current in Israeli, but the primary sense has been lifted from the religious arena of received doctrine to the commercial world: *kabalá* means both 'receipt' and '(hotel) reception'. Israeli שעת קבלה *shat kabalá*, lit. 'hour-CONSTR receipt', means 'office hour' and מבחן קבלה *mivkhán kabalá*, lit. 'exam:CONSTR receipt', is 'entrance exam'.

(27) הדרן [had'rån] → *adrán*

Rabbinic הדרן [had'rån] is Aramaic for the first person plural imperfect of the root הדר √*hdr*, cf. 'we shall return'. The word is recited upon completing a tractate of the Talmud: הדרן עלך מסכת [hădaran ʕălåkʰ massɛkʰɛt] 'we shall return to you tractate ...'. The phrase is a promise made by the readers to the text itself, that Talmud study will continue and so eventually we will return to the same tractate and study it once again.

Israeli הדרן *adrán* is different in two ways:

(a) Morphologically, since its Aramaic morphology obscures its verbal form and makes it look as if it has the Hebrew agentive nominal suffix *-án*, *adrán* comes to be used as a noun, so that one can speak of an *adrán* or the *adrán*.

(b) Semantically, *adrán* shifted from the religious and scholastic usage of the Yeshiva world to the realm of popular concerts: it means 'encore'. The onstage return of the popular singer takes the place of the commitment to ongoing Talmud study.

(28) ראיון [reʔå'jon] → *reayón*

The Mishnah tractate Pe'ah opens with a list of religious categories that have no fixed measure:

These are things for which no measure is prescribed: *pe'ah* (the margins of the field that are to be left unharvested for the poor), first fruits, [reʔå'jon] (the pilgrimage appearance), deeds of loving kindness, and the study of Torah. (Mishnah Pe'ah 1.1)

The 'pilgrimage appearance' [reʔå'jon] refers to the biblical decree that

שלוש פעמים בשנה **יראה** כל זכורך את פני יהוה אלהיך

Three times a year ... all your males shall appear before the Lord. (Deuteronomy 16: 16)

The interpretation of this verse is a matter of some controversy. In the Masoretic vocalization [jerå'ʔɛ], the pilgrim is seen by God. But the linguistically more natural – though theologically problematic – reading [jir'ʔɛ] has the pilgrim seeing God (cf. Shemesh 1997). Whatever its original meaning, Mishnaic Hebrew [reʔå'jon] refers to an encounter between the Israelite pilgrims and God.

In Israeli, however, the face-to-face encounter with the deity is replaced with a much more mundane engagement: *reayón* is an 'interview'.

6.4.4 Pejoration

Another type of transvaluation involves the reversal of the values associated with a word. Thus, words carrying a negative connotation are, for ideological reasons, construed as positive, or vice versa. Consider the debasement, pejoration, exemplified in the following:

(29) בטלן [batˤˈlån] → *batlán*

The Mishnah tractate Megillah (1.2) establishes different schedules for the reading of the Book of Esther on Purim according to the size of the settlement:

> If [the holiday] fell on the day after the Sabbath, villages read it earlier on the day of assembly, large towns on the day itself, and walled cities on the next day.

The Mishnah then goes on to ask what counts as a large town. The answer: 'Any in which there are ten unoccupied men [batˤlå'nim]' (Megillah 1.3). Mishnaic Hebrew [batˤlå'nim] refers to individuals who are free of the need to work, possibly because they are supported by the community as a ready prayer quorum (מנין [min'jån]) and possibly because they are gentlemen of leisure. In either case this is not a negative designation. Jastrow (1903) translates this phrase as 'ten persons having leisure' (see under בטלן).

With the lionization of labour among the early Zionists, *batlán* becomes a pejorative term: 'a loafer, an idler, a lazy person', sometimes implying a parasite.

6.4.5 Mild amelioration (negative→neutral)

But much more often, secularization involves amelioration.

(30) לץ [lesˤ] → *lets*

(31) ליצן [le'sˤån] → *leytsán*

(32) מוקיון [muq'jon] → *mukyón*

These three terms are grouped together because (a) they reflect a similar tendency: resemantization that neutralizes the religiously or theologically negative meaning of a word, (b) they belong to the same semantic domain.

Biblical Hebrew לץ [lesˤ] refers to both of the following:

(a) 'a person bereft of wisdom' – particularly in Proverbs, where the word is regularly contrasted with the sage, e.g. Proverbs 9: 8; 13: 1; 21: 11;
(b) 'a wicked man' – the best known example for it being the opening verse of Psalms (1: 1):

אשרי האיש אשר לא הלך בעצת רשעים ובדרך חטאים לא עמד ובמושב לצים לא ישב.

Happy is the man who has not followed the counsel of the wicked or taken the path of the sinners or joined the company of the insolent (לצים [le'sˤim]).

'Insolent' is here a theological term, implying insolence towards God.

Meaning (b) largely carries over into the Mishnaic cognate ליצן [le'sˤån], which is often used to designate the sacrilegious; whilst those who doubt the veracity of Jeremiah's prophecy are called ליצנים [lesˤå'nim] (Ecclesiastes Rabba 8), Yalqut Shimoni characterizes the serpent who tempted Eve as ליצן [le'sˤån], as evidenced by its heretical statements against God (Yalqut Psalms 613):

> Rabbi Yehoshua of Sakhnin in the name of Rabbi Levi: The serpent besmirched his creator ... thus we learn that was a [le'sˤån].

Similarly, Mishnaic Hebrew מוקיון [muq'jon] is the term for Maccus, one of the stock characters in the Roman theatre (the *ludi*), originally a celebration of the attributes of a pagan god. Not surprisingly, the Tosefta (Avoda Zara 2.6) explicitly prohibits viewing the [muq'jon] (along with other theatrical characters and the pagan diviner), as part of the prohibitions against idolatry.

In Israeli, however, these terms lose this connotation. *Lets* is 'a joker, a kidder', while both *leytsán* and *mukyón* mean 'clown'. That said, *leytsán* and *mukyón* have a colloquial derogatory meaning: 'not serious, loser'.

(33) מנחש [mena'ħeʃ] → *menakhésh*

(34) קסם [qo'sem] → קוסם *kosém*

A similar process is evident in biblical Hebrew מנחש [mena'ħeʃ] and קסם [qo'sem], both referring to 'diviners'. In Deuteronomy 18: 10–11 they appear in a list of practitioners of prohibited religious practices:

לא ימצא בך מעביר בנו ובתו באש קסם קסמים מעונן ומנחש ומכשף

וחבר חבר ושאל אוב וידעני ודרש אל המתים

Let no one be found among you who consigns his son or daughter to the fire, or who is an augur [qo'sem qəså'mim], a soothsayer, a diviner [mena'ħeʃ], a sorcerer, one who casts spells, or one who consults ghosts or familiar spirits, or one who inquires of the dead.

In Israeli both words lose their theological negative meaning: the root נחש √nħʃ refers to 'guessing' so that *menakhésh* is simply an individual who guesses. Israeli *kosém* is 'a magician'.

6.4.6 Extreme amelioration (negative→positive)

(35) עמל [ʕå'mål] → *amál*

Biblical Hebrew עמל [ʕå'mål] is generally negative. Jeremiah (20: 18) asks, 'Why did I ever issue from the womb, to see misery [ʕå'mål] and woe'. The Psalmist asserts that, though the wicked man thinks God is oblivious to what happens in the world, 'You do look! You take note of mischief [ʕå'mål] and vexation!' (Psalms 10: 14). Habakkuk (1: 13) speaks of God as one 'whose eyes are too pure to look upon evil, who cannot countenance wrongdoing [ʕå'mål]'. There are a number of verses – albeit strikingly few – in which the word appears to mean 'hard work, labour', but here too the meaning is consistently negative. Consider Ecclesiastes 2: 11:

> Then I considered all that my hands had done and the toil I had spent in doing it, and again, all was vanity and a chasing after wind, and there was nothing to be gained under the sun.

In Mishnaic Hebrew, the narrower sense of 'labour' becomes more pronounced, as in the following statement from Mishnah Avot 2.14:

> Rabbi Elazar says: be diligent in the study of Torah and know the proper response to a heretic [ʔɛppi'qoros], and know before whom you labour [ʕå'mel], and the supervisor is reliable – he will pay you the wages of your actions.

Here too, however, the sense is largely negative: [ʃåˈmål] is regularly paired with יגע [ˈjɛgaʃ] 'exertion, tiring toil'. Man is sentenced to [ʃåˈmål] and can only redeem this state of affairs by labouring in Torah.

Socialist Zionism, however, strips the term of its negative connotations, and it comes to mean 'productive work, labour', often in an unambiguously positive sense as in the following toponyms:

- תל עמל *tel amál* was the name of a kibbutz (the first of the so-called *khomá umigdál* settlements), established in 1936, today called Nir David.
- נוה עמל *nevé amál* is a neighbourhood in Herzeliyah.
- קרית עמל *kiryát amál* is a settlement near Tiv'on.

Amál is also the name of a national network of technical and vocational schools. In the reflexive form, *amál* is something that people can and should impose on themselves for their health and well-being: התעמלות *hitamlút* means 'physical exercise'.

The shift in meaning is particularly marked in the appropriation of the phrase אדם לעמל יולד [ʔåˈdåm ləʃåˈmål julˈlåd] 'Man was born into (or: to do) [ʃåˈmål]'. In the book of Job (5: 6–7), this sentence stands as an accusation of the inherent wickedness of mankind:

כי לא יצא מעפר און
ומאדמה לא יצמח עמל
כי אדם לעמל יולד

Evil does not grow out of the soil
Nor does mischief spring from the ground
For man was born to do mischief [ʃåˈmål].

The negative force of [ʃåˈmål] is clear from the parallel with און [ˈʔåwɛn] 'evil', so the statement – which is made by Elifaz the Temanite, not Job – stands as a pessimistic assessment of the human condition.

But in the language of Socialist Zionism, this very phrase is employed as affirmation that humanity finds its fulfilment in labour. Turning the semantic, etymological truth upside down, an Israeli who reads Job 5: 7 is very likely to understand it as 'man was born to do productive work' – cf. Section 6.6.

It is important to note that Arabic, where *ʕ.m.l* means 'to work', might have facilitated this semantic choice in Israeli.

(36) הגשמה [hagʃåˈmå] → *agshamá*
The word [hagʃåˈmå] enters Hebrew in the Middle Ages under the influence of Arabic. It is part of the vocabulary of medieval philosophy, and one of the foreign words in Yehudah Ibn Tibbon's list of lexical innovations appended to his Hebrew translation of Maimonides' (1963) *The Guide of the Perplexed*, a philosophical work – written in Arabic – harmonizing and differentiating Aristotelian philosophy and Jewish theology.

Medieval Hebrew [hagʃåˈmå] refers to the attribution of a material reality to God, perhaps the most severe philosophical and theological error possible in this tradition, one that Maimonides addresses in the opening words of the *Guide*:

כבר חשבו בני אדם כי צלם בלשון העברי יורה על תמונת הדבר ותארו, והביא זה אל
הגשמה גמורה.

People have thought that in the Hebrew language *image* [ˈsˤɛlɛm] denotes the shape and configuration of a thing. This supposition led them to the pure doctrine of the corporeality of God [hagʃåˈmå].

Ultimately, the negativity of the word derives from a negative valorization of materiality as such: the ultimate good (God) lies beyond the material world, and any attempt to conceive of this good in terms drawn from lived human experience constitutes a grave philosophical and theological error.

In Zionist discourse, however, *agshamá* is ideologically positive, referring to the immanent physical realization of ideological ideals (usually settlement),[3] for example moving from the city to a co-operative agricultural settlement, a kibbutz. Undoubtedly, it is this sense – rather than the Maimonidean – that is alluded to by the toponym רמת מגשימים *ramát magshimím*, lit. '*Magshimím* Heights', a moshav in the Golan Heights, as well as by the *Magshimím* Zionist youth movement. *Magshimím* are the realizers of Zionist ideology.

Note that there were pre-Zionist trends towards revaluating the term [hagʃåˈmå], particularly in Hasidism. In this case, Zionism sided with and radicalized a pre-existent sense of the word. The semantic shift – which indicates a break with the Mishnaic sense – may have already been evident in Yiddish or literary Hebrew. It is

significant to realize that most often it is the case that the marked
Yiddish meanings – rather than the classical senses – were adopted
by Israeli speakers. This general process, however, was often sub-
conscious – as opposed to most cases of ideological secularization
discussed here.

(37) בית העם [bet hå'ʕåm] → *bet aám*
The phrase [bet hå'ʕåm] 'house:CONSTR DEF-nation', i.e. 'the
house of the people', occurs in the Old Testament once (Jeremiah
39: 8), where it is contrasted with the בית המלך [bet ham'mɛlɛkʰ]
'house:CONSTR DEF-king', i.e. 'the king's house'. In the Babylonian
Talmud (Sabbath 32a), the term is part of a pejorative discussion of
unlearned Jews, עם הארץ [ʕam hå'ʔårɛsʕ]:

> Rabbi Ishmael the son of Elazar teaches: the unlearned Jews [ʕam
> hå'ʔårɛsʕ] die on account of two things: that they call the Torah
> ark 'the ark' and they call the synagogue 'the house of the people
> [bet hå'ʕåm]'.

What, one might ask, is so terrible about calling the synagogue
by that name? Rashi explains that 'This is a derogatory term suggesting that everyone congregates there.' In other words, the term
[bet hå'ʕåm] marks the speaker as part of the unlearned, the antith-
esis of the rabbinic intellectual élite. This is such a derogatory term
for the synagogue that employing it results in the death of the
speaker.

When Zionist settlements – with their strong ideological commitment to populism – established cultural centres, they called them
bet aám, taking on and transvaluing the role of the non-scholastic
and non-rabbinic [ʕam hå'ʔårɛsʕ] (see 'A Song of Praise to '*amey ha-
'aretz*' by Zalman Schneur, 1886–1959, cited in Luz 1987: 382).

(38) חלוני [ħillo'ni] → חילוני *khiloní*
The priestly literature in the Old Testament draws a sharp distinction between the priest and the non-priest, so much so
that there is a technical term for the non-priest: זר [zår]. Thus
we find: 'No lay person [zår] shall eat of the sacred donations'
(Leviticus 22: 10); 'If a priest's daughter marries a layman [zår] ...'
(Leviticus 22: 12); 'When the Tabernacle is to be pitched, the
Levites shall set it up; any outsider [zår] who encroaches shall be
put to death' (Numbers 1: 51). In Onqelos's Aramaic translation

of these verses, biblical Hebrew [zår] is consistently replaced by חלוני [ħillo'ni].
The latter is the basis of Israeli חילוני *khiloní* 'secular'. The semantic shift is telling and, to an extent, emblematic: while the Aramaic word is defined negatively, as the individual who is *not* a priest and does *not* have the rights of a priest, Israeli *khiloní* assumes a positive cultural content or *Weltanschauung* (at least in the circles that adopted this new meaning), one centred around humanity rather than God.

It is worth noting that Israeli *khiloní* was coined by Joseph Klausner, a scholar intimately involved in the establishment of an anti-orthodox counter-history, primarily in his attempt to 'redeem' two Jews marginalized by rabbinic Judaism: Spinoza and Jesus. In a 1927 speech Klausner delivered at Mt Scopus, he addressed the excommunicated philosopher Spinoza saying 'You are our brother! You are our brother! You are our brother!' On Jesus, see Klausner (1922).

(39) תרבות [tar'but] → *tarbút*
A biblical hapax legomenon, [tar'but] appears in Numbers 32: 14 in the phrase תרבות אנשים חטאים [tar'but ʔănåˈʃim ħatˤˈtˤåʔim] 'a *breed* of sinful men', with the root רבה √rbh being understood as referring to the group that was 'raised' in a certain manner. In rabbinic literature it appears almost exclusively in the phrase רעה תרבות [tar'but råˈʕå] 'bad rearing/education' (e.g. Mishnah Niddah 10.8, Babylonian Talmud Hagigah 15a). In Israeli, the valence of *tarbút* changes and it becomes 'culture' in the sense of *Bildung*.

(40) בלורית [bəlo'rit] → *blorít*
In delineating the borders between the Jew and the non-Jew in Roman Palestine, rabbinic literature often draws the line at any action that could involve participation in idolatrous practices. It is generally permitted to trade with pagans, but not immediately prior to pagan holidays lest the Jew's money fund the idolatrous practices; it is generally permitted to purchase food from a pagan, though not wine that could be used for pagan libations; and so on. Interestingly, this distinction is also found in the realm of coiffure: a barber is, as a rule, permitted to cut the hair of a pagan, but there is one exception (Mishnah Avoda Zara 3.6):

A Jew who is cutting the hair of a pagan, as soon as he reaches the [bəlo'rit] he drops his hands.

According to Maimonides's *Mishneh Torah: the Book of Knowledge* (see Hyamson 1965: 78b), [bəlo'rit] refers to the following haircut:

'And I have set you apart from the nations' (Leviticus 20: 26): He shall not put on a garment like that specially worn by them, nor let the lock of his hair grow in the way they do. Thus, he shall not cut the hair of the head at the sides, leaving the hair in the center untouched as they do – this is called [bəlo'rit].

Thus, Mishnaic Hebrew [bəlo'rit] is 'Mohawk', a hairstyle in which the scalp is shaved except for an upright strip of hair that runs across the crown of the head from the forehead to the nape of the neck. But the precise definition is less important than its function as a distinctive marker of the pagan. Consider the following *drashot* (interpretations):

'Or has any God ventured to go and take for himself one nation (גוי [goj]) from the midst of another nation (גוי [goj])' (Deuteronomy 4: 34): Both these and those were uncircumcised; the Egyptians grew [bəlo'rit] and the Israelites grew [bəlo'rit]; those wore garments of mingled fabric and these wore garments of mingled fabric. (*Leviticus Rabba* 23.2; see Slotki 1977: 292)

In describing Israel's exodus from Egypt, Deuteronomy speaks of the departure of 'one nation from the midst of another nation', using the word גוי [goj] for Israel and Egypt alike. The linguistic equation of Israel and Egypt suggests to the interpreter that the Israelites had lost their distinctive identity and adopted that of their hosts. To prove the point, the interpreter cites a number of characteristics which are normally associated with the pagans but which have been adopted by the Israelites: both are uncircumcised, both wear garments of mingled fabric, and both have grown a [bəlo'rit].
Similarly:

These things are prohibited because they savour of heathen practices [the way of the Emorites]: to trim the front of the hair and to grow a [bəlo'rit]. (*Deuteronomy Rabbah* 2.18; see Rabinowitz 1977: 44)

Intriguingly, in Israeli not only does בלורית *blorít* lose its meaning as the marker of the pagan as opposed to the Jew, but it also becomes one of the defining characteristics of the Sabra,[4] the 'new Jew', characterized by 'forelock, hair above the forehead'.

Thus, in Naomi Shemer's classic song about two young men from the same village, who march through life in parallel until one is killed in battle:

אנחנו שנינו מאותו הכפר, אותה קומה, אותה בלורית שיער

We are both from the same village, the same height, the same *blorít* of hair

Israeli *blorít* also appears in Hayim Guri's poem 'Camaraderie' (הרעות *areút*), a paean to the fallen fighters of the *Palmach* brigade:

ונזכור את כולם, את יפי הבלורית והתואר

We shall remember them all, they of the beautiful *blorít* and countenance

And similarly in Haim Hefer's portrait of the *Palmach* fighter Dudu, who is also fated to die:

היתה לו בלורית מקורזלת שיער , היתה לו בת צחוק בעיניים

He had a curly *blorít*, he had laughing eyes

Almog (2003) characterizes *blorít* as the hairstyle of the mythical Sabra.[5] Here we come to the ultimate ideological secularization: the Mishnaic marker of otherness is appropriated by the Sabra warrior. The new Jew is ultimately a pagan.

(41) תל אביב [tel ʔåˈbʰibʰ] → *tel avív*

It is often said that the name *Tel-Aviv*, 'hill:CONSTR spring', i.e. 'Hill of Spring', is a juxtaposition of the old (the ancient *tel*) with the new, an allusion to Herzl's utopian *Altneuland*, which was translated as *Tel-Aviv* by Nahum Sokolov. Both Sokolov's translation and the choice of this name for the 'first Hebrew city' are striking in light of the name's biblical precedent. It appears in the Old Testament only once, in Ezekiel 3: 15. Ezekiel, who prophesied in Babylon after the fall of the first temple, has just heard God's call to speak to Israel, and a mighty wind (or spirit) carries him away:

And I came to the exile, to Tel Aviv [ʔel haggoˈlå tel ʔåˈbʰibʰ] those who settled by the river Chebar [kəˈbʰår] ...[6]

The precise meaning of this transvaluation seems to be that Zionism would take an explicitly exilic location [haggoʻlå tel ʔåʻbʰibʰ] 'the exile, Tel Aviv' and turn it into the centre of Jewish national revival, forcefully reversing the biblical association of Tel Aviv with exile.

6.4.7   Ameliorative recycling of biblical names: using deep-rooted Hebrew forms ignoring their original negative associations

Extreme amelioration is also apparent in Zionist reappropriation of anthroponyms of biblical figures that are disparaged by the Old Testament or later rabbinic tradition.

(42) רחבעם [rəħabʰʻåm] → *rekhavám*

Consider רחבעם [rəħabʰʻåm] 'Rehoboam', Solomon's son, best known for his draconian taxes and impositions on the populace:

אבי יסר אתכם בשוטים ואני איסר אתכם בעקרבים

My father flogged you with whips, but I will flog you with scorpions. (I Kings 12: 14)

Indeed, these policies (at least according to the biblical narrative) contributed to the split of Israel into two kingdoms, Israel in the north and Judaea in the south. For obvious reasons, Rehavam has not been a popular name in traditional Jewish circles, but it has enjoyed a renaissance as a name for Israeli boys – cf. Rehavam Zeevi (nicknamed Gandhi – because on one occasion he looked like skinny Mahatma Gandhi, not because of his politics) (1926–2001), an Israeli general, politician and historian who founded the right-wing nationalist Moledet party.

(43) עמרי [ʻomʻri] → *omrí*

The example of 'Omri is even more dramatic. A king of the northern kingdom of Israel, the Book of Kings recounts that "Omri did what was displeasing to the Lord; he was worse than all who preceded him' (1 Kings 16: 25), a damning appraisal by all accounts. Nonetheless, some Israeli speakers have chosen to name their sons Omri, cf. Omri Sharon (1964–), the son of the former Israeli Prime Minister Ariel Sharon and himself a former member of the Likud party in the Knesset.

(44) ענת [ʕăˈnåt] → *anát*

Hebrew ענת [ʕăˈnåt] 'Anat' was a bloodthirsty Canaanite goddess who slew her enemies and made herself a belt of their heads and hands. The great popularity of Anat as an Israeli girl's name is undoubtedly not in the spirit of the Old Testament.

Names such as Rehavam, Omri and Anat – as well as Hagar, Shamgar, Nimrod and many others – represent a cultural appropriation of biblical names that baldly undermines their (often explicit) biblical axiology. The names maintain a vaguely biblical – and thus authentic, desirable – sense (*Sinn*), but lose their biblical reference (*Bedeutung*). The material is biblical but the connotations are not.[7]

A similar phenomenon is the return of Canaanite divinities such as *Yam* (popular among kibbutz children), *Shákhar* and *Réshsef* as first names for Israeli children. To be sure, there is no cultural appropriation intended here, no conscious desire to reclaim a Canaanite identity. Still, the renewal of these names – meaning 'sea', 'dawn' and 'flame' respectively – may be a reflection of a deep affinity between the explicit identification of nature and the divine in Canaanite mythology, on the one hand, and the nature-worship that is part of the more Romantic strains of Jewish nationalism, on the other.

6.4.8 Trivialization ('Israelis have no God')

(45) תחתונים [taħtoˈnim] → *takhtoním*

In a number of instances the theological sense of a word is done away with by turning the word into a colloquial term. Thus Mishnaic Hebrew תחתונים [taħtoˈnim] designates the material world, literally 'those below', as opposed to the heavenly or supernal world, the latter being the עליונים [ʕeljoˈnim]. Genesis Rabba, for example, discusses at length whether, in the process of creation, God first created the [ʕeljoˈnim], the supernal world, and then the [taħtoˈnim], the material world, or vice versa (Bereshit Rabba section 2; vol. 1, p. 15 in the Theodor-Albeck edition).

In Israeli, however, *takhtoním* means 'underwear, underpants' ('those below'). This is a marked resemantization inasmuch as one would expect the word for 'underwears' to be in the dual form, in analogy with מכנסיים *mikhnasáim* 'trousers, pants'. The semantic shift is particularly jarring considering that the term is perhaps best known from a midrashic statement that played an important role in later Hasidic thought, namely that the divine presence originally resided in the material world (but took refuge in the heavens after Adam's sin): עיקר שכינה בתחתונים 'originally the Divine Presence resided in the lower realm', i.e. in the [taħto'nim].

An Internet search of the Hebrew phrase קרע את התחתונים Israeli *kará et atakhtoním* 'tore [or: parted] the *takhtoním*' will yield two types of sites:

(a) religious sites discussing Rashi's statement (commentary on Deuteronomy 4: 35):

> When the Holy One, blessed be He, gave the Torah, He opened for them the seven heavens. And just as he tore [or: split] the upper regions [ʕɛljo'nim], so too he tore [or: parted] the lower regions [taħto'nim].

(b) Israeli erotica or pornography sites, where *takhtoním* appears in its Israeli sense.

The juxtaposition of the religious and the pornographic websites on the result page represents a striking manifestation of the distance this word has traversed, and of the willingness of Israeli to thumb its nose at the values of earlier strata of Hebrew.

(46) חנות (פתוחה) [ħǎ'nut (pətu'ħå)] → *khanút (ptukhá)*
Both Mishnaic [ħǎ'nut] and Israeli *khanút* means 'a shop, a store'. In Mishnah Avot 3.16, Rabbi Akiva uses the term in a theological metaphor:

> The shop stands open (החנות פתוחה [haħǎ'nut pətu'ħå]) and the shopkeeper gives credit and the account-book lies open and the hand writes.

That is, God keeps open account books in which one's debits and credits are listed.

Calquing Yiddish, the opening phrase, החנות פתוחה [ħǎ'nut pətu'ħå] is appropriated in a distinctly non-theological colloquial sense in Israeli: 'the zipper is open'.

6.4.9   Allusion

Allusion to religious concepts is a very effective rhetorical device, often used by politicians. Consider George W. Bush's use of *axis of evil* or Osama Bin Laden's use of *crusade*. Ophir (2001) claims that Israeli nationalists use interpretation of holy texts and rituals to justify discrimination, segregation and overpowering of the Palestinian people.

Through allusion, in which the new meaning is heir to the older, while at the same time displacing it, Socialist Zionists shrewdly draw on earlier linguistic strata without legitimizing the exilic and religious sensibilities they encode.[8] Consider the following:

(47) מי ימלל גבורות יהוה [mi jəmal'lel gəbʰu'rot JHWH] → מי ימלל גבורות ישראל
mi yemalél gvurót israél
Consider the shift from the religious cry of the Psalmist (Psalms 106: 2) מי ימלל גבורות יהוה [mi jəmal'lel gəbʰu'rot JHWH] 'Who can tell the mighty acts of the Lord' to the lyrics of Menashe Rabina's popular Hanukkah song: מי ימלל גבורות ישראל *mi yemalél gvurót israél* 'Who can tell the mighty acts of Israel'. By replacing 'the mighty acts of the Lord' with 'the mighty acts of Israel', the songwriter is consciously seeking to shift the focus from the worship of the divine to the worship of the national collective.

This model of appropriation of classical Hebrew sources bespeaks a Zionist ambivalence towards earlier strata of Hebrew. The clear allusion to the words of the Psalmist indicates an explicit desire to link the nationalist song to an ancient poetic model. At the same time, the allusion to Psalm 106: 2 involves an important shift: praise of God is replaced by the glorification of the nation of Israel. Indeed, the allusion serves to highlight the place of Israel – that is, of the nationalist ideal – as heir to the religious ideal regnant in the Psalms.

(48) יזכור אלהים [jiz'kor ʔelo'him] → יזכור עם ישראל *izkór am israél*
Another example of such supersessionist secularization is found in the standard memorial ceremony of the Israel Defence Forces (and other state institutions), that opens with the words יזכור עם ישראל *izkór am israél* 'Let the people of Israel remember' – followed by an exaltation of the fallen soldiers. This formula, which was composed by the Zionist leader Berl Katzenelson, is based on the medieval *Yizkor* liturgy, that opens יזכור אלהים [jiz'kor ʔelo'him] 'Let the Lord remember' – often followed by a description of religious martyrs.[9]

(49) תורה ועבודה [to'rå waʃăbʰo'då] → *torá veavodá*
The religious Zionist youth movement, B'nei Akiva, lit. 'Akiva's sons', has תורה ועבודה *torá veavodá* as its motto, an allusion to the well-known Mishnaic statement from Mishnah Avot 1.2:

על שלושה דברים העולם עומד: על התורה, על העבודה ועל גמילות חסדים

On three things the world is sustained: on the Torah [to'rå], on the (Temple) service [ʃăbʰo'då] and on deeds of loving kindness.

Note, however, that the two terms, *torá* and *avodá*, refer in Israeli to the study of Torah and to labour as a Socialist value.

(50)   על המשק, על הנשק ועל החשק ← על התורה, על העבודה ועל גמילות חסדים

In Moshe Shamir's play – adapted from his novel of the same name הוא הלך בשדות *u alákh basadót* 'He Walked through the Fields' – the young prototypical Sabra protagonist, Uri, is taught the following from his rugged platoon commander:

> It is written in the Torah: The world is sustained by three things: the agricultural plot (המשק *améshek*), the weapon (הנשק *anéshek*) and sexual desire (החשק *akhéshek*). (Act 1, Scene 18, p. 53)

This statement parodies the famous Mishnaic statement (see example 49), replacing the values of '*torah*, Temple service and deeds of loving kindness' with a trio that emphasizes the agricultural, military and sexual ethos of Zionism. But unlike 'who can tell the mighty acts of Israel' for 'who can tell the mighty acts of the Lord', the lofty, sublime register of the earlier phrase is not maintained. Similarly, whereas the B'nei Akiva motto, *torá veavodá*, alludes to the Mishnah statement as a way of legitimizing its own (radically new) ideology, here, quite to the contrary, the irreverent Sabra's statement is a parody of the rabbinic dictum, not its heir.

Note that this is the position of the character, not necessarily of Shamir himself. The platoon leader gets his parody wrong by suggesting that he is making fun of a dictum that appears 'in the *Torah*' when, in fact, it is one of the best known statements in the Mishnah. Here Shamir may be subtly expressing his own scorn for the derisive attitude of the Sabra.

(51)   בקי בהטיה [bå'qi bəhat͡ʃt͡ʃå'jå] → *bakí beatayá*

There are instances of enthusiastic appropriation of sexual themes in earlier strata of Hebrew. A literary example appears in Haim Nachman Bialik's children's book 'The Champion of the Onions and the Champion of the Garlics' (*alúf abtsalím vealúf ashúm*), which refers to one of its characters as בקי בהטיה [bå'qi bəhat͡ʃt͡ʃå'jå] 'an expert incliner'. This is an obscure Mishnaic phrase referring to one who is able to have sexual intercourse with a virgin without drawing blood. That Bialik would choose to incorporate the phrase into juvenile literature – without, of course, making its meaning explicit – is an indication of the sexual playfulness that

at least some prominent writers associated with their work – cf.
Be'er (2004: 269–70).

(52) ונתתי את שמיכם כברזל ואת ארצכם כנחשה [wənåtat'ti ʔɛt ʃəme'kʰɛm kabbar'zɛl
wə'ʔɛt ʔarsˤə'kʰɛm kannəħu'ʃå]
Consider the sentence written beneath a portrait of a pilot standing in front of a jet fighter, in a recruitment poster hanging in
some Israeli Air Force bases: ונתתי את שמיכם כברזל ואת ארצכם כנחשה. The
Hebrew pronunciation was [wənåtat'ti ʔɛt ʃəme'kʰɛm kabbar'zɛl
wə'ʔɛt ʔarsˤə'kʰɛm kannəħu'ʃå] but in Israeli it would be pronounced *venatáti et shmeykhém kebarzél veét artsekhém kenekhushá /
kenekhóshet*. The literal meaning of this high-register sentence is 'I
will make your skies like iron and your earth like copper', implying
that the Israeli Air Force makes the skies as impenetrable as iron to
its enemies. But the use of Leviticus 26: 19 as a recruitment slogan
is remarkable considering its original meaning:

> And if, for all that, you do not obey Me, I will go on to discipline
> you sevenfold for your sins, and I will break your proud glory.
> *I will make your skies like iron and your earth like copper*, so that
> your strength will be spent to no purpose. Your land shall not
> yield its produce, nor shall the trees of the land yield their fruit.
> (Leviticus 26: 18–20)

The biblical context is explicitly negative: the iron sky a sign of
drought, the copper land an indication of barrenness – whilst the
air force poster suggests military power and fortitude. Clearly, the
appropriation of the biblical verse involves a shift in the original
meaning. Be that as it may, this shift may simply be due to the
graphic designer's ignorance of the verse's original meaning and
while ignorance is a cultural force in its own right, it is not one of
the manipulative forces treated in this chapter. But it *is* relevant to
Gershom Scholem's 1926 letter to Franz Rosenzweig.

6.5 Confession on the subject of our language (*Bekenntnis über unsere Sprache*)
A letter by Gershom Scholem to Franz Rosenzweig, 26 December 1926

This country is a volcano. It houses language. One speaks here of many
things that could make us fail. One speaks more than ever today about

the Arabs. But more uncanny than the Arab people [*unheimlicher als das arabische Volk*] another threat confronts us that is a *necessary* consequence [*mit Notwendigkeit*] of the Zionist undertaking: What about the 'actualization [*Aktualisierung*]' of Hebrew? Must not this abyss of a sacred language handed down to our children break out again? Truly, no one knows what is being done here. One believes that language has been secularized, that its apocalyptic thorn has been pulled out [*ihr den apokalyptischen Stachel ausgezogen zu haben*]. But this is surely not true. The secularization of language is only a *façon de parler*, a ready-made phrase. It is absolutely impossible to empty out words filled to bursting, unless one does so at the expense of language itself. The ghostly Volapük spoken here in the streets points precisely to the expressionless linguistic world in which the 'secularization' of language could alone be possible. If we transmit to our children the language that has been transmitted to us, if we – the generation of the transition [*das Geschlecht des Übergangs*] – resuscitate the language of the ancient books so that it can reveal itself anew to them, must then not the religious violence of the language one day break out against those who speak it [*gegen ihre Sprecher ausbrechen*]? And on the day this eruption occurs, which generation will suffer its effects [*und welches Geschlecht wird dieser Ausbruch finden*]? We do live inside this language, above an abyss, almost all of us with the certainty of the blind. But when our sight is restored, we or those who come after us, must we not fall to the bottom of this abyss? And no one knows whether the sacrifice of individuals who will be annihilated in this abyss will suffice to close it.

The creators of this new linguistic movement believed blindly, and stubbornly, in the miraculous power of the language, and this was their good fortune. For no one clear-sighted would have mustered the demonic courage to revive a language there where only an Esperanto could emerge. They walk, and walk still today, spellbound [*gebannt*] above the abyss. The abyss was silent and they have delivered the ancient names and seals over to the youth. We sometimes shudder when, out of the thoughtless conversation, a word from the religious sphere terrifies us, just there where it was perhaps intended to comfort. Hebrew is pregnant with catastrophes. It cannot and will not remain in its current state. Our children no longer have another language, and it is only too true to say that they, and they alone, will pay for the encounter which we have initiated without asking, without even asking ourselves. If and when the language turns against its speakers – it already does so for certain moments in our lifetime, and these are difficult to forget, stigmatizing moments in which the daring lack of measure of our undertaking reveals itself to us – will we then have a youth capable of withstanding the uprising of a sacred language? Language is Name [*Sprache ist Namen*]. In the names, the power of language is enclosed; in them, its abyss is sealed. After invoking the ancient names daily, we can no longer hold off their power. Called awake, they will appear since we have invoked them with great violence. Truly, we speak in rudiments; we truly speak a ghostly language [*wir freilich sprechen eine gespenstische Sprache*]: the names haunt our sentences. One or another plays with them in writings and newspapers, lying to themselves or to God that this means nothing, and often, out of the ghostly shame of our language, the power of the sacred speaks out. For the names have their own life – had they not, woe to our children, who would be hopelessly abandoned to the void.

Each word which is not newly created but taken from the 'good old' treasure is full to bursting. A generation that takes upon itself the most fruitful in our sacred traditions – our language – cannot live, were it to wish it a thousandfold, without tradition. The moment the *power* stored at the bottom of the language *deploys itself*, the moment the 'said [*das Gesprochene*]', the content of language, assumes its form anew, then the sacred tradition will again confront our people as a decisive sign of the only available choice: to submit or to go under. In a language where he is invoked back to a thousandfold into our life, God will not stay silent. But this inescapable revolution of the language, in which the voice will be heard again, is the sole object of which nothing is said in this country. Those who called the Hebrew language back to life did not believe in the judgment that was thus conjured upon us. May the carelessness, which has led us to this apocalyptic path, not bring about our ruin [*Möge uns dann nicht der Leichtsinn, der uns auf diesem apokalyptischen Weg geleitet, zum Verderb werden*].

Jerusalem, 7 Tevet 5687
Gerhard Scholem
(Translation by Anidjar, see Derrida 2002: 226–7)

6.6 The Mutual Intelligibility Myth

Modern Greek, for example, boasts many similarities to its ancestor, yet a speaker of the current language must struggle to read ancient texts. The modern Hebrew speaker, however, moves smoothly through the Bible. (Ravitzky 2000: 13–14)

Frequently, new research emerges allegedly demonstrating how 'bad' Israelis are at reading comprehension vis-à-vis pupils in other countries. I wonder whether these exams test reading comprehension in *Hebrew* rather than in *Israeli*. The former might be a second language for Israelis. The Mutual Intelligibility Myth posits that Israeli is Hebrew because an Israeli speaker can understand Hebrew. Edward Ullendorff (pers. comm.) has claimed that the biblical Isaiah could have understood Israeli. I am not convinced that this would have been the case. The reason Israelis can be expected to understand the book of Isaiah – albeit with difficulties – is because they study the Hebrew Bible at school for 11 years, rather than because it is familiar to them from their daily conversation. Furthermore, *Israelis read the Hebrew Bible as if it were Israeli and often therefore misunderstand it.*

(53) When an Israeli reads **ילד שעשעים** *yéled sha'ashu'ím* in Jeremiah 31: 19 (King James 20), s/he does not understand it as 'pleasant child' but rather as 'playboy'.

(54) **באו בנים עד משבר** *Ba'u banim 'ad mashber* in Isaiah 37: 3 is interpreted by Israelis as 'children arrived at a crisis' rather than as 'children arrived at the mouth of the womb, to be born'.

Add to these all the numerous lexical items discussed in this chapter, e.g. in example (35): **אדם לעמל יולד** *ʔådåm ləʕåmål yullåd* (Job 5: 6–7), which is interpreted by Israelis as 'man was born to do productive work' rather than 'man was born to do mischief'. This biblical sentence stands as an accusation of the inherent wickedness of mankind.

Most importantly, the available examples are far from being only lexical (as in the above *faux amis*). *Israelis are usually incapable of recognizing moods and aspects in the Bible. Whereas in biblical Hebrew there is a perfect/imperfect* **aspect** *distinction, in Israeli there is a past–present–future* **tense** *distinction.*T

(55) Ask an Israeli what **אבנים שחקו מים** *'abanim shaḥaqu mayim* (Job 14: 19) means and s/he will most likely tell you that the stones eroded the water. Of course, on second thought, s/he would guess that semantically this is impossible and that it must be the water which eroded the stones. But such an object–verb–subject (A) constituent order is impossible in Israeli.

(56) **נפילה גורלות** *nappila goralot* 'let us cast lots' (Jonah 1: 7) is thought to be rhetorical future rather than cohortative.

By and large, Israelis are the worst students in *advanced* studies of the Bible, although almost all Israelis would disagree with this statement of mine. Try to tell Israel's Ministry of Education that *the Hebrew Bible should be translated into Israeli!* (It will eventually happen!)

Yet, Israeli children are told that the Hebrew Bible was written in their mother tongue. In other words, in Israeli primary schools, Hebrew and the mother tongue are, axiomatically, the very same. One cannot therefore expect Israelis easily to accept the idea that the two languages might be genetically different. In English terms, it is as if someone were to try to tell a native English speaker that his/her mother tongue is not the same as Shakespeare's. The difference is that between Shakespeare and the current native speaker of English there has been a continuous chain of native speakers. Between the biblical Isaiah and contemporary Israelis there has been no such chain, while the Jews have had many mother tongues other than Hebrew.

An example from the Mishnah:

(57) פרס [pəˈrås] → *pras*

Israeli פרס *pras* means 'prize' (cf. *Milón leMunekhéy haHitamlút, Dictionary of Gymnastics Terms*, 1937: 49, Item 625), nativizing the internationalism *prize* – cf. Russian приз *priz* [pris] 'prize', German *Preis* 'prize, price', English *prize* (cf. *price*) and Yiddish פריז *priz* 'prize'.[10] Originally, Mishnaic Hebrew פרס [pəˈrås] meant 'half a loaf' – cf. Mishnah Kritot 3: 3. Consequently it referred to 'payment, reward' – שלא על מנת לקבל פרס [ʃɛlˈlo ʕal məˈnåt ləqabˈbel pəˈrås] 'not motivated by the wish to get a reward/payment' (Mishnah Avot 1: 3). The latter expression is currently understood by many native Israeli speakers I have studied as meaning 'not motivated by the wish to receive a prize'. Their belief that Mishnaic Hebrew פרס meant 'prize' is thus no more than the etymological truth turned upside down.[11]

6.7 The political (ab)use of ambiguity

Ironically, the very same people who may argue that Israelis can easily understand Hebrew often abuse the vagueness or ambiguity resulting from secularization. They nourish grey areas of mutual intelligibility as a means of getting out of a legal or political quagmire. Consider the beginning of the concluding sentence of Israel's Declaration of Independence, construed to pacify both the religious and secular:

מתוך בטחון בצור ישראל הננו חותמים בחתימת ידינו לעדות על הכרזה זו, במושב מועצת המדינה הזמנית,

120   *The Sociology of Language and Religion*

על אדמת המולדת, בעיר תל-אביב, היום הזה, ערב שבת, ה' אייר תש"ח, 14, במאי 1948.

mitókh bitakhón betsúr israél …

Placing our *trust* in the *almighty* / Placing our *security* in the *rock of Israel*,

we affix our signatures to this proclamation at this session of the Provisional Council of State, on the soil of the homeland, in the city of Tel Aviv, on this Sabbath Eve, the 5th day of Iyar, 5708 (14 May 1948)

Biblical Hebrew בטחון [bitˤtˤå'ħon] means 'trust, faith (in God)'. The semantic range of its root בטח √bṭħ is not limited to 'trust/faith in God' but this is certainly one of its main meanings. Indeed, in many instances the biblical text promotes faith or trust in God over earthly persons or institutions. The psalmist exhorts 'O Israel, trust in the Lord! He is their [sic] help and shield' (Psalms 115: 9). Isaiah teaches 'Trust in the Lord for ever and ever' (Isaiah 24: 4). The phrase 'Happy is the man who trusts in You' (Psalms 84: 13) is incorporated into the *Havdalah* liturgy.

The question of earthly versus divine trust indeed comes to the fore in the nominal form בטחון [bitˤtˤå'ħon]. When Hezekiah King of Judah (eighth century BC) rebels against Senacherib, the latter sends an emissary, Rabshakeh, to convince the Jerusalemites to lay down their arms. Rabshakeh sends the following question to Hezekiah: הבטחון הזה אשר בטחת מה 'What is this confidence [bitˤtˤå'ħon] you have?' (Isaiah 36: 4), then asserts the futility of claiming 'we are relying [batˤ'åħnu] on the Lord our God' (Isaiah 36: 7). But of course the [bitˤtˤå'ħon] was not misplaced, as God does turn back the Assyrians and Hezekiah remains on the throne.

In later strata of literary Hebrew, the specific sense 'faith in God' is the dominant, almost exclusive meaning. Thus, Shlomo Ibn Gabirol (eleventh century AD) devotes a chapter in his ethical treatise *The Improvement of the Moral Qualities* (*tikkun middot hannefesh*) in Yehudah Ibn Tibbon's translation of the moral attribute [bitˤtˤå'ħon]. The opening statement of the chapter is 'This is the exalted trait by which an individual comports himself according to his faith in God and his reliance on Him.'

In Israeli, however, בטחון *bitakhón* no longer derives from God but rather from military power. The word means 'military power' as in the phrase מערכת הביטחון *maarékhet abitakhón* 'the military' and כוחות הביטחון *kokhót abitakhón* 'the security forces', while the minister charged with the army and other security forces is שר הביטחון *sar abitakhón* 'Minister of Defence (literally: security)'.

6.8 Concluding remarks

Israeli society is riven. Ironically, as well as being a highly symbolic common language, Israeli has come to highlight the very absence of a unitary civic culture among citizens who seem increasingly to share only their language (and enemies). The nexus which allegedly binds all Israelis together is an illusion. The existing continuum between the ultra-orthodox and the ultra-secular does not mitigate the divide, and mutual hostility is apparent in the two camps.

In line with the prediction made by the Kabbalah scholar Gershom Scholem in his letter to Franz Rosenzweig, some ultra-orthodox Jews have tried to launch a 'lexical vendetta': using secularized terms like 'dormant agents', as a short cut to religious concepts, thus trying to convince secular Jews to go back to their religious roots (cf. Walzer 1965, Ravitzky 1993).

The study of Israeli cultural linguistics and sociophilology may cast light on the dynamics between language, religion and identity in a land where fierce military battles with external enemies are accompanied by internal *Kulturkämpfe*.

Notes

1. Thanks to Grace Brockington, Simon Overall, Uri Eisenzweig, Ken Moss, Erez Cohen, Gary Rendsburg, Jeffrey Shandler and Yael Zerubavel, who read and commented on an earlier version of this chapter.
2. See the discussion of Weiss (1977), Kantor (1992) and Zuckermann (2003: 75).
3. On the shift toward an 'earthly' reinterpretation of Jewish history in Zionist thought (and Eastern European *Haskalah*), see Luz (1987).
4. Sabra 'prickly pear' (widespread in Israel) – cf. צבר *tsabar* – is a nickname for native Israelis, allegedly thorny on the outside and sweet inside. This is analogous to the use of the word kiwi to denote a New Zealander, not after the delicious fruit but rather after the nocturnal, wingless bird which has a long neck and stout legs.
5. Thanks to Yael Zerubavel for reference to Almog's article.
6. Biblical Hebrew [haggo'lå] most likely meant 'exile community' rather than 'the exile'. However, the relevant issue is how the phrase was understood by those who associated this Babylonian location with the Israeli city – cf. Section 6.6.
7. Though the differences are obvious, the use of the Bible may be compared to what Schwarz (1995: 38) calls the 'talismanic and evocative' use of Hebrew in the post-AD 70 Jewish Diaspora, inasmuch as it is not the biblical meaning that generates these names (and which may be quite unknown to, for

example, parents naming their daughters 'Anat), but their biblical *feel*. They serve to connect the bearer of the name with a vague and ill-defined biblical 'heritage', the precise details of which are much less significant. Thanks to Andrea Berlin for referring us to Schwarz's article.

8. Don-Yehia (1980) discusses Socialist Zionism's appropriation of a number of traditional Jewish terms. His focus is more on the overtly ideological use of the terminology of, for example, redemption, covenant and sacrifice.

9. See the discussion in Azaryahu (1995).

10. Cf. also Yiddish פרײַז *prayz*, Polish Yiddish *prās*, 'price', that has recently gained the additional meaning 'prize'. Thus, *dóvid hófshteyn prayz* means 'Dovid Hofshtein Prize' – see *Fórverts 'Yiddish Forward'*, 28 July 2000, p. 16. This is an incestuous phono-semantic matching by semantic shifting of English *prize*.

11. Cf. the 1999 advertisement (in the UK) for Toblerone chocolate (which 'inspires the world'), which showed a photo of pyramids in Egypt, asking: 'Ancient Tobleronism?'

References

Akadém (*The Bulletin of the Academy of the Hebrew Language*) (1993–2000) (Issues 1–15) E. Gonen (ed., 5–15). Jerusalem: The Academy of the Hebrew Language.

Almog, O. (2003) 'From Blorit to Ponytail: Israeli Culture Reflected in Popular Hairstyles'. *Israel Studies*, 8.

Azaryahu, Maoz (1995) *pulkhanéy medina: khagigót haatsmaút vehantsakhát hanoflím beisraél 1948–1956* [State Cults: Celebrating Independence and Commemorating the Fallen in Israel, 1948–1956]. Beer Sheva: Ben-Gurion University of the Negev Press.

Bar-Asher, M. (1995) 'al kharóshet hamilím beváad halashón uvaakadémya lalashón haivrít' ['Fabrication' of Words by the Hebrew Language Council and the Academy of the Hebrew Language]. *Leshonenu La'am*, 47 (1), 3–18.

Be'er, H. (1992) *Their Love and Their Hate: H. N. Bialik, Y. H. Brenner, S. Y. Agnon – Relations*. Tel Aviv: Am Oved.

Ben-Yehuda, E. (1909–59) *milón halashón haivrít hayeshaná vehakhadashá* [A Complete Dictionary of Ancient and Modern Hebrew]. Tel Aviv: La'am; Jerusalem: Hemda and Ehud Ben-Yehuda; New York/London: Thomas Yoseloff (16 vols plus an introductory volume).

Ben-Yehuda, E. (1978) *hakhalóm veshivró: mivkhár ktavím beinyenéy lashón* [The Dream and Its Fulfilment: Selected Writings], Reuven Sivan (ed.). Jerusalem: Dorot; Bialik Institute. (*shivró* could also mean 'its realization/meaning/ breaking'.)

Derrida, J. (2002) *Acts of Religion*, G. Anidjar (ed.). New York/London: Routledge.

Don-Yehia, E. (1980) 'khiúv, shlilá veshilúv: tfisót shel hayahadút hamasortít umusagéha batsionút hasotsyalístit' [Affirmation, Negation and Integration: Perceptions by Socialist Zionism of Traditional Judaism and Its Concepts]. *Kivuním*, 8, 29–46.

Even-Shoshan, A. (1970) *hamilón hekhadásh* [The New Dictionary]. Jerusalem: Kiryath Sepher (7 vols).

Even-Shoshan, A. (1997) *hamilón hekhadásh – hamahadurá hameshulévet* [The New Dictionary – the Combined Version]. Jerusalem: Kiryat-Sefer (5 vols).

Horvath, J. and Wexler, P. (eds) (1997) *Relexification in Creole and Non-Creole Languages – with Special Attention to Haitian Creole, Modern Hebrew, Romani, and Rumanian* (Mediterranean Language and Culture Monograph Series, vol. xiii). Wiesbaden: Otto Harrassowitz.

Hyamson, M. (1965) Translation of Maimonides, in *Mishneh Torah: the Book of Knowledge*. Jerusalem: Qiriya Ne'emana.

Jastrow, M. (1903) *A Dictionary of the Targumim, the Talmud Babli and Yerushalmi, and the Midrashic Literature*. Jerusalem: Horev.

Kantor, H. (1992) 'Current Trends in the Secularization of Hebrew'. *Language in Society*, 21, 603–9.

Klausner, J. (1922) *Jesus of Nazareth: His Life, Times, and Teachings*. New York: Block Publishing.

Klausner, J. G. (1940) 'khamishím shaná shel váad halashón' [Fifty Years of the Hebrew Language Council]. *Lešonénu*, 10 (4), 278–89.

Klein, E. (1987) *A Comprehensive Etymological Dictionary of the Hebrew Language*. Jerusalem: Carta.

Kuzar, R. (2001) *Hebrew and Zionism: a Discourse Analytic Cultural Study* (Language, Power and Social Process 5). Berlin/New York: Mouton de Gruyter.

Laméd Leshonkhá [Teach Your Language]: New Series. 1993–2000 (Leaflets 1–34). Sh. Bahat (ed.: Leaflets 1–2), R. Gadish (ed.: Leaflets 3–10), R. Selig (ed.: Leaflets 11–34). Jerusalem: The Academy of the Hebrew Language.

Luz, E. (1987) 'Spiritual and Anti-Spiritual Trends in Zionism', in Arthur Green (ed.), *Jewish Spirituality II: From the Sixteenth Century Revival to the Present*, New York: Crossroad, pp. 371–401.

McMahon, A. M. S. (1994) *Understanding Language Change*. Cambridge: Cambridge University Press.

Maimonides, M. (1963) *The Guide of the Perplexed*, Shlomo Pínes (trans.). Chicago: University of Chicago Press (2 vols).

Ophir, A. (2001) *avodát hahové: másot al tarbút israelít bazmán hazé* [Working for the Present: Essays on Contemporary Israeli Culture]. Hakibbutz Hameuchad.

Pínes, Y. M. (1893) 'davár laoskéy bitkhiyát sfaténu' [Something for Those who Deal with the Revival of Our Language]. *Haór*, 9 (18).

Rabinowitz, J. (1977) Translation of *Deuteronomy Rabbah*. London/New York: Soncino.

Ravitzky, A. (1993) *hakéts hamegulé umedinát hayehudím: meshikhiút, tsionút veradikalízem datí beisraél* [Messianism, Zionism and Jewish Religious Radicalism]. Tel Aviv: Am Oved.

Ravitzky, A. (2000) 'Religious and Secular Jews in Israel: a *Kulturkampf*?' Position Paper, The Israel Democracy Institute.

Sapir, Y. and Zuckermann, G. (2008) 'Icelandic: Phonosemantic Matching', in Judith Rosenhouse and Rotem Kowner (eds), *Globally Speaking: Motives for Adopting English Vocabulary in Other Languages*, Clevedon/Buffalo/Toronto: Multilingual Matters, pp. 19–43 (Ch. 2) (References: 296–325).

Schwarz, S. (1995) 'Language, Power and Identity in Ancient Palestine'. *Past and Present*, 148, 3–47.

Shemesh, A. (1997) ' "The Holy Angels are in their Council": the Exclusion of Deformed Persons from Holy Places in Qumranic and Rabbinic Literature'. *Dead Sea Discoveries*, 4, 178–206.

Slotki, J. (1977) Translation of *Leviticus Rabba*. London/New York: Soncino.

Walzer, M. (1965) *The Revolution of the Saints: a Study in the Origins of Radical Politics.* Harvard University Press.

Weiss, R. (1977) 'From Sanctity to Secularization' [Israeli]. *Leshonenu La'am*, 28, 1–32.

Zikhronot Va'ad HaLashon [Proceedings of the Hebrew Language Council] (1912–28) Jerusalem/Tel Aviv (6 vols – at irregular intervals: 1912, 1913, 1913, 1914, 1921, 1928; it can be regarded as the predecessor of *Lešonénu*, as well as of *Zikhronot Ha-Aqademya LaLashon Ha-Ivrit*).

Zuckermann, G. (1999) Review Article of N. Sh. Doniach and A. Kahane (eds), *The Oxford English–Hebrew Dictionary.* Oxford/New York: Oxford University Press, 1998. *International Journal of Lexicography*, 12, 325–46.

Zuckermann, G. (2003) *Language Contact and Lexical Enrichment in Israeli Hebrew.* London/New York: Palgrave Macmillan.

Zuckermann, G. (2004) 'Cultural Hybridity: Multisourced Neologization in "Reinvented" Languages and in Languages with "Phono-Logographic" Script'. *Languages in Contrast*, 4(2), 281–318.

Zuckermann, G. (2006a) 'A New Vision for Israeli Hebrew: Theoretical and Practical Implications of Analysing Israel's Main Language as a Semi-Engineered Semito-European Hybrid Language'. *Journal of Modern Jewish Studies*, 5(1), 57–71.

Zuckermann, G. (2006b) ' "Ety*myth*ological Othering" and the Power of "Lexical Engineering" in Judaism, Islam and Christianity. A Socio-Philo(sopho)logical Perspective', in Tope Omoniyi and Joshua A. Fishman (eds), *Explorations in the Sociology of Language and Religion* (Discourse Approaches to Politics, Society and Culture series), Amsterdam: John Benjamins, pp. 237–58 (Ch. 16).

Zuckermann, G. (2006c) 'Complement Clause Types in Israeli', in R. M. W. Dixon and Alexandra Y. Aikhenvald (eds), *Complementation: a Cross-Linguistic Typology* (Explorations in Linguistic Typology, vol. III), Oxford: Oxford University Press, pp. 72–92 (Ch. 3).

Zuckermann, G. (2007) 'di isróeldike shprakh: hebréish lebt víder, yídish lebt váyter' [The Israeli Language: Hebrew Revived, Yiddish Survived]. *Afn Shvel*, 337–338, 24–7 (in Yiddish).

Zuckermann, G. (2008a) ' "Realistic Prescriptivism": the Academy of the Hebrew Language, its Campaign of "Good Grammar" and *Lexpionage*, and the Native Israeli Speakers'. *Israel Studies in Language and Society*, 1.

Zuckermann, G. (2008b) *Israelít Safá Yafá* [Israeli – a Beautiful Language. Hebrew as Myth]. Tel Aviv: Am Oved.

Zuckermann, G. (2008c) 'farmaskírte antláyung: yídishe léksishe hashpóe af ivrít' [Camouflaged Borrowing: the Lexical Influence of Yiddish on Israeli]. *Yerusholaimer Almanakh* (*Journal of Yiddish Literature, Culture and Society*), 28, 418–28 (in Yiddish).

Zuckermann, G. (2009) 'Hybridity versus Revivability: Multiple Causation, Forms and Patterns'. *Journal of Language Contact*, Varia 2: 40–67.

Appendix: reference chart: proposed periodization of Hebrew and Israeli

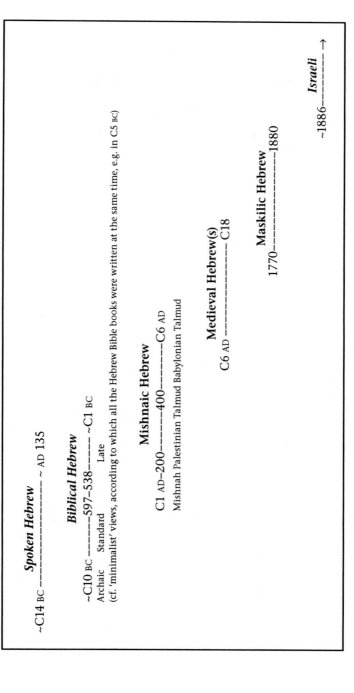

Spoken Hebrew

~C14 BC ————————— ~ AD 135

Biblical Hebrew

~C10 BC ———— 597–538 ——— ~C1 BC
Archaic   Standard   Late
(cf. 'minimalist' views, according to which all the Hebrew Bible books were written at the same time, e.g. in C5 BC)

Mishnaic Hebrew

C1 AD–200———400————C6 AD
Mishnah Palestinian Talmud Babylonian Talmud

Medieval Hebrew(s)

C6 AD ———————— C18

Maskilic Hebrew

1770———————1880

Israeli

~1886————— →

7
Society, Language, History and Religion: a Perspective on Bangla from Linguistic Anthropology

James M. Wilce

Introduction

The sociology of language and religion explores some of the same terrain as linguistic anthropology, this author's disciplinary home. Anthropology is increasingly engaged in analysing history (change), a major concern of SLR (Fishman Decalogue principle No. 2). Anthropology has for at least two decades discarded reifying approaches to 'culture' in favour of those approaches that focus on contestation as well as the situational production and 'dialogic emergence' of culture (Tedlock and Mannheim 1995), and the complex relationship of culture to discourse. Linguistic anthropologists have rejected simplistic equations of culture with text arising out of the humanities and cultural anthropology, preferring instead to explore *natural histories of discourse*. These explorations reveal processes by which discourse comes to appear, momentarily, as text-like (Silverstein and Urban 1996). This linguistic anthropological perspective on conflict, history and everyday and macrosocial process, complements some of Joshua Fishman's principles (Decalogue), as I will point out from time to time below.

Comparing approaches to 'accommodation' in the two allied fields is a bit more complex, but perhaps even more interesting. As implied above, linguistic anthropologists (Silverstein 2004, Wilce 2006b) tend to focus less on 'religion' – a noun vulnerable to criticism as an abstraction – and more on empirically analysable processes such as rituals, and particularly, *specific ritual events* in which speech and other semiotic systems are deployed at particular times and places to achieve particular sociocultural ends as locally understood. Following Durkheim (1965[1915]: 54), anthropologists treat rituals – 'political' or 'religious' (and we often are hard pressed to distinguish between the two) – as forms of social action that sometimes reproduce the status quo but are quite often transformative. Among the transformations they may effect are those we may call new 'accommodations'. Put differently, rituals have conventionally been means by which polities have adjusted to new circumstances, such as the death of a leader (Silverstein 2004: 627 [commenting on Fox 1989]). In an age of mass communication, ritual almost inevitably surrounds and defines those occasions when leaders virtually address whole nations, or physically address mass gatherings – as in the speech of the 'Father' of independent Bangladesh, Sheikh Mujibur Rahman, at Ramna Racecourse on the eve of Bangladesh's *Mukti Juddho*, Liberation War, 7 March 1971 (discussed below).

Transformative power is not equally distributed throughout a polity. Michael Silverstein and many of his students (e.g. Errington 1988) have persuasively argued that the production of signs (semiosis) in political systems involves not a uniform distribution of semiosis within a polity, but centres and peripheries – 'ritual centers of semiosis', 'authority' or 'institutionality' (Silverstein 2004: 623, 632, 645). Errington has described 'exemplary centers' from whence 'the ideally refined, ritualized forms of conduct' (including *priyayi* speech, the 'highest' form of Javanese) emanate, e.g. from 'the royal palace in a traditional Javanese kingdom' (1988: 24). The term 'ritual center of semiosis' (Silverstein 2004) is perhaps more generally applicable, since not all such centres act as examples for conduct outside of the centre.

Hanne-Ruth Thompson argues that East Bengal/East Pakistan went through two major linguistic accommodations in the middle of the twentieth century; relatively speaking, it is now in a period of stability. When East Bengali mullahs, 'religious leaders', realized in the lead-up to the independence of India that a Muslim state was also achievable, they changed their standoffish attitude toward the Bangla (*bāṅlā*, baŋla, but hereafter, Bangla) language (richly documented by Ahmed [1981]) – sometimes known as Bengali in the Anglophone world – and decided to engage in an effort to reform Bangla. That is, they decided to remake it as an Islamic language (Thompson 2007, Ahmed 1981, Fishman Decalogue IX [see reference to the Arabization of non-Arabic vernacular languages spoken by Muslims]). This chapter tells a theoretical story by way of a history – of change, conflict and accommodation. The theoretical story is that which I sketched out above. It is a semiotic vision, a linguist–anthropological vision, in which empirical ritual moments, particularly in ritual centres, play key roles precisely in relation to the tensions embodied in the trio of key terms this book addresses.

An overview of the recent political history of Bangla

After Pakistan emerged as a result of India's Partition in 1947, most of East Pakistan's citizenry came to experience their political situation as West Pakistani domination, including linguistic domination. In 1948 Pakistan had parliamentary debates about which language, or languages, to constitutionally legitimate. Bangla speakers dominated numerically – but certainly not politically – in the geographically bizarre bipartite nation, representing 57 per cent of Pakistani citizens, followed by Punjabi speakers at 29 per cent. Only 3.5 per cent spoke Urdu, Pakistan's official language, natively. Yet the non-Bengali Prime Minister, Liaqat Ali Khan, rejected even a moderate proposal arising in the parliamentary debates that Bangla be given co-equal recognition alongside Urdu and English (Thompson 2007: 41). Khan insisted on Urdu's dominance.

On 21 February 1952, an increasingly restive Bangla-speaking East Pakistani population, led by the Awami League party, engaged in a strike 'to publicly protest against [current moves by West Pakistan] "to dominate the majority province of East Bengal linguistically and culturally"' (Thompson 2007: 43). Heavy-handed police action culminated in the killing of five protestors, including four Dhaka University students. Almost immediately, a memorial was erected on the site – 'a Shahid Minar ('Tower of Witness')' (Thompson 2007: 44), commemorating this action on behalf of the mother tongue. The day has been ritually observed since then as *Shahid Dibas*, 'Martyrs' Day' – and now has been consecrated by UNESCO as a global Mother Language Day 'in recognition of the sacrifice of life for language that was made by the Bengali activists in 1952' (Thompson 2007: 44).

During periods of my fieldwork in Bangladesh (particularly 1991–92), however, such observances had become prototypical sites of conflict (Fishman Decalogue principle X, the ebb and flow) between Islamists, for whom the event and site's label – *Shahid*[1] – are illegitimate appropriations of an Islamic concept for secular (national-language-oriented) purposes, and linguistic nationalists (secularists). To Islamists, a *shahid* is strictly a martyr (or witness, literally)[2] in the cause of Islam; they see linguistic nationalism as an affront to Islam. On the other side, present-day Awami League and other left-leaning party activists see Islamists as illegitimate actors on the Bangladeshi political stage, and hear their rhetoric as a complete betrayal of Ekushey (21 February, *Shahid Dibas*) and of the Liberation War.

This brief description of relatively recent political history provides a backdrop for understanding both the long history of Bangla I am about to describe, and contemporary state rituals in which speech must do what ritual speech must nearly always do – carry those within its purview into the 'sacred' space that the ritual language magically/textually 'figurates' (Silverstein 2004: 626) in its words, poetic structure, and non-linguistic signs (Wilce 2006b).

It is difficult to recuperate, retrospectively, even the words of ritual in the distant past, let alone the other signs that made rituals come alive. My argument thus depends, in part, on some degree of speculation.

Language and the rituals of statecraft in Bengal: change, conflict, and accommodation in the last millennium

Although the Bengal region did not start speaking a language that was widely *known* as *bāngālā* until the seventeenth century, Old Bangla arose out of Middle Indo-Aryan around 1100 (Bhattacharya 2001) or earlier (Huq and Sarkar 2009). However, polyglot influences have helped define the region, and purism is well-nigh impossible to maintain here as in many other cases of language history. Bangla reflects the influence of the Dravidian and Munda languages (compare Huq and Sarkar 2009) in its lexicon, its tendency toward sound symbolism, and certain morphosyntactic features, particularly its use of reduplicative forms such as *mārā-māri* to express reciprocal ideas, in this case, 'hitting-hitting (i.e. hitting each other)' (see discussion in Wilce 1996a).

Very soon after (Bhattacharya's date for) the emergence of Old Bangla, it came under the influence of Persian and Arabic, when Turkish Muslims invaded Bengal. 'Although the Bengal sultans continued to inscribe most of their monuments and coins in Arabic, from the mid fourteenth century on, they began articulating their claims to political authority in *Perso*-Islamic terms' (Eaton 1993: 47; emphasis added). Sultan Jalal al-Din (1415–32), however, cultivated *local* language and culture – Sanskrit, but particularly Bangla, which was 'the language in universal use there' (in court) even though Persian was understood by some courtiers, as we know from reports by Chinese travellers to Jalal al-Din's court (1993: 60). 'In short, apart from the Persianized political ritual that survived within the court itself, from the early fifteenth century on, the sultanate articulated its authority through [Bangla] media' (1993: 66–7). The sultans' cultivation of Bengali literati led to reciprocal benefits. 'In the early 1550s [a] Vaishnava poet,[3] Jayananda, refers in his Caitanya-Mangala to the Muslim ruler not only as raja but as *isvara* ('god'), and even as Indra, the Vedic king of the gods. The use of such titles signals a distinctly Bengali validation of the sultan's authority' (Eaton 1993: 68, citing O'Connell 1983).[4]

This is an early form of linguistic accommodation at the very ritual centre of power in Mughal Bengal. It is of course impossible at this remove to reconstruct either what I am calling the ritual role of Bangla literature in the court of the sultans or its role in the broader task of ruling over Bengal. However, the sultans must have made some calculation as to the utility or even necessity of supporting Bangla.

A significant challenge one faces in understanding medieval Bengali history is deciphering relationships among 'religious communities' in an era radically different from our own. Following Harjot Oberoi's history of Sikhism (1994), we should be cautious about projecting backwards into the medieval era anything like rigid communal identity boundaries, indexed by language or otherwise. Hindus at the sultans' court used a Persianized style of Bengali, and Muslims were also known to write *Vaiṣṇava* 'Hindu' poetry (Haq 1957: 51, Dimock 1960). No form of Bangla had communalist connotations, since communalism per se emerged much later.

During my own linguistic–ethnographic fieldwork in Bangladesh I had an encounter with a man I call Munir (described in detail in Wilce 2000), who was markedly voluble, acting in a manner that earned him a local reputation as *pāgal*, 'mad, insane'. Munir told me that his father had died quite recently, and that now his own body was divided in two, that one half being Hindu and the other Muslim. I asked him what happens to his duplex, trans-communal body when he attends public prayers at the mosque. He confirmed that his Hindu left side goes along; Munir is thus able to lift two hands and successfully follow the required Islamic bodily discipline of prayer.

The loss of his father was fresh in Munir's mind, presumably causing him much distress. At least in that time of distress, he was falling apart, fragmenting. But the idiom in which he depicted his fragmentation was fraught with cultural–historical particularity. It reflects, *inter alia*, the historic shift in just over a century from a 'porous and fluid' relation – one of unity in diversity (Eaton 1993: 303) between 'Hindu' and 'Muslim' life and thought – to one of clear distinction and mutual Othering, mutual alienation. The unity in diversity of the earlier era was consummated throughout South Asia in rites known as *urs* – carnivalesque (Bakhtin 1984) commemorations of the births or deaths of holy men. Those who attended such carnivals were 'Hindus' or 'Muslims' – but the point is, they were both or either, depending on the occasion, since the distinction was not enforced (Ahmed 1981). Thus, no one's language was guarded as to what sort of religious–communal 'membership' it indexed, for such 'membership' was not exclusive. Fortunately, records of how this changed are quite available. The next section is devoted to those.

Dobhāshi Bāṇlā and the British Rāj

In the two centuries leading up to the 1757 Battle of *Palāsi* (Plassey), after which the British impact on, and ultimately rule over, South Asia began to be felt in its greatest intensity – first through the East India Company, later in direct rule – debates arose among Muslims as to whether or not Bangla was a suitable language for sacred use.

Between 1584 and 1586, the Chittagong-based Sufi poet, Syed Sultan (1550–1648 [Haq 2009b]), composed a Bangla account of the prophets' lives and deeds (Sultan 1960), a monumental and bold work of cultural translation in which prophets were portrayed in terms of a Hindu 'dynamic equivalent' to the category of prophet – the *avatāra* or various 'descents of gods' – and figures such as *Śiva* were portrayed in terms of their Arabic–Islamic dynamic equivalent, i.e. *nabi*, 'prophets' (Stewart 2001). Sultan expressed confidence, in the third colophon of *Nabi Bangsa [Nabi Vaṁśa]*, that his preaching in Bangla ('an Indic [*'hinduwani'*] language') would help Bengalis toward ritual propriety: *hinduwāni bʰāsā pāi ācāre rahila* ('[but] once accessed in this Indic language, proper ritual conduct has been [= will be] established')[5] though their ignorance of Arabic had previously left them 'ignorant [of] the wisdom of scripture'. Note that the term he used for scripture was itself Sanskritic – *sāstra*. It seems clear that Sultan wrote with a ritual end in view. It is equally clear, however, that he used a Bangla register that was (quite consciously, explicitly) the same as that used by Hindu authors. Sultan's mission to make Islam accessible to Bengalis led him to translate Islamic ideas using dynamic equivalents, rendering them in the Bangla he knew they spoke.

Thus the opinion expressed by historian Rafiuddin Ahmed – that a subset of Bengalis (those who at least tried to trace their descent back to the prophet of Islam, the *ashraf*) 'never accepted Bengali as a proper language for the Muslims and always considered it a Hindu language' (1981: 23) – must be understood vis-à-vis the limited time Ahmed covers, viz., 1871–1906.[6] That is, Islamist rejection of Bangla developed long after Sultan composed the *Nabi Bangsa* (1584 [Badiuzzaman 2009]).

Between 1584 and 1871 Hindu as well as Muslim writers developed a register of Bangla (called *dobhāṣi*, two-languaged, 'mixed diction' – that (at least at first) largely reflected court patronage.

In the label *dobhāṣi* and the phenomenon we can recognize a clear affinity to Bakhtin's notion of double-voicing or heteroglossia (1981). Thus, at no point in the history of Bangla does it become possible to judge whether an author/speaker's voice is more 'Muslim' or 'Hindu' by merely measuring the proportion of Sanskrit vs Perso-Arabic lexemes in his or her discourse; the potential for double-voicing prevents this. Easily recognized forms of double-voicing include irony; one can invoke a Perso-Arabic voice for ironic reasons (or many others), and play that voice off against any number of other voices – even within the same utterance, as Bakhtin and others have shown.

Qazi Abdul Mannan, author of a groundbreaking study of *dobhāṣi* Bangla (1966), found the earliest examples in the early sixteenth century CE (1966: 51). 'Though no work written by [pre-eighteenth century] Muslim poets reveals the [grammatical and lexical] influence of the ruler's language, the works of Hindu poets unquestionably do, and that from a comparatively early period … not later than the end of the fifteenth century' (Mannan 1966: 59).

It is useful to see how an eighteenth-century Hindu poet, Bhārat Cāndra Rāy (1712–60),[7] actually mentions the mixed idiom, attributing it to courtly influence:[8]

The passage comes from *Annadāmaṅgal*:

Mansimha Padsar haila ye baṇi	When before the Emperor, Mansimha,
Ucit ye Pharsi Ārbi Hindustani	(One) should use Persian, Arabic and Hindustani.
Pariāchi ye mata barṇibāre paṟi	Since I studied these languages I could use them.
Kintu se sakal loke bujhibāre bhāri	But they are difficult for people to understand.
Na rabe prasād guṇ nā habe rasāl	They lack grace and poetic quality.
Otaeb o kahi *bhāṣā yābaṇi misāl*	I have chosen, therefore, *the mixed language of the Muslims.*
Pracīn paṇḍitgaṇ giyāchen kaye	The ancient sages have declared:

Ye hok se hok bhāṣā kavya	Any language may be used. The
ras laye	important thing is poetic quality.
	(Mannan 1966: 69–70, emphasis
	added)

This 'mixed idiom', as Mannan calls it, reflects not just Muslim influence but the influence of the *ritual centre*, the court itself. Mannan confirms that, for Hindu poets who were patronized by the sultans of Bengal, 'to write in a partially Persianised Bengali would redound to their credit in the eyes of the patrons' (1966: 249).

Although Mannan finds no Muslim writers using this mixed idiom until the eighteenth century, but rather using 'the traditional literary language of Bengal' in a manner indistinguishable from Hindu writers (1966: 58), this changed after 1753 or so. That is the date at which Mannan fixes the *Yusuf-Zulekhā* (the love story of the two characters in the title) of Fakir Garibullah (1670–1770; compare Ahmed 2009), the birth year of *puthi* literature (from Bangla, *pustika*, 'book', but specifically a book in *dobhāṣī*, mixed idiom – 'a mixed vocabulary drawn from Bangla, Arabic, Urdu, Persian and Hindi' [Ahmed 2009]).

It is significant to see the extent to which, real or imagined, this pioneer of Muslim *dobhāṣī* literature linked his text to the ritual continuation of particular Muslim rulers in Bengal:

Āllātālā chālāmate rākhen *bādśāre*	May *Allah*-the-Transcendent grant *peace* to the *Emperor*,
cher *chālāmate* rākhe *bādsār wazire*	Grant *peace* to the *Emperor's ministers*
dojakh ājāb haite tvarāo karatār	From the *torments of hell* preserve
imān bajāy rākha *mamin* sabāre	the *faithful* and grant that they remain steadfast in their *faith*
bajāy *chālāmat* rākha rajār *deoāne*	Grant that the Rājā, his *Deoān*,
sikdār copdār ijārādār jane	*Sikdār, Copdār and Ijārādār* continue their rule and reign.[9]

The italicized words – an overwhelming proportion of the nouns – are Perso-Arabic loanwords in Bangla. Thus it is obvious that Garibullah's Bangla is not at all that of Syed Sultan.

But whose Bangla was this Perso-Arabized vernacular (Fishman Decalogue IX)? Was it artificial, or did it reflect speech forms in common use in some part of Bengal?[10] Ahmed's view is clear:

> Bharatchandra [Bhārat Cāndra Rāy, author of *Annadāmaṅ gal*] and Garibullah came from the same region of Bhurshut Pargana at about the same time. The spoken language of the common people, irrespective of whether they were Hindu or Muslim, was the language of puthi literature and thus cannot be termed as an artificial literary language. The ordinary educated Muslim liked it because of the mixture of Arabic and Persian vocabulary. (Ahmed 2009)

Questions about the accuracy of Ahmed's statement persist to this day and occupy me for the remainder of this chapter.

However, a brief word about ritual and accommodation. First, the nature of linguistic accommodation shifts over time (Fishman Decalogue X), exemplified in the shift from Syed Sultan's Bangla to that of Garibullah over the course of just under two centuries, from a concern to present Islam so that Bengalis could understand it, to a concern to transform Bangla into a purified Islamic language. Second, very different sorts of persons in the penumbra of the ritual centre – enjoying the patronage of the Bengal sultans' court and thus in at least some fictitious geographic proximity to it – worked out the discursive accommodations favoured by the court, from Bhārat Cāndra Rāy to Garibullah (whose eighteenth-century lives completely overlapped).

The colonial impact: complementary schismogenesis

As far back in time as we might project, all varieties of all languages, and all speech acts, have had ideological or social–indexical significance.[11] However, *some* speech acts, like those issuing from Bengal's ritual centres of semiosis in emergently prestigious varieties of Bangla, possess a clearer and greater social–indexical significance than do other speech acts.

> [R]itual centers of semiosis come to exert a structuring, value-conferring influence on any particular event of discursive interaction with respect to the meanings and significance of the verbal and other semiotic forms used in it. (Silverstein 2004: 623)

If 'performativity' represents the creative force of utterances, texts, and linguistic ideologies (Silverstein 1985), this certainly includes their potential to shape history, as linguistic ideologies have clearly done (Silverstein 1985).

Though no era was free of ideology or indexical value attaching to forms of Bangla, it is safe to say that not only *dobhāṣī* but perhaps all forms of Bangla – particularly the counterpart of *dobhāṣī*, the *Sanskritized* form that emerged out of collaborative work on Bangla in Kolkata [formerly transliterated 'Calcutta'] by British Orientalists and Hindu pundits – had clear indexical value. Some called this Sanskritized form *sādhu bhāṣ ā*, 'chaste language' (Ahmed 1981: 91) or the language of sages, while others called it 'pedantic language'. The conflict-laden development of *sādhu bhāṣā* and *dobhāṣī* or *Musālmāni* ('Muslim') Bangla can be best understood by reference to Gregory Bateson's notion of *complementary schismogenesis*,

> a process of differentiation in the norms of individual behaviour resulting from cumulative interaction between individuals [or groups] ... [or the study of] the reactions of individuals to the reactions of other individuals. (1958: 175)[12]

Given some of the 'purifying' tendencies of ideologies of language at work in Europe at the same time (Bauman and Briggs 2003), it should not surprise us that one of the earliest linguists to serve the British Raj, Nathaniel Brassey Halhed (1751–1830, Qayyum 1982, 2009, Schwarz 1997) considered foreign elements pollutants in the 'pure Bengalese'. Halhed admitted that in Bengal 'at present those persons are thought to speak this compound idiom with the most elegance, who mix with pure Indian verbs the greatest number of Persian and Arabic nouns' (1969 [1778]: xi). Although this compound idiom, whose reform Halhed made the goal of much of his work, was part of the common speech and even valued in some circles, he discovered and embraced a group that clung to another form of Bangla – 'he cites a small but influential band of "Bramins and all other well-educated Jentoos ... [who] adhere with a certain conscientious tenacity to their primeval tongue, and have many ancient books written in its purest style" ' (Schwartz 1997, citing Halhed 1969 [1778]: xii). Halhed acknowledged 'the modern [mixed] jargon of the kingdom', but declared the loanwords unintelligible outside large cosmopolitan towns (p. xiv).

Halhed's vision of the origins of Bangla in resistance to 'Muslim invaders' must have coloured his judgement of the intelligibility of loanwords in the countryside. But this particular ideology of language had a great impact insofar as it helped determine the formation of the

Sanskritized *sādhu bhāṣā* and its fortunes, i.e. its ability to achieve wide circulation by virtue of colonial state sponsorship. Following Halhed's lead, British Orientalists and Hindu pundits working in Fort William College, Kolkata, produced a Sanskritized register successfully promulgated as 'standard Bengali', and industries of text production – writing as well as printing and distribution – sprung up in that centre of semiosis (Kopf 1969), one defined as a *'ritual* centre' in relation to the rituals of colonial governmentality.

Some of Halhed's successors – e.g. the famous British Baptist missionary to Bengal, William Carey (1761–1834) – at least for a time rejected linguistic purism. 'A multitude of words, originally Persian or Arabic, are constantly employed in common conversation, which perhaps ought to be considered as *enriching* rather than corrupting the language' (Carey 1801a: iii; emphasis in original). Qayyum (1982) notes that later editions of Carey's *Grammar* omitted these words.

The colonial impact was profound and complex. The Orientalists at Fort William College – Warren Hastings, William Jones, John Gilchrist and W.W. Hunter – at least paid lip service to the goal of reviving purer, older forms of India's religions. Analogously, their approach to the language probably combined some desire to Anglicize with stronger conflicting tendencies either to purify and standardize Bangla or to romanticize and glorify vernacular forms (Kopf 1969). At any rate, there arose at the College a class of pundits whose Bangla self-consciously eliminated borrowings from Islamicate languages.[13] Sanskritization of Bangla proceeded apace.

We have seen disparate scholarly judgements as to what sort of Bangla was actually spoken beyond the courts, and later, beyond the cities. Scholars differ as to the intelligibility of Islamicate loanwords in Bangla to the common speaker. It is worthwhile at this point to mention what is claimed, as well as what is not known, about these matters. There are no large corpus-based linguistic studies of Bangla, let alone of the frequency of Perso-Arabic terms in actual instances of contemporary Bengali discourse. Writing in pre-Partition Kolkata, Suniti Kumar Chatterji was a giant of a figure in the 1930s and 1940s as India transitioned from colony to independent postcolonial state. He counted 2500 Perso-Arabic terms in Bengali (Chatterji 1934: 210, Ahmed 1981: 121). Writing 30 years later in Islamic East Pakistan, Hilali and Haq (1967) listed 9000 such loanwords. Billah (2009) claims 'more than two thousand such words have come to have a permanent place in Bangla vocabulary'. These different claims probably reflect shifting scholarly ideologies more than shifts in Bangla speech practices. Moreover, the relation of such 'counts' to actual *usage* is an even greater mystery.

The relative proportion of Perso-Arabic loanwords in my own small corpus of carefully transcribed, naturally occurring Bangla speech varies greatly by *register*. In 'Latifa's' 1992 lament (Wilce 1998) only 6 per cent of total word tokens were Perso-Arabic loans. By contrast, in the Bangla 'translation' of an Arabic prayer offered at a 1991 wedding (Wilce 2006a), about 33 per cent of the total words are Arabic loans.[14]

Returning to the historical situation in the early nineteenth century, although we do not know the particulars, it is quite clear that *sādhu bhāṣā* differed from the common speech of Muslims, and that whatever the frequency of loanwords and the popularity of *puthi* literature and its 'mixed diction' had been to that point, *colonial language policies favouring sādhu bhāṣā* provoked a counter-reaction, a middle-class movement fostering a Muslim form of speech. To summarize: under British influence, elite Hindus undertook to 'purify' Bangla of 'foreign' (Muslim) elements, which provoked counter-steps by Muslims to 'purify' Bangla of Sanskritic influence, if that were possible. And so the cycle of complementary schismogenesis originated.

Another layer of complexity: the relation of class-based variation to communally based variation

The theme of class stratification has been present, albeit implicit, from the outset of this essay. Those Hindu poets who gained court sponsorship enjoyed at least some benefits that set them apart from the great bulk of their compatriots, benefits that were presumably material and not only symbolic. My argument about ritual centres of semiosis can be reconceptualized in terms of concentric circles of status or prestige moving away from the centre of power – the royal court, and later, Fort William, Kolkata, the centre of British imperial power (Chattopadhyay 2009). Fort William College and its industry of text production must be seen as the early-modern counterpart, in Bengal, of the medieval production of Bangla texts translating the wisdom of Islam.

But along with any wisdom produced by Fort William came a language ideology characterizable in terms of 'communicability'. Linguistic anthropologist Charles Briggs has recently argued that notions of communication are just as 'productive' (in a Foucaultian sense) as are notions of race. Briggs remarks that 'power is derived partly from ideologies of communication with which notions of race and health are imbricated' (2005: 271). Just such a complex emerged when colonial forces produced a hybrid of language (written and spoken) and race, that determined which 'natives' could communicate with 'Europeans'. In the following passage, Schwarz writes about the British vision of 'incorporating' India into Empire, and in the second paragraph, takes on the temporal perspective of a man like Halhed:

> Since it was widely reported (however inaccurately) that Bengal had no indigenous tradition of prose writing, both Europeans and European-trained Indians began to experiment with forms that could be used for efficient communications in linking the outposts of company administration.
>
> ...
>
> The empirical difficulty facing the government ... seems to be that no collective audience as yet exists to hear its declaration of sovereignty (Bengal has only [been] 'professedly incorporated' [into the Empire]). Strictly speaking, the empirical speaker of that 'Bengal Language' for which Halhed is writing his Grammar does not yet actually exist [at the time Halhed is writing it]. (Schwarz 1997: 513–14)

Schwarz argues that setting up inequality between 'natives' and 'Europeans' was part of the task of writing the grammars, producing the texts, and everything else that Fort William College did.

But that inequality surfaced elsewhere as well – not only between 'Europeans' and 'natives' but reproduced by *fractal recursion* (Gal and Irvine 1995, Irvine and Gal 2000) *among* 'natives'. Fort William was producing *śādhu bhāṣā* to fill the slot of 'standard Bengalese' at the same time European philologists were producing standard versions of European languages. Philological efforts at home co-opted (as 'folklore') the discursive resources of Europe's peasants and women, while denying that such persons could analyse – or even continue to produce – the discourse that was said to characterize them, because the folk and their lore were said to be perishing, necessitating collecting efforts by elites (Bauman and Briggs 2003: 222). Also, the home efforts at least pretended to produce clear boundaries between (reified visions of) 'languages' (and between languages and 'dialects' in what linguists think of as the layman's pejorative sense of the term, as if we could control meanings in public discourse).[15] The production of inequality was thus not only foundational at the periphery of empire (in the colonies) but at its core, at home.

Thus William Carey was perplexed, almost panicked, when he found no 'universally accepted standard of language in Bengali' (Qayyum

1982: 137) – a terrible problem from the perspective of one coming from Europe, where an ideology was emerging in which there was *always* a 'standard' form of any language, and that it corresponded neatly with boundaries of a Volk ('people') that could become a modern nation state.[16] And Carey projected invidious distinctions onto what he did find. He remarked on how 'different is the language called Bengalee (which is spoken by the higher ranks of Hindoos) from the common language of the country which is a mixture of Bengalee, Hindostanee, Persian, Portuguese, Armenian, and English, that is a mere jargon' (Qayyum 1982: 137–8, citing Carey's letter to S. Pearce, dated 31 December 1795, *Periodical Accounts*, vol. I, p. 222). The distinction between a language and a 'mere jargon' should sound very familiar to us.[17]

Carey did even more to elevate (high caste) Hindu forms of speech through the book of dialogues he published to facilitate European learning of Bangla, and in doing so, became entangled in hardening and projecting onto the larger stage of colonial statecraft what might, prior to his publications, have been more locally relevant categories. I refer in particular to the category of *bhadrolok*, which Carey renders, quite literally, as 'gentle people'. The gloss, of course, glosses over the ways in which Carey and other foreign actors participated in making these members of *bhadrolok* into an intelligentsia in the sense of a cosmopolitan elite, an elite whose loyalties were no longer local. In Carey's *Kathopakathan* ['Dialogues' 1801b], one gains the direct impression of

> 'gentle folk' [bhadralok] [speaking] in [what Carey called] a 'grave style,' characterized by heavy Sanskritic borrowings. Others employed a more racy patois replete with foreign borrowings ... As far as he could see, the only style of speech that would serve his purpose was the 'grave style' of 'the higher ranks of Hindoos'. (Qayyum 1982: 139, citing Carey's letter, dated 31–12–1795, collected in *Periodical Accounts*, vol. I, p. 222)

The missionary-linguist had become an instrument of the Sanskritization of Bangla – using 'instrument' advisedly, because Carey was influenced by the Hindu classes he describes here, according to Qayyum. Here the particular history of local agency vis-à-vis Carey and the missionization of Bengal complicates the portrayal of 'missionization' as an agent of language change mentioned in Fishman (Decalogue VI).

Dobhāṣī Bangla was thus never on an equal footing with *sādhu bhāṣā* in terms of the metadiscourse of Fort William, and that inequality persisted into the twentieth century. Although Suniti Kumar Chatterji, the linguist active in Kolkata in the 1930s, recognized that 'Musalmani' Bangla was 'the Maulavi's reply to the *Paṇḍit's sādubhāṣā'*, implicitly blaming Fort William College rather than Muslims as a whole, it *was* indeed for him a question of *blame*. 'The literature in [Musalmani or *dobhāṣī*] Bengali has no merit and some of the deathless tales of [Persia and Islam]...have been ruined by the hack versifiers of Calcutta and Chittagong in rendering them in this jargon' (Chatterji 1934: 211f.). There may indeed be a direct lineage between Carey's and Chatterji's disparaging use of 'jargon', indeed in relation to roughly the same variety of Bangla.

Were this simply a matter of communal taste, one would expect the roughly contemporary Muslim authority on the history of Bangla literature, Enamul Haq, to sharply disagree with Chatterji. Instead, Haq shares his Hindu counterpart's disdain for the Bangla variety others describe as 'mixed diction': '...Dobhashi...was an inferior poetic medium to standard Bengali' (Haq 1957: 175, cf. 192). This is evidence that one's evaluation of *dobhāsi* indexes not just one's religious community but one's *social class/aspirations*.

The ongoing question of *what to do* with the Sanskritic 'nature' of Bangla became periodically controversial between Muslims and Hindus. In an Appendix to a Government of India Report, Chatterji (1943) made clear that (a) based on the source of lexical borrowings, 'the grouping of Indian languages into the two groups of (i) Sanskritic and (ii) Perso-Arabic alone seems reasonable because based on facts and on avowed and declared tendencies', (b) Bangla is among the former ('Sanskrit has been the unquestioned supplier of new words for the Aryan languages', which he sets against Urdu, lexified primarily with Perso-Arabic borrowings), and (c) the dominance of the Sanskritic origin for the languages of India ought to be intentionally maintained by state intervention, which he justifies as 'practical'.

Despite charges made even by some Muslims (Abdul Majid Khan, in the *Proceedings of the Bangiya Sahitya Sammilan* 1910: 74, as quoted by Ahmed 1981: 122 and note 79) that a highly Islamized Bengali was unintelligible to the masses, for a short period in the early twentieth century the British colonial administration supported the development of a vernacular (Islamized) literature and even toyed with a proposal for the development of ' "a separate language for the Muslims"... "an Islamized Bengali" ' (Resolution by the Government of India, Home Dept. [Education], No. 3000, Simla 7 August 1871, as cited by Ahmed 1981: 124, and note 93). The fact that some Bengali Muslims *opposed* this proposal probably indicates the status distinctions I have been describing, including the influence of one phrase, perhaps attributable to W.W. Hunter, calling Musalmani Bangla 'an unsophisticated ... *patois*' (Ahmed 1981: 126).[18] As far as I know, no one ever called *sādhu bhāṣā* an unsophisticated patois – at least not vis-à-vis Musalmani or *dobhāṣī* Bangla. What twentieth-century Bengal had inherited was a system of sociolinguistic value oriented to historic centres of power. For indeed, radiating out from ritual centres of semiosis are concentric circles of value – in this case, from the English spoken by officers of the Raj, to *sādhu bhāṣā*, to mere 'jargon' and 'patois'. The class sentiments attaching to Bangla varieties went on to undermine, as I argue two sections below, a Pakistan-era 'Simple Language' campaign. First, however, we must consider whether the relationship between status and linguistic usage in Bengal is best conceived of under the rubric of 'diglossia'.

'Diglossia'

Previously (Wilce 1996b) I discussed the literature that argues that the Bangla sociolinguistic situation is best treated as a case of 'diglossia',

> a relatively stable language situation in which, in addition to the primary dialects of the language (which may include a standard or regional standards) there is a very divergent, highly codified (often grammatically more complex) superposed variety [H], the vehicle of a large and respected body of written literature, either of an earlier period or in another speech community, which is learned largely by formal education and is used for most written and formal spoken purposes but is not used by any sector of the community for ordinary conversation [L]. (Ferguson 1959: 336)[19]

To summarize Ferguson's argument: some speech communities are characterized by a particularly stable relationship between forms of a language in which one variety adheres fairly closely to a literary tradition and derives prestige from it, while another – a spoken variant – is considered inferior but intimate. Diglossia is said to entail a structural and functional gap between an H and an L variant, in which no one speaks the H natively.[20]

Most discussions of Bangla diglossia have reckoned the divide along the folk distinction between *sādhu bhāṣā* and *calit bhāṣā* (e.g. Dimock 1960). I have introduced the former earlier. The latter arose as a matter of reform and morphological simplification particularly in the writings of the first non-European Nobel laureate in literature,

Rabindranath Ṭhākur (commonly transliterated Tagore, 1861–1941). As Suhas Chatterjee (1986) points out, the distinction is/was crucially lexical. H speech is full of lexemes drawn directly from Sanskrit, while L speech drew on a much more limited lexicon that had undergone more nativization (so-called 'tatsmama' forms, Chatterjee 1986: 297).

In fact the H–L divide cross-cuts the *sādhu-calit* or S–C split, as Chatterjee (1986) demonstrates. There are – or were – H and L forms of both *sādhu* and *calit*. Mimi Klaiman (1993) marshals evidence that Bangla diglossia is disappearing.

My 1996b paper made claims that I wish to revise here. I argued that scholars of Bangla who approached the problem of linguistic varieties from divergent disciplinary perspectives – particularly historians, linguists and sociolinguists – had in effect talked past each other. I claimed that historians who paid any attention to Bangla, while they may have attended to religious or ethnically based linguistic variation (which is rare – for the most part they have tended to treat Bangla as one reified linguistic entity)[21] had missed the social facts that occupy sociolinguists, particularly class-based linguistic diversity, and for the most part that argument stands. But I was wrong in claiming that the sociolinguists concerned with Bangla diglossia – typically analysed as a situational, but also class-linked, phenomenon – had altogether missed the extent of its entanglement with communal or religious identities (e.g. Klaiman 1993).

More importantly, with a few exceptions (Makihara 2004), most anthropologists concerned with language and related sign systems have – following Herzfeld (1987) – now distanced themselves from the diglossia concept (Haeri 2000: 67), and I wish to do the same. It is as hard to fit Bangla into two variant forms as it is Greek (which Herzfeld was describing). Moreover, there are typically more sign systems than just language that participate in determining the sort of status hierarchies associated with diglossia (Herzfeld proposed the term *disemia* to evoke other semiotic forms). Finally, the ranking of H and L forms is not objective but ideologically fraught – related to currents of Orientalism, myths of purism, and myths of decline and rebirth.[22]

One good reason for rejecting the diglossia model is that doing so liberates us from some unfortunate limits. Bangla diglossia may, as Klaiman argues, be disappearing, but linguistically indexed social inequality will never disappear. More sophisticated sociocultural models are needed to work on this broader issue.

How class undermined East Pakistan's Simple Language campaign

After the Partition of India and Pakistan, between roughly 1948 and 1950, the provincial East Pakistan government appointed an East Bengal Language Committee (EBLC) whose policy goals were summarized under the banner *sahaj bāṇlā* (Simple Bangla). Mawlana Akram Khan was its chair (Umar 1970: 275).[23] Those were heady days, with Bengali Muslims feeling liberated from the superposed Kolkata-based, Hindu-indexing *sādhu bhāṣā* – a standard in which, according to committee members, East Bengalis could never become fluent (Chowdhury 1960: 75). The 'Simple Bangla'-related policy goals that the committee promulgated were as follows:

i) that the Sanskritization of the language be avoided as far as possible by the use of simple phraseology and easy construction..., ii) that the expressions and sentiments of Muslim writers should strictly conform to the Islamic ideology; and iii) that the words, idioms and phrases in common use in East Bengal especially those in the Puthi and the popular literatures be introduced in the language more freely.

After this direct quote, Dil goes on to paraphrase other goals: (iv) to simplify the orthography and (v) simplify the grammatical metalanguage, involving a decision paralleling (i), that 'unintelligible technical terms of Sanskrit...be substituted by the simple non-technical terms of Bengali language...' (Dil 1986: 454, citing and translating Chowdhury 1960).

H forms, including HCB (H *calit* Bangla, Chatterjee 1986) carries a prestige not to be sacrificed. Dil tells of an interview she conducted with the same Munier Chowdhury whose work she cites (above). Admittedly, Chowdhury himself had not been an advocate of *sahaj* Bangla. Nonetheless, it is interesting that Chowdhury's speech during the interview included elements of H *śādhu bhāṣā*, HSB. When Dil pointed this out, Chowdhury 'did not defend himself or contradict' the observation (Dil 1986: 460). He explained that he and others of his class were prone to use the supposedly written 'pedantic' standard on '*attanta śiṣṭa paribeś* meaning "very strictly formal occasions", [or] for discussing *duraha biṣay, kaṭhin praśanga* meaning "difficult subjects"' (Dil 1986: 460f.). Together, such settings, genres, participant structures, and act sequences form a whole (at least in the imagination of such speakers) that Hymes says should be linked in 'ethnographies of communication' (1972). I stand by my (1996b) statement that Dil's work leaves such questions as the restrictions on access to such speech events as 'strictly formal occasions' radically undertheorized.

Notions like 'diglossia' are bound up with ideologically charged perspectives on the social practice of writing. Situations that have been represented as 'diglossic' crucially entail attitudes toward written and spoken language. To illustrate this, we return to Chowdhury's colleagues who advocated 'Simple Bangla'. Why did they call for publications in Simple Bangla but, for the most part,[24] fail to write such works themselves? There was so little response following the EBLC's specifications that no accepted model of simple Bangla ever emerged. Dil insightfully acknowledges that one reason for this failure was that 'Shahaj Bangla' emerged from a government-appointed committee rather than from *the people* themselves.

A more or less unconscious class-based ideology of language, one that rationalized the current sociolinguistic situation, coloured the policies of the EBLC. Like all ideologies of language, that of the committee reflected their relation to power. For the analysis of conflict, competition among socially significant linguistic variants, and the reproduction of social inequality in greater Bengal, an approach grounded in work on language ideologies (Schieffelin et al. 1998, Kroskrity 2000), has real advantages over theories of diglossia.

Political speeches as ritual events: Sheikh Mujib's pre-war Ramna Racecourse speech, March 1971

Whatever sense we attribute to 'accommodation', the Pakistan era did not produce one in terms of a resolution of the tension between a rhetoric of egalitarianism among national language planners on the one hand – which reached its zenith in the 'Simple Bangla' campaign – and practices that reproduced inequality on the other. Moreover, despite the Pakistani state's vision that (a reified notion of) 'religion' would dominate ethnicity, and despite its mullahs' feeling that religion must have supremacy over language (Thompson 2007), ethnolinguistically based political agitation within East Pakistan reached a boiling point in 1971 (the ebb and flow Fishman recognizes in Decalogue X). It is worthwhile to examine Sheikh Mujibur Rahman's speech at Ramna Racecourse (now Ramna Park) on the eve of his arrest and of the Liberation War, 7 March 1971 (available 'in full' audio at http://www.mukto-mona.com/1971/7th_march/index.htm),[25] because of (a) its relative 'L-ness' vis-à-vis a diglossia model, (b) its relative 'Hindu' or 'Muslim' flavour, and (c) its extreme historic importance. For the most part, this speech by Sheikh Mujib is in *calit bhāṣā*, CB. It is quite consistently so in morphology and syntax. From the first paragraph come the verbs *hayechi* and *karechi* (rather than *haiyāchi* and *kariāchi*. From the third paragraph from the end, we find the verb *thākbe* (rather than *thākibe*). The lexicon is also consistent with L from the perspective of both Klaiman (1993),[26] and Thompson – it is, in plain terms, *familiar* to his audience, rather than stilted. It differs, for example, from the H lexicon typical of newspapers of the Sheikh's era. Sheikh Mujib uses simple, evocative terms like *kaṣṭo* ('hardship' – rather than *āyās*), *rakto* ('blood' – rather than *ranjit*), and *mukti* ('liberation' – rather than *moksha*).

The Sheikh uses quite a few neutral-to-Hindu terms when he could have used Perso-Arabic loanwords – *mukti* (instead of *nājāt*), *nar-nāri* 'men-women' (instead of *insān*). However, he does use a sprinkling of clearly Islamic expressions such as *inshallah*, 'God willing'. Significantly, he uses *sahid* – the Arabic loanword for martyr discussed earlier – for *all* who had died thus far in the (secular, ethno-nationalist) liberation struggle. It is important to understand that it is the *particular* use-in-context of any Sanskrit- or Perso-Arabic-derived form, beyond the mere fact that one *does* use more of one or the other, that indexes 'identity', if anything does (for example, speech use also indexes situation). We must move beyond simple notions of indexicality,[27] beyond the claim that 'language' indexes 'identity' to a more nuanced recognition that emergent and variable forms of speaking may index dynamic, ever-shifting *processes of identification*.

Crucially, Sheikh Mujib's historic performance mimics the pattern of all ritual speech events in that its power derives in part from the arc of its overall unfolding. It is *not* words, or the ideas that a few keywords call up, that are sources of power or persuasion in politics or any other form of magic. The magic of ritual speech works by iconically/indexically figurating on the textual plane what it must achieve on the cosmic plane (Silverstein 2004). Rituals work, that is, by both pointing to, or reminding participants of, pre-existing sacred features of the surround, and effectively bringing others into being, often through signs that individually or collectively (as a 'diagram') imitate the cosmic end being ritually enacted. A crucial form of iconism in ritual speech – diagrammatic iconism – is the stepwise relation of parts of the text mirroring steps in the transformation to be achieved.[28]

The schema emergent in Sheikh Mujib's speech is really quite simple, but it was *successful* in the here and now of delivery, at that dangerous moment of historic defiance in the face of vastly greater military force, a delivery that for many reasons (including prosody) was profoundly moving. This schema entailed dwelling on the past (Pakistani atrocities) for most of the speech, and then flipping to the boldly envisioned future of defiance and ultimate liberation at the end.

Among the reasons for labelling the speech event 'ritual' rather than merely political or rhetorical are these: first, *Jai Bāṇlā* (Victory to Bengal/Bengalis/ Bangla! – the phrase with which he ended) resonates across contexts. The related phrase *Jai-Dev!* (Victory to the god!) can be found on the lips of Hindus. It is an optative, a performative. Uttering the phrase in some sense brings about the victory, or at least adds to its probability. Second, the degree to which Sheikh Mujib *incorporates the congregation into the speech event* by addressing them as *bhāyerā āmār,* 'brothers mine', bespeaks ritual. Finally, the speech's (diagrammatic) iconic–indexical pattern typifies ritual semiosis.

Ritual transforms. In a sense, this speech by the leader of the Bangladesh Awami League, even though that party has since then often been out of power, helped to seal the transformation of East Pakistan into Bangladesh,[29] and the transformation of a situation in which loyalty to Islam coincided with suspicion toward Bangla as a whole into a situation in which the legitimacy of Bangla in Bangladesh was never again seriously questioned. Although it has adopted ever more Perso-Arabic elements, and even evinced increasing concern to denativize borrowed elements so that Arabic words are increasingly pronounced 'accurately', there would never be another political movement based on the rejection of Bangla. Given Muslim (or *ashraf*) suspicions toward Bangla in the nineteenth century, this does indeed represent accommodation.

Ritual speech: prime ministers Begum Khaleda Zia and Sheikh Hasina Wazed

A marked Islamization of political rhetoric in Bangladesh began with the rise to power of General Ziaur Rahman and increased during the dictatorial rule of General Ershad through the 1980s. When democracy was restored in 1991, the Bangladesh Nationalist Party of Zia's widow, Begum Khaleda Zia, won the February elections and maintained control of Parliament until 1996, when the Awami League won their first election since the Sheikh's time. In 2001 the Awami League lost in a landslide victory to a four-party coalition involving the BNP and an avowedly Islamist party, the Jamaat-e-Islami, which had been banned from politics under some previous regimes because of its alleged association with atrocities during the Liberation War. Still, changing the language was never a priority for the coalition.

The opening and closing of Prime Minister Khaleda Zia's address to the nation on 10 October 2004 departed little from that of her late husband, Ziaur Rahman. She opened with the Arabic formula with which devout Muslims begin any activity – *Bismillāhir Rāhmānir Rāhim*, 'In the name of Allah the merciful, the compassionate'. There follows the typical Arabic greeting used by Muslims in many countries – *Āssālāmu Ālāikum*, 'Peace be upon you.' To some extent these Arabic ritual forms distinguish BNP political speech events from Awami League events.

Before going further with the analysis of Prime Minister Zia's speech, let me put its ending – *Āllāh hāfez* – in context. In the late 1980s Arabic expressions began displacing Persian ones among Muslim Bangladeshis. I did my doctoral fieldwork in Bangladesh in 1991–92. When I returned in 1996 I noticed a new discourse fashion on the rise – some people took their leave with *Āllāh hāfez* instead of *Khodā hāfez*, different forms of 'go[o]db[ewith]ye'. In 1995 Monsur Musa, then Director of the Bangla Academy, wrote,

> Nowadays, in certain Bengali newspapers, an eagerness to substitute Arabic words for prevailing Persian terms can be seen. These newspapers use *ṣalāt* instead of [*nāmāz*, ritual prayer observance], *ṣiyām* instead of [*rajā*, 'fast'] – and *Allah* is considered better than *Khoda*. (1995: 92; translation mine)

The speech by Prime Minister Zia ends, *Āllāh hāfez – Bānglādesh Zindābād*, 'Go[o]db[ewith]ye', long live Bangladesh!'[30]

Zia's counterpart, the daughter of Sheikh Mujib (murdered in 1975), and recent Awami League leader, Sheikh Hasina Wajed, gave a speech on 10 October 2004 that contrasts with Zia's style. I have only the (mostly) English version; she might or might not have made the address in Bangla, given the presence of foreign diplomats in the audience. We can still glean significance, however, from the speech's closing (thanks to the mixed code of the transcript):

> Please accept my greetings for the upcoming month of Ramadan. I also greet my Hindu brothers and sisters on the eve of the Durga

Puja. Khoda Hafez. Joy Bangla. Joy Bangabandhu.[31] Long Live Bangladesh.

Sheikh Hasina's party, the Bangladesh Awami League, makes available the full Bangla text of another address to the national press corps on 4 February 2006. She opened with 'Honourable members of the press, friends, *Āssālāmu Ālāikum*' and closed with '*Sobāike dhannabād. Jai Bāṇlā. Jai Bangabandhu. Bangladesh cirajībī hok*': 'Thanks to you all. Victory to Bangla. Victory to Bangabandhu [Sheikh Mujib]. May Bangladesh live forever.'

Clearly, the expression *Jai Bāṇlā* in Awami League ritual speech takes the place of *Bānglādesh Zindābād* in its BNP counterpart. The closing *is* the ritual moment par excellence. And the fact that the two parties' representatives close in such different ways, drawing on different linguistic traditions (Persian in the one case, Indo-Aryan in the other) underscores the degree to which an accommodation (between certain religiously inspired linguistic reformists and others satisfied with the ethnic indexicality of Bangla) has *not* been reached. There are ongoing tensions over Bangla as a language that is, or is not, so secular that (from an Islamist perspective) it requires rampant Arabic borrowing to sanctify it.

Ah, but the story does not end there. Some accommodate more than others. On the one hand, Prime Minister Zia budged not an inch vis-à-vis her linguistic choices even when the occasion was Shahid Dibas, (Language) Martyrs' Day. Bangladeshis living in Tokyo, it seems, were able to build a Shahid Minar ('Tower of Witness' [to the 1952 martyrs]) in Ikebokoro Park. On 12 July 2005, when the foundation was being laid, Prime Minister Zia was present – along with the Mayor of Toshima-k'u, Tokyo, Yukio Takano. Zia began with the same Arabic greeting used in her national address. She closed with *āpnāder sabāike dhannabād* followed by the precise formula represented above.

On the other hand, Sheikh Hasina's 4 February 2006 press conference began with *Assalamu Alekum* (Arabic, 'peace be with you'), accommodating the BNP-led shift. It was not her father's habit to begin speeches with this Muslim greeting, ever conscious as he was of the multi-ethnic nature of Bangladesh.

Conclusion

The evolution of Bangla resists reduction to a unified narrative. It is rather the story of multiple shifting forms of accommodation. But accommodation with what? The story may not be one of Bangla being remade to fit this or that 'religion'. We might better conceive of the domain of SLR as one in which ritual *performance* really matters. It matters in creating, and not merely reflecting, matters of status and identity. Ritual speech performances, be they by court poets or by recent prime ministers, matter. They matter, not independent of the social dynamics of space and power, but in dialectic with them, i.e. in a geometry of ritual centres of semiosis, from royal courts in medieval Bengal, to the colonial-era Fort William, to the elusive electronic centres of broadcast power in (post) modern statecraft in Bangladesh. Through all of these permutations, Bangla never manages to be completely co-opted. As Bakhtin taught us, 'the word' is never fully owned by any speaker, but always has double-voiced potential – vis-à-vis competing objectified religious communities as in relation to anything else.

Notes

1. The place is designated Shahid Minar and the observance, Shahid Dibash, Martyrs' Day.
2. To become a Muslim, one recites the *shahada*, one 'bears witness', that there is no god but Allah, and Muhammad is his Apostle. The Arabic noun *Shahid* derives from that Arabic verb; it is one of perhaps thousands of Perso-Arabic borrowings in Bangla use today, particularly as Bangla is spoken in Bangladesh.
3. *Vaiṣṇavas* form that sect of Hindus who worship Kṛṣṇa as an *avatāra* of *Visnu*, the root of *Vaiṣṇava*.
4. It is impossible to distinguish the ethnic from the linguistic sense of 'Bengali' here, just as it is impossible to delineate what precisely is the object of the prayer-like performative utterance, *Jai Bānglā*, 'Victory to (Bangla, the language? Bengal?) popularized during the Liberation War.
5. The translation is Tony Stewart's (personal communication: March 2006).
6. For evidence of an earlier, deeper Muslim sentiment against Bangla, see Mannan (1966).
7. He is also known simply as 'Bharatchandra' (Haq 2009a).
8. That is how I interpret this possessive: 'the mixed language of the Muslims'. Note that Haq (1957: 174) cites this author as the one who coined the term *dobhāṣi bānglā*.
9. This translation is adapted from Mannan's (1966: 76) based on my own sense of the text.
10. Were its use and spread subject to limits like those on English (Fishman Decalogue VI)?
11. By ideologies I do not mean anything dark and nasty – though they *are* always tinged with power – but simply notions of language, and values attached to various forms of it, that help determine the future evolution of those forms.
12. This explanation of the divergence of communal forms of Bengali is foreshadowed in the works of Haq and Chatterji. Haq claims that 'Hindu–British

hostility to Muslims resulted in a recrudescence of Muslim consciousness of their separate identity and the Muslims especially of lower Bengal, filled their language with more and more Arabic, Persian and Urdu words' (Haq 1957: 175). As for Chatterji, despite his denigration of Musalmani (see n. 7), by calling this variant of Bengali 'the Maulavi's reply to the *Paṃḍit's sādubhāṣā.'*, he implicitly 'blames' Fort William College rather than the Muslims.

13. It is not at all clear that the Orientalist-trained pandits wrote uniformly in a Sanskritized Bengali from the earliest days of the nineteenth century. In fact, Dil (1986: 453) describes the great contrast between the Sanskritized style of Mrytunjoy and the heavily Perso-Arabized lexicon of Ramram Basu.

The term 'Islamicate' is borrowed from Hodgson (1974), who rejected the practice of labelling any particular language an 'Islamic' language, i.e. fully participating in the religion of Islam, but wanted to acknowledge that some languages had certainly been caught up in the history of Islamic civilization.

14. Neither of these is an accident. Latifa's lament performances drew on 'folk' traditions – *bilāp*, 'lament, weeping, dirge' – while the man who offered the prayer was one of the elite imams of Bangladesh (since the wedding guests included a former Prime Minister and many high-ranking military officers) who was extremely well versed in Arabic. Their ideologies of language (and of gender, etc.), and their performance 'stances', differed markedly.

15. The discussions of Ebonics in the US in 1997 prove scholars can scarcely control public discussions and distinctions.

16. See Bauman and Briggs (2003), in particular, their perspective on the work of Herder and the brothers Grimm.

17. At least in the US it is common to hear people refer to 'all of the "unwritten dialects" [not worthy of the dignifying label "languages"] spoken in Africa'.

18. Haq (1957: 174) himself uses this label.

19. Most scholars who write about diglossia in the Bangla speech community believe that *sādhu bhāṣā* occupies the H position, but linguist and Bangla expert Probal Dasgupta (1993) has argued that English occupies it, throughout South Asia.

20. The popularity of the concept of diglossia owes much to Fishman's (1972: 92) broadening of it.

21. For example:

> The two wings [of Pakistan] were also linguistic and cultural contrasts, for while the West Pakistanis proudly proclaimed their martial character, the East Pakistanis similarly flaunted their literary and poetic pedigree made world famous by Nobel laureate Rabindranath Tagore. What one saw as a natural endowment, the other vilified as an insignificant, even deplorable, trait. (Devotta 2001: 86)

The political football here is Bangla, demonized by one side and the hero of the other. But Devotta fails to realize that Bengalis were somewhat divided about Bangla, and that there were many forms of 'the language' to be divided about. This is the problem with the sort of folk Whorfianism to which Devotta appeals; as Duranti points out (1997: Ch. 3), it needs to be complemented or countered by a sophisticated sociolinguistic analysis of variation within speech communities.

22. I acknowledge the fruitful reworking of the notion of diglossia that Abel traces, and for which she is partly responsible (1998). However, I find other theoretical traditions still more fruitful, particularly the complex semiotic approach to analysing 'speech levels' (Errington 1988).
23. Such campaigns are nothing new, but reflect language ideologies put in place by Bacon and Locke (Bauman and Briggs 2003). Silverstein (1996) has warned of the Trojan horses concealed in reform agendas going by labels of 'plain' or 'simple' language.
24. Principal Ibrahim Khan did indeed publish books in 'a very simple Bengali' for children, 'though his simple Bangla is not the "Shahaj Bangla" recommended by the East Bengal Language Committee' (Dil 1986: 456).
25. Neither the 'Mukta Man' (Open Mind') website nor Sheikh Mujib's own party's website's version of the audio file is complete according to the Bangla typescript (pdf) of the speech one can download from http://www.albd.org/bangabandhu/bangabandhu.htm. Moreover, the English version one can download does not follow the audio or the Bangla typescript (at least at the end, where the order of lines varies quite a lot; in fact the English version starts with the penultimate lines of the speech: 'The struggle this time is for emancipation! The struggle this time is for independence!').
26. Klaiman speaks of a 'general preference in H for *tatsama* (direct borrowings from Sanskrit) as opposed to the L preference for *tadbhavas*, or lexemes which have gone through the regular diachronic sound change process characteristic of Bengali as a New Indo-AP language' (Klaiman 1993: 153; see Chatterjee 1986: 287).
27. On this point, see Samuels (2004), especially the concluding chapter.
28. Icons resemble their objects. Diagrammatic icons involve not simple object-to-sign resemblances but real patterns (or part-to-part relations) and sign patterns (or sub-sign to sub-sign relations) (Jakobson 1987 [1965], Silverstein 2004: 626). Fans of American football might picture a football coach's sketch of a play – no sign signifying a player is intended to resemble him; it is the pattern that is iconic.
29. Bangladesh's name loosely signifies 'the land constituted as that of ethno-linguistic Bengalis', rather than a land constituted as a religious entity, as the pure (Pak) land of Muslims.
30. *Jindābād, zindābād* – from Persian *zinda*, 'alive, living' + *bād*, 'be he' (Hilali and Haq 1967: 106).
31. Victory to the Friend of Bengal/Bangladesh, i.e. Sheikh Mujib (or his spirit, or his party).

References

Abel, P. Rekha (1998) 'Diglossia as a Linguistic Reality'. *Yearbook of South Asian Languages and Linguistics*, 83–104.

Ahmed, Rafiuddin (1981) *The Bengal Muslims, 1871–1906: a Quest for Identity.* Delhi: Oxford University Press.

Ahmed, Wakil (2009) 'Puthi Literature', Asiatic Society of Bangladesh-Banglapedia (http://www.banglapedia.org/httpdocs/HT/P_0336.HTM).

Austin, John L. (1962) *How to Do Things with Words*. Cambridge, Mass.: Harvard University Press.

Badiuzzaman (2009) Nabi Bangsha, Asiatic Society of Bangladesh-Banglapedia. http://www.banglapedia.org/httpdocs/HT/N_0006.HTM. Last accessed 4 September 2009.

Bakhtin, Mikhail M. (1981) *The Dialogic Imagination*. Austin: University of Texas Press.

Bakhtin, Mikhail M. (1984) *Rabelais and His World*. Bloomington: Indiana University Press.

Bateson, Gregory (1958 [1936]) *Naven*. Stanford: Stanford University Press.

Bauman, Richard and Briggs, Charles (2003) *Voices of Modernity: Language Ideologies and the Politics of Inequality*. Cambridge: Cambridge University Press.

Bhattacharya, Tanmoy (2001) 'Bangla', in J. Garry and C.R.G. Rubino (eds), *Facts about the World's Languages*, New York and Dublin: New England Publishing Association, pp. 65–71.

Billah, Abu Musa Mohammad Arif (2009) 'Persian', Asiatic Society of Bangladesh-Banglapedia (http://www.banglapedia.org/httpdocs/HT/P_0148.HTM).

Briggs, Charles L. (2005) 'Communicability, Racial Discourse, and Disease'. *Annual Review of Anthropology*, 34, 269–91.

Carey, William (1801a) *A Grammar of the Bengalee Language*. Serampore: Mission Press.

Carey, William (1801b) *Kathopakathan (Dialogues Intended to Facilitate the Acquiring of the Bengalee Language)*. Serampore: Serampore Mission.

Chatterjee, Suhas (1986) 'Diglossia in Bengali', in B. Krishnamurti, C.P. Masica and A. Sinha (eds), *South Asian Languages: Structure, Convergence and Diglossia*, Delhi: Motilal Banarsidass, pp. 294–302.

Chatterji, Suniti Kumar (1934) *The Origin and Development of the Bengali Language*, Vol. I. London: George Allen Unwin.

Chatterji, Suniti Kumar (1943) '[Chatterji Contributions to] Appendix A: Observations of the Members of the Reference Board on Scientific Terminology' (Central Advisory Board on Education, 8th Meeting, 1943). C.A.B.o. Education (ed.), Vol. 2006: 2006 Government of India, Ministry of Human Resource Development, Department of Education.

Chattopadhyay, Basudeb (2009) 'Fort William', Asiatic Society of Bangladesh-Banglapedia (http://www.banglapedia.org/httpdocs/HT/F_0169. HTM).

Chowdhury, Munier (1960) 'The Language Problem in East Pakistan', in C.A. Ferguson and J.J. Gumperz (eds), *Linguistic Diversity in South Asia: Studies in Regional, Social, and Functional Variation*, Vol. 13, Bloomington: Indiana University Research Center in Anthropology, Folklore, and Linguistics, pp. 64–80.

Dasgupta, Probal (1993) *The Otherness of English: India's Auntie Tongue Syndrome*. New Delhi, Newbury Park and London: Sage.

Devotta, Neil (2001) 'The Utilisation of Religio-Linguistic Identities by the Sinhalese and Bengalis: Towards a General Explanation'. *Commonwealth and Comparative Politics*, 39(1), 66–95.

Dil, Afia (1986) 'Diglossia in Bangla: a Study of Shifts in the Verbal Repertoire of the Educated Classes in Dhaka, Bangladesh', in J. Fishman (ed.), *The Fergusonian Impact*, Vol. 2, *Sociolinguistics and the Sociology of Language*, Berlin: Mouton de Gruyter, pp. 451–65.

Dimock, Edward C. (1960) 'Literary and Colloquial Bengali in Modern Bengali Prose'. *International Journal of American Linguistics*, 26(3), 43–63.

Duranti, Alessandro (1997) *Linguistic Anthropology*. Cambridge: Cambridge University Press.

Durkheim, Emile (1965 [1915]) *The Elementary Forms of the Religious Life*, J.W. Swain (trans). New York: The Free Press.

Eaton, Richard Maxwell (1993) *The Rise of Islam and the Bengal Frontier, 1204– 1760*. Berkeley: University of California Press.

Errington, J. Joseph (1988) *Structure and Style in Javanese: a Semiotic View of Linguistic Etiquette*. Philadelphia: University of Pennsylvania.

Ferguson, Charles A. (1959) 'Diglossia'. *Word*, 15, 325–40.

Fishman, Joshua (1972) *The Sociology of Language: an Interdisciplinary Social Science Approach to Language in Society*. Rowley, Mass.: Newbury House.

Fox, James J. (1989) ' "Our Ancestors Spoke in Pairs": Rotinese Views of Language, Dialect, and Code', in R. Bauman and J. Sherzer (eds), *Explorations in the Ethnography of Speaking*, Cambridge: Cambridge University Press, pp. 65–85.

Gal, Susan and Irvine, Judith T. (1995) 'The Boundaries of Language and Disciplines: How Ideologies Construct Difference'. *Social Research*, 62(4), 967–1001.

Haeri, Niloofar (2000) 'Form and Ideology: Arabic Sociolinguistics and Beyond'. *Annual Review of Anthropology*, 29, 61–87.

Halhed, Nathaniel Brassey (1969 [1778]) *A Grammar of the Bengal Language*. Yorkshire: Menston/Scolar Press.

Haq, Khandker Muzammil (2009a) 'Bharatchandra', Asiatic Society of Bangladesh -Banglapedia (http://www.banglapedia.org/httpdocs/HT/B_0459. HTM).

Haq, Khandker Muzammil (2009b) 'Syed Sultan', Asiatic Society of Bangladesh-Banglapedia (http://www.banglapedia.org/httpdocs/HT/S_0647.HTM).

Haq, Muhammad Enamul (1957) *Muslim Bengali Literature*. Karachi: Pakistan Publications.

Herzfeld, Michael (1987) *Anthropology through the Looking-Glass: Critical Ethnography in the Margins of Europe*. Cambridge: Cambridge University Press.

Hilali, Shaikh Ghulam Maqsud and Haq, Muhammad Enamul (1967) *Perso-Arabic Elements in Bengali*. Dhaka: Central Board for Development of Bengali.

Hodgson, Marshall G. S. (1974) *The Venture of Islam: Conscience and History in a World Civilization*. Chicago: University of Chicago Press.

Huq, Mohammad Daniul and Sarkar, Pabitra (2009) 'Bangla Language', Asiatic Society of Bangladesh-Banglapedia (http://www.banglapedia.org/httpdocs/ HT/B_0137.HTM). Accessed 4 September 2009.

Hymes, Dell (1972) 'Models of the Interaction of Language and Social Life', in J. Gumperz and D. Hymes (eds), *Directions in Sociolinguistics: the Ethnography of Communication*, New York: Basil Blackwell, pp. 35–71.

Irvine, Judith and Gal, Susan (2000) 'Language Ideology and Linguistic Differentiation', in P. Kroskrity (ed.), *Regimes of Language: Ideologies, Polities, and Identities*, Santa Fe: School of American Research, pp. 35–83.

Jakobson, Roman (1987 [1965]) 'Quest for the Essence of Language', in *Language in Literature*, Cambridge, Mass. and London: Harvard University Press, pp. 413–27.

Klaiman, Miriam H. (1993) 'The Demise of Diglossia in Bengali', in A. Davison and F. Smith (eds), *Papers from the Fifteenth South Asian Language Analysis*

Roundtable Conference 1993, Iowa City: South Asian Studies Program, University of Iowa, pp. 151–66.

Kopf, David (1969) *British Orientalism and the Bengal Renaissance: the Dynamics of Indian Modernization 1773–1835*. Berkeley and Los Angeles: University of California Press.

Kroskrity, Paul (ed.) (2000) *Regimes of Language*. Santa Fe: School of American Research Press.

Makihara, Miki (2004) 'Linguistic Syncretism and Language Ideologies: Transforming Sociolinguistic Hierarchy on Rapa Nui (Easter Island)'. *American Anthropologist*, 106(3), 529–40.

Mannan, Qazi Abdul (1966) *The Emergence and Development of Dobhāṣi literature in Bengal (up to 1855 A.D.)*. Dhaka: Department of Bengali and Sanskrit, University of Dacca.

Musa, Monsur (1995) *Bāṇlādesher Rāstrabhaṣā* [The State Language of Bangladesh]. Dhaka: Bangla Academy.

Oberoi, Harjot (1994) *The Construction of Religious Boundaries: Culture, Identity, and Diversity in the Sikh Tradition*. Chicago, Oxford: University of Chicago/Oxford University Press.

O'Connell, J.T. (1983) 'Vaisnava Perceptions of Muslims in Sixteenth-Century Bengal', in M. Israel and N.K. Wagle (eds), *Islamic Society and Culture: Essays in Honour of Professor Aziz Ahmad*, New Delhi: Manohar, pp. 298–302.

Qayyum, Muhammad Abdul (1982) *A Critical Study of the Early Bengali Grammars: Halhed to Haughton*. Dhaka: Asiatic Society of Bangladesh.

Qayyum, Muhammad Abdul (2009) 'Halhed, Nathaniel Brassey', Asiatic Society of Bangladesh-Banglapedia (http://www.banglapedia.org/httpdocs/HT/H_0031.HTM).

Samuels, David (2004) *Putting a Song on Top of It: Expression and Identity on the San Carlos Apache Reservation*. Tucson: University of Arizona Press.

Schieffelin, Bambi B., Woolard, Kathryn A. and Kroskrity, Paul (eds) (1998) *Language Ideologies: Practice and Theory*. New York: Oxford University Press.

Schwarz, Henry (1997) 'Laissez-faire Linguistics: Grammar and the Codes of Empire'. *Critical Inquiry*, 23(3), 509–36.

Silverstein, Michael (1985) 'Language and the Culture of Gender: At the Intersection of Structure, Usage, and Ideology', in E. Mertz and R. Parmentier (eds), *Semiotic Mediation: Sociocultural and Psychological Perspectives*. Orlando: Academic Press, pp. 219–59.

Silverstein, Michael (1996) 'Monoglot "Standard" in America: Standardization and Metaphors of Linguistic Hegemony', in D. Brenneis and R.K. Macaulay (eds), *The Matrix of language: Contemporary Linguistic Anthropology*, Boulder: Westview, pp. 284–306.

Silverstein, Michael (2004) ' "Cultural" Concepts and the Language–Culture Nexus'. *Current Anthropology*, 45(5), 621–52.

Silverstein, Michael and Urban, Gregory (1996) 'The Natural History of Discourse', in M. Silverstein and G. Urban (eds), *Natural Histories of Discourse*, Chicago: University of Chicago Press, pp. 1–17.

Stewart, Tony K. (2001) 'In Search of Equivalence: Conceiving Muslim–Hindu Encounter through Translation Theory'. *History of Religions*, 40(3), 261–88.

Sultan, Syed (1960) (1584–86) 'Nabi Bangsa' (p. 225, no. 222, MS 656). Dacca: Asiatic Society of Pakistan.

Tedlock, Dennis, and Bruce Mannheim (eds) (1995) *The Dialogic Emergence of Culture*. Champaign/Urbana: University of Illinois.

Thompson, Hanne-Ruth (2007) 'Bangladesh', in A. Simpson (ed.), *Language and National Identity in Asia*, Oxford: Oxford University Press, pp. 33–54.

Wilce, James M. (1996a) 'Reduplication and Reciprocity in Imagining Community: the Play of Tropes in a Rural Bangladeshi Moot'. *Journal of Linguistic Anthropology*, 6(2), 188–222.

Wilce, James M. (1996b) 'Diglossia, Religion, and Ideology: On the Mystification of Cross-Cutting Aspects of Bengali Language Variation'. *Proceedings of the 1995 Bengal Studies Conference*, University of Chicago. Electronic document. http://www.lib.uchicago.edu/LibInfo/SourcesBySubject/SouthAsia/James.1.html

Wilce, James M. (2000) 'The Poetics of Madness: Shifting Codes and Styles in the Linguistic Construction of Identity in Bangladesh'. *Cultural Anthropology*, 15(1), 3–34.

Wilce, James M. (2006a) 'Arabic Loanwords in Bengali', in K. Versteegh (ed.), *Encyclopedia of Arabic Language and Linguistics*, Leiden: E.J. Brill, pp. 146–9.

Wilce, James M. (2006b) 'Magical Laments and Anthropological Reflections: the Production and Circulation of Anthropological Text as Ritual Activity'. *Current Anthropology*, 47(6), 891–914.

8
Metaphors of Change: Adolescent Singaporeans Switching Religion[1]

Phyllis Ghim-Lian Chew

8.1   Introduction and background

One may suppose that in a 'competitive, lean and modern state' such as the Republic of Singapore, with a relatively high per capita gross domestic product and a reputation for efficiency and enterprise, the religious aspiration would be presumably secondary to the material one or non-existent. But such a presupposition is surprisingly off target. Religion is an important ingredient in the lives of the 4 million. Indeed, religiosity may be said to be a dominant feature of Singapore, and for many of its citizens religion is a source of spiritual, social and even cultural nourishment. In addition, for Singaporean Sikhs, Malays and Parsis, religion is a definition of their identity. For the Chinese and Indians, it is a major part of their cultural life, as seen in the mass celebrations of annual local festivals such as the Moon Cake Festival, Deepavali and Thaipusam.

   Singapore's population is extremely diverse: 76 per cent are Chinese, 14 per cent Malays, 8 per cent Indians, with the remaining 2 per cent made up of Eurasians, Arabs, Jews and other minority groups. Correspondingly, Singapore's religious composition is also very diverse: 51 per cent are Buddhist or Taoists, 15 per cent are Muslims, 15 per cent are Christians and 4 per cent are Hindus and the remainder (15 per cent) consisting of freethinkers, Sikhs, Jews, Zoroastrians, Baha'is and others (Leow 2000). Such an ethnic and religious profile presents a potentially volatile situation, more so because religion, ethnicity and language tend to overlap. Muslims generally are of Malay, Indian or Arab ethnic backgrounds and tend to speak Malay. Among the Chinese there is both linguistic and religious diversity. Indians are, however, generally Hindus, with a minority being Christians, Sikhs and Zoroastrians.

To complicate this picture further, religion also correlates with age and language. Dialect speakers are mainly Taoists and Buddhists; Hindi speakers are mainly Hindus while English speakers could be Hindus, Buddhists and Christians (Clammer 1991). Hence, when one speaks of religious identity, it is often conjoined with racial, ethnic, linguistic and cultural identities as well (Alatas et al. 2003). Religion is naturally an extremely sensitive subject. Hence, although Singapore is a multilingual, multiracial and multireligious society, discourse on religion has been noted to be often characteristically dense and ambiguous (Sinha 2003). To keep racial and religious harmony intact, the Inter-religious Council is a state-recognized non-governmental organization. Its members come from the Taoist, Jewish, Muslim, Zoroastrian, Christian, Sikh, Muslim, Jain, Hindu, and Baha'i faiths. It is an active organization which highlights the similarities and downplays the differences between the ten independent religions in Singapore.[2]

Tong (2002) has conducted anthropological and sociological studies on Hinduism, Christianity, Hinduism and Chinese religion in Singapore written in English in the last 150 years. These studies have mostly focused on more apparent aspects such as rituals or festivals. Although Christianity is practised by 14.6 per cent (Leow 2000) of the population, it has attracted greater research attention than other religions. Much of that research has included very few systematic surveys if at all. Also, while there has been some research of religious conversion among students in tertiary institutions, mostly on Christianity and Buddhism (e.g. Tamney and Hassan n.d., 1987), no study of religious switching in the demography of the adolescent school-going population has been done. Thus, this chapter fills a gap in the research literature in spite of its preliminary and exploratory nature.

One reason for the scant research in religious switching and conversion is the assumed involvement of supernatural phenomena. We also do not know, for instance, when someone says that they have 'switched', whether this is an authentic or inauthentic conversion as it is difficult to distinguish between the two. While we are aware of this problem, in this study we will accept all declarations of switching as authentic and sincere.

A study of change, conflict and accommodation in adolescents' religious behaviour is important because their behaviour, attitudes and beliefs potentially affect the political, economic and social future of a nation. Adolescence is characterized by many cognitive and social changes, which constitute the transition into adult life. It is a time of extreme biological change that carries implications for social and cognitive development. Growth can spur changes in how adolescents are viewed and treated by their parents and peers as well as changes in how adolescents view themselves. It is a period where there is a strong need to discover not only society's expectations of them, but also intimacy and friends. Religion or more generally, religiosity, begins to play a large part in how a potential adult views the world. Important questions of identity and meaning begin to surface. However, research on religious development in adolescence is an often neglected area, as can be observed by the lack of research and surveys available until recently.

More specifically, this study is a study of Singaporean adolescent use of English metaphors to describe their switch of religion. The majority of adolescents in our study have switched from Taoism to Christianity and Buddhism. This is not particularly surprising since such a trend has already been noted in the past Census reports. The censuses of 1980, 1990 and 2000 (Dept. of Statistics 1991, 2000) have shown a striking decline in the number of Taoist adherents – from 38.2 per cent in 1980 to 28.4 per cent in 1990 to 10.8 per cent in 2000. Two religions have absorbed the departing Taoists adherents – namely Christianity and Buddhism. For example, Christianity grew dramatically from 10.9 per cent in 1980 to 14.3 per cent in 1990 to 16.5 per cent in 2000. Buddhism has also grown steadily from 34.3 per cent in 1980 to 39.4 per cent in 1990 to 53.6 per cent in 2000. Ostensibly then, there has been a marked switch of the Singapore populace from Taoism to Christianity and Buddhism in the last two decades; and it is also a trend that is apparent in our study. While there are obviously macro and sociopolitical reasons behind such a trend, this study focuses on the more micro and individualistic reasons as revealed by adolescents' use of metaphors in their oral and written discourse. More specifically, this is a study focusing on the change, conflict and accommodation which adolescents go through. It is a study of metaphoric use in English as our adolescents attend English-medium schools in Singapore, communicate fluently in the language and use English for the greater part of their time.

8.2   A genre of adolescent religious switching

In analysing both written and oral data, we found a certain systematicity, giving rise to what one may discern as a 'genre' or supra-individualistic structure of religious switching. The structure may be said to first begin with the realization of a mental conflict, which ultimately leads the subjects to a 'switch' of religion as a means of 'resolving' their internal conflict. In examining the metaphoric linguistic expressions used we found many to cluster under what may be termed as 'push' and 'pull' factors. 'Push factors' are factors existing in the respondents' system of beliefs in which a sense of dissatisfaction and alienation is experienced. These expressions are usually negative in connotation since they must provide the 'push' for the switch. Hence, images of Taoism are predictably, negative, such as:

> *Taoism*: Funereal, dark, smoky, obscure, hazy, cloud, dim, dense, thick, frightening, old, lonely

On the other hand, *pull* factors are the attractions or 'rewards' offered by the target religion to which our subjects feel an attraction. These are usually positive in connotation, leading the subjects to experience a 'pleasant' and 'happy' sensation. Because most of our respondents were attracted to Christianity and Buddhism, the metaphoric linguistic expressions relating to these religions were positive ones. For example:

> *Christianity*: friendly, companionship, success, helpful, singing, uplifted spirits, wings of knowledge
>
> *Buddhism*: steady, upright, good character, friendly, detachment, peacefulness, calmness

Besides the above more concrete metaphoric linguistic expressions, there is also a predominance of what may be termed spatial–orientational metaphors, often described in the literature as 'dead' metaphors – that is, metaphors alive at one point but became so commonplace that they had lost their vigour and ceased to be metaphors at all. However, while these may be highly conditional and effortlessly used, they are still alive in a most important sense – as they still govern our thoughts and are metaphors 'we live by' (Lakoff and Johnson 1980). As can be seen the phrases below, spatio-orientational metaphors used in discussing Taoism have to do with rather negative events and states such as the loss of consciousness, lack of attention, something breaking down, inward-looking, being left behind. They give us additional insights into the change, conflict and accommodation processes in religious switching. Some commonly used metaphors from the data include:

> Go *under*
>
> Everybody look *inwards* and doesn't care about others
>
> *Against* my interests … feelings
>
> *Break down* the superstitions and idols

I don't want to be left *behind*
Backward type of religion

On the other hand, the 'pull' religions of Christianity and Buddhism attracted movement metaphors which were frequently deictic, oriented towards the direction of itself. In the following example, the spatial orientation of *forth, around* and *forward* are associated with positive feelings and events:

Christianity is *forward*-looking
I look *forward t*o the prayer meetings
To bring *forth* good thoughts and deeds in our lives
I reach *forward* for it.
I *come around* to my senses

Adolescents also tend to see happiness in terms of being spatially 'up' or 'down'. This may be because the rapid biological growth during this period helps them to be more visual and physical, as a means of releasing physical and emotional tensions:

I want to build *up* myself
My marks went up and so did my grades
I cry and felt so *down.*
I *sink* deeper and deeper with sadness...

There was also significant usage of the spatial metaphor 'out' in both written and oral discourse. 'Out' was found in both dimensions of push and pull:

Push: I am *out* of sorts with all the joss sticks...
All this makes me want to *pass out.*
Pull: *Set out* to *build*...a friendship circle...
I have to reach *out* for my future good...
Set *out* to help others...

The interplay between the push and pull factors leads – predictably – to an emotional conflict in the minds of our respondents. This conflict, seen in terms of a series of potent metaphoric images, leads inevitably to attempts at accommodation. It is a period which may last any time from one week to a few years, after which our subjects made their decision

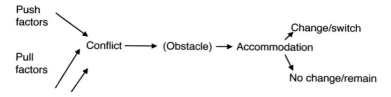

Figure 8.1 Push and pull factors

to switch. In our data, 25 per cent of interviewees switched religion within a month of finding a new religion; 37.5 per cent switched within three months; 12.5 per cent switched within a year; and 25 per cent switched after a year. Adolescents extricated themselves from the confluence of push and pull factors by either walking a path (as in the case of Buddhism) or taking the hand of 'a friend' (as in the case of Christianity). It must be noted however that not all subjects chose to switch. Our study was designed to capture only cases where a switch had occurred – and it was unfortunately not able to go deeper into cases where the choice was to remain in the original religious affiliation.

Figure 8.1 illustrates the push-and-pull factors which preceded change. An internal conflict results from the push–pull tension, which in turn leads to efforts at accommodation. Accommodation will take the form of a change and/or switch to a new religion or no change at all.

It is interesting to note that in his study of personal transformation, Campbell (1968: 245) argued that all inner quests, such as the quest for truth or the ideal belief (in our study, a religious path), are simple multiple forms of the 'monomyth'. Campbell (ibid.) wrote of the 'centring and unfolding of the individual' to the heart of inner life. Suddenly, 'the call' (in our case the 'pull' factors) is the beginning of the 'hero quest' which is followed by supernatural assistance from 'the helper' or 'the guide' (in our case the Christian or Buddhist 'friend') who offers some protection or direction towards the 'threshold of adventure' (in our case the 'conflict') at which there may occur 'battles with dragons or evil brother, crucifixion, abduction, sea journey', followed by 'the test' (in our case 'the obstacles') before winning 'a prize' (in our case, the 'switch').

8.3   Methodology

The subjects of this study comprise 102 adolescents from 6 secondary schools between the ages of 13 and 17 who had switched out of Taoism and other religions into another religion of their own choice; 90 out of 102 (or 88.2 per cent of our sample) had switched from Taoism to Christianity and Buddhism and will comprise our data sample. Out of the 90, 68 (or 75.6 per cent) had switched from Taoism to Christianity and 22 (24.4 per cent) had switched from Taoism to Buddhism. This chapter presents a discussion of these switchers' explanation of their own conversion process through a study of their use of metaphors in a short descriptive essay and through a spontaneous interview.

8.3.1   The short descriptive essay

In the short descriptive essay, 90 subjects professing Taoism were asked to write as much as they know on the religion they had switched from (Taoism) and the religion they had switched to (Buddhism and Christianity). They were given 30 minutes (one class period) to write on any aspect of the religion, including main teachings and principles, e.g. festivals, ceremonies, administrative structure and any stories associated with that religion. They were asked to leave the spaces blank if they knew nothing about the particular religion. The instructions for the descriptive essay, which subjects were asked to complete on a prescribed sheet of paper, are shown in Figure 8.2.

Out of 90 subjects, 78 (86.7 per cent) wrote something under every heading while the rest (13.8 per cent) left it blank. Some wrote up to more than 50 per cent of the space allotted while others wrote only a short phrase here and there. While the greater part of their essays were

---

How much do you know of these religions? Write as much as you can in the space below. (You may leave a blank if you do not know anything about it). You can include things such as main teachings; main practices e.g. festivals, ceremonies, administrative structure and stories associated with religion, etc.

Taoism is
....
....
....

Buddhism is
....
....
....

Christianity is......
....
....

Note: the actual form includes more space(10 lines) for adolescent switchers to write their responses to each of the above-mentioned religions

---

Figure 8.2   The descriptive essay

literal, it was striking that many similar metaphorical linguistic expressions were used in their essays. My assistants and myself read through the short descriptive essays, identified and counted the metaphors used in their descriptions as a means of understanding the perceptions adolescents possess towards different religions which had played a significant part in their lives.

8.3.2 The spontaneous interview

The spontaneous interview was conducted for around 20 minutes with 72 subjects. The interviews were tape-recorded and the findings subsequently transcribed. The interview data, which were more dynamic in nature, complemented those found in the short descriptive essay, which were more descriptive and static. The interview also allowed us to cross-reference and/or verify information from the same respondent. It also allowed us to probe more intimately into the connection between metaphor and action – in other words, what happens after the respondent had identified a conflict. Is there a 'tipping point' just before the switch? (See interview question 3.) Finally, it gave us a chance to see how particular manifestations of metaphor might be motivated in spontaneous discourse contexts since metaphors are as much an interactional phenomenon as a conceptual one (Wee 2005).

The interview was guided by three categories of questions:

1. Warm-up questions: Describe yourself. What makes you happy? What are your pastime activities? Do you like your school?
2. General questions: How many religions are there in Singapore? Do you or your friends ever mention that any religion is not a good one? If so, which one? What are their reasons?
3. 'Switch' questions: Tell me about your new religion and what you like about it. Why did you switch? Was there a tipping point? What do you do in your new religion? Who brought you there? Are you the first in your family to become …. (name of new religion)? Were there any obstacles which prevented you from switching? How long did it take for you from the time you heard of the new religion to switch?

Question 1 aimed to put the interviewee at ease and to establish a comfortable conversational relationship. 'Warm-up questions' such as 'Describe yourself' and 'What makes you happy?' helped begin the interview in a personable and friendly manner. It also provided the necessary backdrop for the interpretation of each individual's data.

Question 2 was more specifically oriented to the focus of this study and brought in the subject of religion in Singapore and in adolescent life. Just as in the short descriptive essay, it also tested (and reconfirmed) adolescents' impressionistic knowledge of the religions of Singapore. Question 3 centred on the assumption that switching always has a context – possibly a 'pull' (solution) or 'push' (problem) factor – and tries to uncover these.

It should be noted that the above questions were only meant as a guide as I wanted the respondents to take control of the interview as far as possible. As it turned out, not all the questions were always asked in the same order; sometimes the interviewee would provide an answer to a specific question listed at a later stage, therefore making the question schedule redundant. Although my assistants and I had a list of questions at the interview, we did not hold it in front of us or referred to it frequently – in some cases, we did not use the list at all. In analysing the transcripts and listening to the taped voices, I was concerned not just with what is said but also how the implementation of specific linguistic choices, primarily metaphors, operates to bring about a specific interpretation. Often, interviewees were unable to express all that they meant in a fully explicit way and most of the assumptions they expected their readers to share with them were left implicit. It is unlikely that the subjects had any particular awareness of metaphoric usage at the time of speaking, beyond the normal awareness which native speakers might have in spontaneous speech.

We used a range of corroborative evidence to ascertain the role of metaphors in these contexts: the frequency of occurrence of the same, or very similar, metaphors in the data; the discoursal context in which the metaphors were used, the number of speakers who gave these metaphors. Once there is a token of at least ten similar metaphors in the data by different subjects in both the oral and written discourse, it is taken as a metaphor of note and becomes part of our sample for analysis. Often the minimum limit was superseded.

8.4   Dominant images in Taoism, Christianity and Buddhism

Within this push–pull superstructure, there are discernible clusters of similar metaphoric expressions. In this section, we discuss how such expressions tend to cluster around a conceptual metaphor or image schema. The method of analysis is basically an application of Lakoff and Johnson's (1980) theory that language and thought tend to be structured around certain metaphoric concepts.

Theorists generally agree that metaphor involves a relationship between conceptually distinct entities so that the characteristics associated with one conceptual entity often described as 'source' or 'vehicle' are used to represent another conceptual entity, often described as the 'target' or 'topic'.[3] In this study, the conceptual domain from which we draw metaphorical expressions to understand another conceptual domain is called a *source domain,* while the conceptual domain that is understood in this way is called the *target domain.* Source domains are typically more concrete or physical and more clearly delineated concepts than the targets, which tend to be fairly abstract and less delineated ones. We usually make use of, for example, *death, life, sick, happy, animals, bodies, sickness, movement, travel, objects in physical environment, emotions one feels for our source domain* (Kovecses 2002). This source domain is an extremely simplified world, but it is exactly the simplified nature of this world that enables us to make use of parts of it in creating more abstract ones. Target domains such as Taoism, Christianity, Buddhism and the phenomenon of switching are abstract, diffuse and lack clear delineation and therefore 'cry out' for metaphorical conceptualization.

Conceptual metaphors differ from metaphoric linguistic expressions in the sense that the latter are words or other linguistic expressions that come from the language or terminology of the more concrete conceptual domain, that is, domain 'B' or the source domain. In other words, while a conceptual domain is any coherent organization of experience, the metaphorical linguistic expressions make manifest particular conceptual metaphors. Just as we will find how metaphoric linguistic expressions cluster to form a conceptual metaphor, we will later in this section also attempt to find what kinds of conceptual metaphors cluster together to form a root metaphor. The root metaphor is identified as the one which most easily unifies or unites all the other conceptual metaphors and is often referred to in other studies as 'thematic domain' or 'key scenario'.

8.4.1 'Push' metaphors in Taoism

As the switchers in our study come predominantly from the Taoist background, references to Taoism were negative in connotation. The following are common metaphoric linguistic expressions used to describe Taoism; with the total number of tokens taken from the short descriptive essays in brackets. The most commonly used metaphoric expressions are listed first, followed by the second most commonly used ones and so on. The conceptual metaphors, which the linguistic expressions support, are in bold.

Taoism is funereal/deathlike (T = 270)

Burning... Need to burn paper money to the dead (52)[4]
The Hungry Ghost Month (29)[5]
Ghosts (29)
Many priests for funeral (28)
Cheng Ming[6] (22)
Visit graveyards (and/or crematoriums) (21)
Long funereal rites at the void decks (20)
Ancestor's tablets for worship (19)
Mediums go into trance (14)
Communicate with dead (13)
Dark and reminds me of night time (13)
Gates of Hell (10)

Taoism is idolatry (T = 211)

Idols – there are too many gods and goddesses... (34)
Altar... Many gods on the altar (33)
You need to clean the altar and refill the lamps (21)
You need to feed the gods all the time (20)
Statues (19)
It is so dark and smoky in the temple (17)
Loud talking worshippers (12)
Tua Pek Kong (12)[7]
Fighting gods (12)
Ugly and fierce-looking gods (10)
The eyes in the idols' faces are very frightening (10)

Taoism is loneliness (T = 157)

No friends there; unfriendly (29)
You need to do everything yourself (23)
Nobody talks to you in the temple (20)
Confusion (20)
Sadness (19)
Everybody is so old (18)
... all the ancient furniture everywhere (17)
Taoism is a bore (11)

Taoism is gambling (T = 84)

You need to offer food and drink to get good luck (28)
We cannot eat beef, only vegetables for purity (22)
To kneel to ask for lucky numbers (19)
Worshippers go to gamble there and it's for personal gain (15)

Taoism is confusion (T = 79)

Superstitions (30)
Too many festivals and processions (20)
Beggars outside the temple (19)
Feng shui (10)

Taoism is to do with spirits of animals (T = 70)

Animal images (30)
Spirits of tigers, monkeys, are revered (18)
Spirits of many living things (13)

We can see that Taoism is predominantly viewed through the metaphoric lenses of things 'funereal' and 'deathlike'. Both conceptual metaphors receive over 200 references in the written discourse of our respondents. References to 'burning paper money to the dead' are uppermost in the minds of respondents, probably because this practice is very visible in housing estates during certain times of the year. References to the various gods in Taoism are replete with references to the 'ugly-looking gods' and it is 'idolatry' rather than 'cultural variety' which is viewed through the lens of our young respondents. Youths also view Taoism as 'a bore' as 'you need to do everything yourself' – and hence Taoism is equated as an 'unfriendly' and 'lonely experience'. Taoist worshippers are not only 'elderly' and appear to be concerned not with 'cordiality' or 'hospitality' but with a penchant to obtaining lucky lottery numbers from their patron saints in the temple. Another youthful perspective into Taoism is the conceptual metaphor of 'confusion' with references to its entailments such as superstitions, festivals, processions and feng shui in their written descriptions.

The metaphors gleaned from the short descriptive essays complemented those in the spontaneous interviews. In the following, a respondent was asked to elaborate on why he had switched from Taoism to Christianity. While he described Taoism in the written discourse as:

...a religion for the old people and they worship many gods and animal spirits. There are many altars in the temple and smell of joss sticks (CC19) he explained the reasons behind his switch of religions as:

> ... First, the question of Gods also comes into mind because in the Taoist background there are so many other different types of *deities* and *images* that you pray to, so the question of God is a bit *hazy* and there is a lot of *unanswered questions.* Second, these gods are all *spirits* of *animals* and they have *ugly* faces. Also, I am allergic to the smell of *jossticks.* (CC 19 321–41)

In the essay, another respondent wrote of Taoism as:

> Taoism is a religion where you go to a temple, burn paper to the spirits and there are many gods you must feed. (CC 24)

In the spontaneous interview, however, the same respondent explained his switch in the following way:

> Because the Christian always saying that the Gods of the Buddhist and the Taoists are false and therefore they will not go to heaven and there *are so many gods I am so confused.* (CC 24: 98–9)

> very scary e.g. 'God goes into your body when you are in a trance and things like that'. (CC 24: 201–2)

These adolescents appear to be overwhelmed by the numerous deities and the ritualistic practices of burning and praying. Besides data from the descriptive essay (above), the interview data also found many references to *lottery, burning of incense, idols, mediums and trances, hells, ancestors,* etc. Perhaps the exposure to the more rational and materialistic discourse in schools have caused adolescents to view these as 'irrelevant', 'illogical' and 'irrational'. Indeed, our interviews with adolescents found them appalled by Taoist practices such as that of going into a trance, bodily mutilation and occultism. The effects of such practices, which used to contribute to part of the dynamic mysticism of Taoism, are unfortunately no longer fashionable to a more modern, Western-educated, and materialistic generation. Indeed, among youths in Singapore, Taoism is regarded as a religion of the elderly, with temples functioning as old man's or old woman's clubs. It is popularly viewed as one more centred on the 'dead' than the living, with its elaborate funerary rites conducted conspicuously on the void decks of the housing estates.[8]

The conceptual metaphor of loneliness also appeared often in the interview discourse and played a prominent part in youths' reminiscence for acceptance and belonging:

> I don't like to go to temple because there, you have to do everything yourself. Everyone keeps to themselves. Nobody talks to you including the priest.

> They (Taoists) want to become rich, buy lottery ticket, my father always does that ... (CC 22: 112–13)

There is also a set of correspondences between the source and target in the sense that constituent conceptual elements of the source and the target correspond neatly to one another. In our study, the targets of Taoism, Christianity and Buddhism are characterized by mappings and correspondences from source domains. We found that metaphors from the source domains such as *medium, spirits, demons, gods, festivals and processions*, etc., all of which clustered around the notion of 'death', could be mapped easily to the target of Taoism (Table 8.1).

The constituent mappings and correspondences suggest that Taoism is centrally concerned with the various entailments of death as listed above. While the preoccupation with death is the *raison d'être* of all religions, Christianity and Buddhism are able to background this in their

Table 8.1 Source and target domains in Taoism

Source: hell/death/or the 'other' dimension	Target: Taoism
Medium	Intermediary for spirits in other worlds
Spirits	Those who live in the other world
Demons	Spirits who give you a hard time
Gods	Deities who have power in the other world
Festivals and processions	Commemorative occasions for spirits
Graveyard visits	To visit those who have departed to the other world
Burning paper	To give money to those in the other world
Lottery	A gift to the living from those abiding in the other world
Chambers of hell	A place to go to upon death
Joss sticks	A tool to use while communicating with the other world
Mediums, etc.	An agent (usually paid) you may use to communicate with a spirit

efforts at spreading their faith. In contrast, Taoism has foregrounded this phenomenon. In the first blush of youth, Taoist adolescents are more attracted to life rather than death, the light rather than darkness, and this may explain the inner conflict they feel. Our study shows that Taoism is perceived by youths through the metaphors of: *altar, offerings, temple, funeral, destruction, night/darkness, loneliness, confusion, aged/loneliness, conflict,* all of which contribute to their disillusionment. One adolescent summarizes Taoism as follows:

> There is only death to look to in Taoism. Actually there is no God there and the believers are only interested in spirits, death and funerals and protection from evil spirits. (CC 21: 80–2)

We would like to agree with this youth that the conceptual metaphors of Taoism do tend to cluster around the root metaphor of death.

8.4.2 'Pull' metaphors in Christianity

In our sample, 75.6 per cent of adolescents from the Taoist background had switched to Christianity. Hence, unlike those associated with Taoism, the metaphoric linguistic expressions gathered from the interviews on Christianity are predominantly positive. Once again the conceptual metaphors are listed in bold, and the linguistic expressions that cluster around them are listed directly beneath. The number of times the expression appears in the transcript is bracketed:

Christianity is friendship and/or togetherness (T = 137)

Christianity is a relationship (33)
Friends – we laugh and cry together (22)
The church is like my family (20)
Someone there to hold your hand (18)
So many people to talk to (17)
Singing together... being together.. (15)
A lot of people united in love and sweetness (12)

Christianity is a helpmate (for progress) (T = 129)

Cell group – we belong to a cell group where we have a leader
    who will help us with our problems (25)
... and teach us how to lead a better life (22)
It's friends – there are people to help you and talk to you (19)
Helps to transform and love one another (19)
Helps to make the world a better place (12)

A way to brush up my skills (12)
Jesus said don't worry, I will help and strengthen you. I will
    uphold you with my hand (10)
Don't be afraid. If you are dismayed, I will be here. Don't cry,
    just pray (10)

Christianity is healing (T = 110)

Blessed by the grace of God (19)
Clean our sins and renew us (19)
Drink water of life (15)
Jesus I believe and trust – I feel secure and confident (16)
I see my brother healed ... to heal us all (16)
Forgiveness of all our past sins (15)
Eternal life (17)

Christianity is a rescue ship (T = 92)

People help you (32)
Stories tell me how to solve my problems (19)
I can win the battle (18)
Learn how to improve my character (12)
My grades improved (10)

Christianity is a gift (miracle) (T = 87)

Jesus was dead, now he is alive (28)
A virgin birth/miracle birth/Christ born of a virgin (26)
Resurrection – an amazing miracle and a gift to us (13)
The wise men brought gifts to the stable and this shows Jesus'
    special status (11)
A great gift for believers – the rupture[9] (10)

As indicated by the number of tokens, the conceptual metaphor of
Christianity tended to cluster around that of *friendship, helpmate, healing, rescue ship* and as a *gift*. Of these, the first four appear to be intrinsi-
cally related since they do connote the desire of youths for friendship,
closeness of ties and a helpmate in times of problems. These metaphors
are relevant for adolescents at a time when they are most in need of
friends in shaping their identity and values. Adolescence is a period of
where the quest for self-esteem and self-confidence is uppermost. It can
also be a period of confusion – a time of 'identity crisis' – as postulated
by the work of Erickson in the 1960s. The self-centred need to be 'saved'
is psychologically more appealing, rather than the need to save others.
The proportion of 'this-worldly' needs in this period loom larger than

that of 'other-worldly' ones. A gospel of prosperity – something in which they can 'get' from, rather than one where they have to 'give' – is attractive to Singapore adolescents, many of whom have problems with their self-concept, their relationship with their parents and their studies. Any religious organization which recognizes this important transitional phase will fare well in attracting and keeping them as a congregation. Our study also found that the most common time to switch is between the ages of 15 and 16, a period that could lead to either a solidification of their inherited faith or a departure from it.

As for the last conceptual metaphor – 'Christianity is a gift' – this often involves something mystical or magical for youths – with notions such as *eternal life, virgin birth, resurrection, personal salvation, the rupture,* etc. which are necessarily metaphorical, since we have no experience of them. Of course, one must be careful here that conceptual metaphors and their entailments should not be confused with the truth. Nevertheless, many adolescents do tend to confuse the metaphoric vehicle with the message, and they tend to read their own myths as facts, for example the rupture and the resurrection are taken as factually real by our respondents.

While the above were quantitative counts of metaphoric linguistic expressions from respondents' descriptive essays which tended to cluster around a conceptual metaphor, the following are longer excerpts from the interviews which give us an opportunity to hear the interviewees' voice and the discoursal context in which they operate:

> We have a Christmas party, welcoming party, youth fellowship – pastor tells us what to learn and we can make friends there. Otherwise, at home I am tightly controlled, studies at home, no going out with peers – so this is my opportunity. I love friends, going out and meeting people – there is a life in church and there is none at home. (CC 45 232–5)

> xxx church. – I am so scared and embarrassed but they are so friendly. They ask 'do you find this nice?' 'Don't be scared if we speak in tongues', they put words across in a nice manner – well spoken and like ordinary people. Very friendly. They tell me what is going on in church (I don't even have to ask); Pastor xxxx is strict but very caring and loving. He looks after us like we are children. Makes us feel at home. First time I was awkward but everybody there makes me feel I belong. I treat xxxx church as my home and when I go down there to study, sit in café, take study materials, revise, eat and drink.

With my cell group members, I play games, praise and worship, sermons, testimonials of what God has done for us since we last met and refreshments. (CC 56: 275–83)

It's the easiest religion to know – many people teach you there, can make friends...you are not alone. They buy bible for me and teach me and hold my hand...(CC 15: 189–93)

The problem of 'embarrassment', 'being scared' or 'being lonely' is a recurring theme in our interview discourse. It is a state where youths desire to meet peers but are unable to do so because they are shy, withdrawn or introverted. Loneliness appears to be quite a widespread phenomenon among Singapore adolescents. Weekends and holidays are the loneliest time for the students and these periods find adolescents on the phone chatting up friends (Low et al. 1991). The absence of an attachment figure(s) is solved when there is a successful network which helps take away the feeling of marginality and meaninglessness. As one adolescent puts it when asked whether there is any special teaching that she likes in Christianity:

There's no special teaching I like. It's like a personal one-to-one. Special relationship: like a best friend relationship.

Kau et al.'s (2004) study on the value, lifestyle and aspirations of Singaporeans shows that 'warm relationship with others' has the highest value for those aged 15–24, their youngest group surveyed. The positive imagery of life helps explains why when there is a switch; adolescents tend to go from Taoism to Christianity (60 per cent):

I was very frightened. I was new but everyone was friendly. It's a Chinese church – youth group very nice – strong belief and friends around me. I was traumatized by family but my friends and seniors help me. 'Do not be afraid I will uphold you with my hand and I will straighten you.'

The Christian faith seems to be the overwhelming choice for adolescents. The spontaneous interviews found interpersonal influences, in particular, peer group support and 'fellowship' as the primary 'pull' factor behind the switch. Positive 'pull' factors include Christian friends, from organizations such as the Boys' Brigade and Christian friends in worship services in schools. Friendship is very important and adolescents seem to need company in order not to feel 'lonely' or 'inferior'.

Adolescents switch not because they have commenced on a personal quest for truth but usually because of peer-group influences and the need to 'progress' or 'be healed'. Peer group influence is uppermost and emotional support is crucial for switching to occur. Switching allows a rapid integration into a network of relationships. The time taken to switch is often short – within the first three months. The switching is almost always an 'emotional' rather than an 'intellectual' one:

> Is Christianity important? Don't know. I just want to believe it.

> Jesus Christ is God's only son and he is a Messiah. He died on the cross to save our sins. Without Jesus Christ, man and God cannot communicate. Songs, bonding, hold hands; feel some kind of relief – when you can tell problems to God.

> I am outgoing and fun loving so Christianity is for me. I was exposed to Christianity I grew up in a Christian school I am a dreadful person who lost my directions and indulge in alcohol. But God changed me and make me help people and bless those who do wrong to me instead of eye for an eye Jesus wash away my sins and I realise that by the grace of god and by the blood of Jesus, I am transformed into a better person.

It is seldom that a switcher can explain theosophically or theoretically why it is a particular faith that they have chosen over that of another. Not a single switcher from our interview data referred to the holy writings or scripture as the reason for their switch although some admitted that they liked the inspiring stories in the scripture.

The predominant metaphors used by the respondents such as 'refuge', 'friends' and 'the promised one' tended to cluster around the root metaphor of 'life' or 'the assurance of being saved from death' (Table 8.2).

In the interview, an adolescent compares the two faiths from his perspective:

> I am allergic to Taoism – they burn incense. I follow my parents but I stay outside the temple. But Christ gives me the best things – he keeps me warm, cosy, whenever you need him, you can pray. You can look up the bible; you can feel he's just beside you. Not like Taoism – you've to do everything yourself. (CC2: 183–6)

Table 8.2 Source and target domains in Christianity

Source: Life	Target: Christianity
Refuge/haven	Place to go when things not going well in life
Friends	People who help you get by
Second coming/rupture	The final reward for your belief
God	Someone to pray to when you are in trouble
Personal salvation: Jesus as pilot, as a harbour, as captain of the ship	The assurance of being saved from death
Eternal life	To live forever
Virgin birth, resurrection, promised one	The guarantors (or 'the magic') that what is revealed is true
Pastor	The guide in this life
Shepherd/captain	The ultimate guide in your life
Bible	The book of life

Despite such negative perceptions of Taoism, all religions in reality do foster an alliance with God or the supernatural. It is obvious then that in the homes where the switchers came from, there was a failure of caretakers to convey this to their children. It does appear that the church, much more than the temple, is interested in youths as complete people and as a distinctive group. A closer investigation into the activities of churches in Singapore reveals the presence of all groups in churches which prioritize the building of relationships. There is also the teaching of a God who is personal and caring – something like a friend. Compared to a temple, the church offers a liturgical experience, communion and mission involvement. Churches offer the singing of hymns and pastoral care services. Youths are often drawn to dynamism and charisma of youth-centred activities which are open, attentive, caring, needs-oriented events, where there are friendly people to talk to. In contrast, Taoist/Buddhist parents, many of whom are lowly educated or semi-literate, do not know much about their own religion and hence are unable to explain the main tenets of their beliefs to their children. There is also the 'do it yourself' attitude in syncretistic Taoism/Buddhism. The lack of written canonical scriptures also does not help the situation as syncretistic practices depend a lot on oral tradition. As one youth puts it:

> I prefer to be Christian although my mother takes me to temples because I trust them (the Christians) more. Whenever I ask my parents what this or this mean or why they do such thing, they usually don't know the explanation. (CC3: 83–6)

It is not surprising then to find that Christianity is perceived to be: a 'harbour' or 'rescue ship' from 'loneliness'; a 'gift' vs a 'death'; a 'refuge' from 'hell'; a 'helpmate' for progress' – all in all, leading to a diametrically opposite contrast to Taoism.

8.4.3   Pull metaphors in Buddhism

Twenty-four per cent of our subjects preferred the Buddhist to the Christian faith. Hence, the descriptive essays on Buddhism also carried positive connotative imagery, although not as plentiful those found in the description of Christianity. The dominant metaphors associated with Buddhism are:

Buddhism is a refuge (T = 78)

Change my karma and up my station (19)
Free myself from rebirth (18)
To receive blessings (17)
To rest beneath the lotus flower and lotus feet (14)
It is my mantra (10)

Buddhism is forgetfulness (T = 70)

Free from worries (21)
Free from the loathsome nature of everything (20)
I am blissfully detached (15)
Chanting to be happy (14)

Buddhism is a journey of discovery (T = 68)

Enlightenment, a way to discover about oneself (19)
I just walk along the same path as Buddha (17)
Good speech, good action, good thought (12)
To discover the compassion (10)
To reach nirvana and/or Western pure land[10] (10)

Buddhism is unity (within) (T = 54)

I feel free and powerful (16)
I can become self-reliant and a better person (16)
I search for my inner self (12)
To find the light within (Mediation) (10)

The most popular metaphor of 'refuge' and 'forgetfulness' may be said to be similar to those of 'healing', 'rescue ship' and 'helpmate' found in the data on Christianity. Youths are seeking something which they have not been able to find in Taoism – so a helping hand and a friendly voice is a great attraction. However, what is striking is that Buddhism is perceived not just as 'a haven of refuge' and 'forgetfulness' but also the abstract notion of 'unity within' which may be associated with a sense of 'forgetfulness'. For youths, this appears more palatable than the dark, unwieldy, hazy structure of Taoism. Something quite unique is also the perception not so much of an immediate 'rescue' from their problems by a 'saviour' but more a 'journey of discovery' which all must undertake. There is an awareness of the need to overcome self and passion as a means to be 'free and powerful'. The Buddha is viewed not so much as a physical saviour but a mental beacon along a spiritual path which He too has walked. The Buddha is also not 'the only true one' but 'one of many Buddhas yet to come'.

Our interview data revealed that Taoist switchers to Buddhism usually come from a troubled past and have found a sense of relief, calmness and freedom, translated into what has been termed 'bliss', 'detachment', 'nirvana', 'freedom' and 'power' in our written data.

> problems with mother ... always quarrel – I am very upset – it affected my studies ... I lost all my confidence ... I do badly in school ... My teachers send me for counselling. But I don't want to go anymore because it is so crowded and there are so many students ... long queue. But my mother say, 'However they do it, mother still care', so then my Auntie say 'come with me to xxxx (Buddhist) temple it will solve your problems', so I go.

> I used to cry every night. It is always very dark. I am always alone. I am scared of all the voices I hear. Chanting is good for all kinds of problems ... especially in the night. When I talk to xxxxx Buddha, I feel so much better. I'm peaceful now. I am not afraid of night time.

> I came to the end of the road and was drowning but auntie help me to say ... It was touch and go but I managed to survive I was in a jail term, I wanted to solve my problem.

Similar to those who had switched to Christianity, a switch to Buddhism is more often an emotional experience, rather than an intellectual one:

> I see that my friend has so much success in her study and everything in her life went smoothly. I asked her to help me. She introduced me to prayers, chanting and meditation which help her. It helps me also.

But what make me want to know what Buddhism is about? What got me to ask that question? I think it was from the very beginning the person who answered my question had a lovely voice and you can feel the spirit of loving kindness from that voice. I had no choice but seek the answer to that loving kindness which I found.

There is also a set of correspondences discernible between source and target. References in Buddhism, for example all the commonly recurring metaphors such as *mantra, Western pure land, blessings, sufferings*, etc. are related to the source of 'path' which refers to a kind of way, road or journey to be taken. Table 8.3 shows the systematic set of mappings.

Although Buddhism and Taoism are part of the family of Chinese religions (the other being Confucianism), the metaphors used by the switchers are startlingly different. While Taoist conceptual metaphors are dominantly associated with death, Buddhist conceptual metaphors are primarily to do with walking the path, and staying on it as a means of gaining 'freedom' and 'power'. The basic preoccupation of Buddhist temples appears to be the accumulation of merits and sutra-chanting to improve their karma. It is appealing to youths because there is a feeling of journeying towards a great goal. There is a destination of the blissful paradise of nirvana, a place away from the present world of pain and uncertainty:

I want to be Christian but my parents say I am born with Taoist blood in me, saying it is better for me to be Taoist. In the end, I decided to be a Buddhist as I can still burn offerings to all the idols. (BC 11: 111–13)

In the above, the youth is more inclined to Christianity since he has referred to Taoism as 'idols' but he has made a pragmatic choice by switching to Buddhism since it is more 'flexible' than Christianity, for example it does not categorically object to the adherent continuing with Taoist practice. In relation to parental objection, there will ostensibly be fewer obstacles to the switch since Buddhism is perceived as a 'sister' of Taoism in the family of Chinese religions (Chew 2000).

While we have focused on conceptual metaphors in Taoism, Christianity and Buddhism, it should be noted that orientational metaphors also featured in our sample. Such metaphors have skeletal image-schemas, such as those associated with 'out'. They have very few details filled in and they also tap very little from source to target (see Section 8.2). They are like one-shot images, not based on recurrent

Table 8.3   Source and target domains in Buddhism

Source: Path	Target: Buddhism
Mantra	Something to take with you on the journeys
Nirvana, Western pure land	The destination of the path
Good speech, good action, good thought	Things to bring on the path
Amitabha[11]	The future guide on the path
Buddha	The past guide on the path
Blessings	Good fortune along the path
Sufferings, karma, rebirth	When you stray from the path
Loathsome nature of everything	Things that grow outside the path
Compassion	What you should feel when you meet creatures along the way
Free and powerful	The empowerment you feel walking along the path
Chanting	Solace along the path

experience with a general structure. The first two in the following list are by Taoist converts to Christianity while the next two are by Taoist converts to Buddhism:

> I am feeling *up* with my church friends,
> My spirits *improved* when I am in church
> I *sank* to depths of despair with my fears
> I was *down* in the dumps until I found the way.

To summarize, here are three prototypical voices on the three root metaphors from our sample:

Taoism is *death*	I don't know why I dislike Taoism but it frightens me and reminds me of spirits and ghosts. Especially Taoist funerals are frightening for me. (CC 14 line 60)
Christianity is *life*	I want to be saved and happy and to always have a friend. (CC 15 line 23)
Buddhism is a *path*	Buddhism is Chinese and Taoism is Chinese so we are born good and there is nothing to be saved from. Therefore I find Buddhism is more rational and tells us not to stray from the path. (BC 12 lines 73–5)

8.5　Conflict and accommodation in religious switching

It is unfortunate for Taoism that its root metaphor of death conjures the following thought processes in the minds of adolescents:

> Taoism is concerned with death – We are interested in life and living – Hence we should depart from it

In contrast, the thought processes connected with Christianity, its apparently diametrical opposite, are:

> Christianity is concerned with life – We are interested in life and living – Hence we should go towards it

Naturally, a conflict ensues from the contrast, giving rise to the following metaphoric linguistic expressions, as evidenced in the oral data:

> My head want to burst (26)
> I feel hemmed in (18)
> I am angry until I found my friend in Jesus (14)
> I felt spent up and frustrated then I found the one true god (14)
> I had a sore head (14)
> I was stuck in … (13)
> I was lost and very frighten (10)
> I was a broken being before Jesus came along (10)

The conceptual metaphor around which the above impressions clustered was the embodied metaphor of 'containment' (cf. Gibbs 1999: 44). References to anger, of being 'stuck', 'broken', 'hemmed in', 'spent up', 'frustrated', 'lost', are related to the body, in the sense of being imprisoned or 'contained within'. It is ostensibly a situation of encircled discomfort and one which presupposes a strong urge for 'release'. Expressions such as *stuck in, hemmed in, very frighten, spent up, frustrated,* etc. are also sensorimotor and suggest a state of disequilibrium and perhaps of chaos, and may be quite similar to those used by psychotherapy patients (cf. McMullen and Convey 1996).

The conflict is exacerbated by obstacles which may be internal, as apparent in the embodied metaphors above, but which may also be external. External factors act as environmental 'obstacles' to an impending change of faith. They stem from family opposition to the new faith:

> I was just concerned my parents because as you know my parents are quite staunch Taoists, Buddhists background and they have also very negative feelings about Christianity. They began to get worried, but my father confronted me…in a way his disappointment that I change my religion and that I be very careful and I think. at the end of the day, I get the idea that they are so concerned that…by changing the religion, we are sort of neglecting the parents and ancestors…we are going away from the family…that new religion will take me away from the closeness of the family so what I did is stop seeing my Christian friends. (CC55: 200–10)

The obstacles will cause the subject to 'block out' the pull factors from the new faith and remain in the Taoist tradition, as a kind of filial piety, a value encouraged in traditional Chinese family. In the following, however, a subject recounts not just the external obstacle but also how the demise of that obstacle, enabled her eventually to make the switch:

> My mother had said earlier when I was a child was that should any of her children become a Christian, she would break their leg – this came from a very loving, loving mother. So I didn't become a Christian until after she passed away. After my mother died, I asked my father for permission – my siblings were unhappy. However, my father was very loving and close to 12 midnight, before my baptism, he actually consented and he was sick at that time. I went for baptism early in the morning at 6 am. So that itself show that they gave out of their love for their daughter. My father is very active in the (Taoist) temple and I thank him as well that the daughter should become a Christian. I tried my very best not to disturb his peace in the sense that I would continue to participate in Taoist prayers. (CC14: 230–51)

Once these obstacles are removed, a switch inevitably takes place propelled along by root metaphors. Such metaphors activate a follow-up action and are powerful forces for change. They are dynamic for they portray truth vividly and simply. Their key images and entailments become a symbol fuelling inner turmoil, leading the subject to some form of action. They transform the individual by clarifying the transaction from one to the other. The push–pull tension propels our respondent to either remain in the faith or transit to another. Hence, in considering the 'reality' of these metaphors – whether they are only verbal devices or whether they have cognitive and social validity for switchers – we found that once the respondent has undergone the experience of containment which leads to a search for some kind of release, they do often switch. Hence, these metaphors are in a sense 'real' since they are accompanied by related actions or behaviours.

The switch is often perceived in the following ways: as *breakthrough, escape route, growth,* or *battle.* Certainly, the embodied metaphor of containment gives rise to interesting entailments, for example of 'growing up', 'moving to the light', 'growing out of a problem'. The view of 'switching as growth' is related to escape and breakthrough in the sense that one has to 'grow' out of an embodied contained state into wider more breathable spaces. The more unusual metaphor of 'switching as a battle' probably derives from the obstacles faced by adolescents in their efforts to switch religion. Here, in the examples below, it is apparent that these adolescents have not chosen the path of resignation but rather than of Christians in pious battle.

Once again, the metaphoric linguistic expressions from the interview discourse are counted and listed under each conceptual metaphors (in bold) to which they are drawn.

Switching is a breakthrough or a light at the end of a tunnel (total = 150)

The light at the end of a tunnel (25)
All of a sudden, it was clear to me (24)
A moment of recognition as to what I can do (20)
It is through enduring all the pain and confusion that I wake up (18)
It strikes me hard and I know I like to be a Christian (18)
I am born again (15)
Awareness, dawn, truth I suddenly realise ... (15)
Suddenly, it came on it began like this (15)

Switching is an escape route (total = 119)

Find a way out (45)
To escape from (the problem) (38)
Ride out (the problem) (21)
Sail through (the problem) (15)

Switching is growth (total = 118)

I wish to make a fresh start (27)
My heart set out to change (24)
We can help get a better karma (19)
We need to go from child to adult (18)
An opportunity to move on (15)
To build a new society (15)

Switching is a battle (total = 117)

We need to fight the devil (23)
We are soldiers against the evil (21)
We must turn from being a mouse to a lion (19)
People's eyes turn towards me and help me to face the battle (16)
I need to step out of myself and so I decide to take the plunge
    and go for it (16)
I need to face the situation and take what I want (12)
We are Christian soldiers ... (10)

One notes too the presence of many spatio-orientational metaphors
which are related to a need to escape from the experience of containment. Here, the switch is commonly described as one of facing reality:

We need to *face* reality
To *face* the facts
We need to *stand up* and *be strong*
Once in our life we must *look* at ourselves and *come* to a decision

or of progress and a journey to a goal:

Go *through* the life
What I am *after* in my life is
At 17, I make *headway* with ...
Switch to make progress
A need to move forward

The prototypical adolescent is obviously part of the 'me-first orientation'. That is, the adolescent cultural orientation is one where they
view themselves as functioning from an 'upright' position and moving 'forwards', spending most of their time performing 'actions', viewing themselves as basically 'good' and avoiding the 'bad' things, which
prevents them from making 'headway'. Once the switch has occurred,

adolescents usually experience a sense of relief. Buddhist converts talk about peacefulness and calmness while embarking on a journey, while Christian switchers feel happy and secure and look forward to what promises to be an ideal and happy life.

8.6   Conclusion

This study has been devoted to an understanding of what has been commonly perceived as an abstract and emotional arena, namely, the motivation behind adolescent switching as revealed by adolescents' use of metaphoric discourse both oral and written. It should prove fruitful to those interested in the sociocultural and psychological factors during adolescence – a period of dramatic biological and emotional changes. This has taken place in Singapore – a sociolinguistic paradise where much can be studied and analysed.

Why and when would a person prefer to use figurative statements when the same point can be made by the use of literal statements? It is because metaphors are compact and efficient ways to state the intended meaning, for example the concept of the 'black hole' in science (Ortony 1975). It also adds dramatic effect to thought processes and in our study has been shown as a catalyst for strategic change. There is a human tendency to make use of material things and sense perceptions to create realities, especially social realities – hence the prevalent use of metaphors either at the conscious or unconscious level. Metaphors are therefore 'necessary and not just nice' (Ortony 1975).

A study of metaphor becomes especially invaluable in more private domains of study. It is an indispensable medium used to understand the truth of our emotions because, very often, the mystery of our emotion is not describable in direct language or in simple sentences stating that such and such is so. Religious switching is a value-laden field, often cognitively and perceptually removed from the immediacy of everyday experience. It is also not a common or public phenomenon – it may happen only once in an individual's lifetime, if at all. Certainly then, the attempt to understand a phenomenon by referring it to other phenomena both similar and dissimilar is one of the basic human activities. Not surprisingly, a study of metaphors has traditionally been an important part of discourse theories.

Our study shows that adolescents gravitate towards imagery connected with life rather than death. Hence, in the last two decades in Singapore, there has been a significant movement of the general populace, and not just adolescents, towards the life metaphor of Christianity.

Correspondingly, there is a human tendency to view ourselves as more up than down, more front than back, more active than passive and more alive than dead and more good than bad (Lakoff and Johnson 1980). Hence, a religion which crafts its religious and conceptual apparatus round the motif of life, rather than death, will be much more appealing to the populace, and especially to youths.

While the predominant thematic domains in Taoism and Christianity are 'death' and 'life' respectively, Buddhism's key scenario is perhaps something a little more abstract and less of a diametrical opposite – it is represented predominantly as a 'path' or 'journey' to a better future. Perhaps that may account for why Buddhism is often referred to elsewhere as 'the middle way'. Switching is commonly represented as an 'escape route' or the 'light' vs the 'night' of Taoism. The tipping point is explained as a 'breakthrough' although the reasons given by our respondents are never quite rational or clear.

While the use of metaphors may reveal the internal emotions preceding change, there are also external factors which also play a significant role. Why, for example, have Singapore adolescents chosen to switch to Christianity rather than other faiths? Obvious reasons such as instrumental rewards or useful economic contacts have been proposed in the past by Tamney and Hassan (1987), but theirs was a study of slightly older individuals in a university. In our study of school-going adolescents, we found that peer group influence and crisis management help were the primary factors affecting a switch, at a period of time where parental monitoring and control were greatly threatened. Certainly, there can be other valid reasons other than those given by the switchers themselves, as to why Christianity was their prime choice. There is, for example, the missionary or proselytizing nature of the Christian faith. Christianity has also been transplanted so often that it now appears to be an acultural religion and therefore the most obviously 'modern' and 'global' choice. Relative to the other faiths, Christianity in Singapore is also reputably the best organized with a network which allows youths to develop personal relationships with unusual speed.

In addition, Chew (2006, 2008) refers to the widespread use of the English language as a key reason for the switch. In Singapore, the 15 per cent Christians are overwhelmingly English-educated. The more English a person uses, the more likely they are to lose affinity with native religion, because language is by its very nature ideological and plays a major part in moulding our values and the way we perceive our world. Chew argues that embedded within the English language are

'Western' values such as meritocracy and scientific rationality. Allowed to follow a natural cause, the hegemony of English has the potential power not only to diminish the use and value of native languages but also to replace or displace their religio-cultural framework altogether. The decline of Chinese dialects within a generation in Singapore has led to the loss of discursive practices which are essential in the transmission and maintenance of folk religions such as Taoism. Without Hokkien, Teochew, Cantonese and Hainanese (Chinese dialects), Taoists can no longer experience the immediate relevance and emotional reality of the faith. Hence, the ascendancy of the English language and the rise of Christianity at the expense of Taoism.

The intrinsic nature of Taoism also contributes to the 'push' factors. We recall adolescents' disenchantment with Taoist rites/rituals, which they deemed 'superstitions', and the lack of available information on Taoism either from the temple authorities or their parents. The lack of a central authority or scriptural doctrine in Taoism will certainly have a part to do with their disillusionment. The fact that the Taoist priesthood is random and anyone can set up a 'Taoist' temple may explain the 'hazy' or 'obscure' understanding by the general populace. Last but not least, the common problems which the elderly men and women bring to the temple have to do with mundane domestic affairs, illnesses, emotional and psychological problems, social and marital discord – something quite different from the modern adolescents' array of interests (Kuah-Pearce 2005).

We live in an increasingly competitive world and even in matters of faith, it is a zero-sum gain where rivalry for religious membership is concerned – one group's gain is often another's loss. Bolinger (1980) writes of how different interest groups seek to publicize their rival metaphors as a means of persuading the public to subconsciously accept the entailments of these metaphors. To stem the tide of adherents moving to greener pastures elsewhere, the Taoist and Buddhist groups need to accelerate their move towards a more canonical context by stripping away the more random and superstitious elements of their faiths. The creation of Internet sites, forming clubs in schools, use of music and chanting, and the use of English in their services, would certainly be of appeal to youths. One notes, however, that Buddhism has risen to the challenge. The past few years have seen a resurgence in Buddhism in Singapore and it is now regarded as an effective competitor to Christianity in attracting adherents from Taoism (Chew 2008).

To conclude, this study has highlighted the processes of change, conflict and accommodation in the highly delicate and subjective context of adolescent religious switching. Negative and positive mental images merge and interact to produce an emotional conflict which ultimately results in accommodation and change. Change, however, may not result if the obstacles present are insurmountable. In such a scenario, there is a retreat from the pull factors, back to square one, where the adolescent was originally. Change is uncomfortable and is often either a result of conflict or a prelude to conflict. Conflict is of two kinds: internal, where the adolescents are gripped, trapped and cajoled to accommodate, by seeking a way out. On the other hand, external conflict is manifest in the environmental obstacles encountered. Here then is a preliminary study which has attempted to traverse the inner landscape of the heart. An array of subconsciously used metaphors lights the way and reveals an intricate interplay of life, death and path imagery in a generic superstructure of change, conflict and accommodation.

Notes

1. I would like to acknowledge the help given by my two research assistants: Yeo Yew Hock and Betty Wee; as well as the grant from the Institute of Policy Studies, Singapore for part of the data collected in this study.
2. See e.g. *Straits Times* 16.1.1995, p. 19: 'Singapore First World Religion Day Draws 1000'.
3. Lakoff and his associates use the term 'source' or 'target' while Glucksbert and his collaborators prefer 'vehicle' or 'topic'. In this essay, I use 'source' and 'target'.
4. This 'burning' is associated with the burning of paper money or 'spirit paper' for the benefit of the dead. This happens at the Hungry Ghost month as well as other auspicious occasions during the year.
5. The Hungry Ghost Month is a yearly festival celebrated by the Taoists in Singapore. In this month, it is believed that the spirits of the deceased will visit earth. To 'appease' the spirits, the offering of food and the burning of spirit paper are practised by Taoist adherents throughout Singapore.
6. Cheng Ming is a festival for the dead. During this period, it is important for the Chinese to visit members of their family or clan who have passed away. Usually practised by the older or more conservative members of the family, who come from a Taoist–Buddhist background.
7. One of the gods in Taoism.
8. Most Singaporeans live in high-rise flats. The 'void decks' are the ground floor of such flats, which are wide open spaces, which can be rented for public functions such as parties, funerals and weddings.
9. Rupture – a time in the future awaited by Christians who believe literally that Christ will come down from the heavens.
10. 'Nirvana' refers to a pleasant 'nothingness' while 'Western pure land' is an imaginary heaven.
11. Amitabha – the fifth Buddha (some Buddhist groups are awaiting this Buddha – that is yet to come).

References

Alatas, Syed Farid, Lim Teck Ghee and Kuroda, Kazuhide (eds) (2003) *Asian Inter-Faith Dialogue: Perspectives on Religion: Education and Social Cohesion*. Singapore: Rima Singapore and World Bank, pp. 203–34.

Bolinger, D. (1980) *Language; the Loaded Weapon. The Use and Abuse of Language Today.* London: Longman.

Campbell, Joseph (1968) *The Hero with a Thousand Faces*, 2nd edn. Princeton: Princeton University Press.

Chew, Phyllis G.L. (2000) 'Brothers and Sisters: Buddhism in the Family of Chinese Religion'. *The Singapore Baha'i Studies Review*, 5 (1), 1–33.

Chew, Phyllis (2006) 'Language Use and Religious Practice: the Case of Singapore', in Tope Omoniyi and Joshua Fishman (eds), *Explorations in the Sociology of Language and Religion*, Amsterdam: John Benjamins, pp. 212–34.

Chew, G.L.P. (2008) 'Religious Switching and Knowledge among Adolescents in Singapore', in A.E. Lai (ed.), *Religious Diversity in Singapore*, Singapore: Institute of Southeast Asian Studies, pp. 381–410.

Clammer J. (1991) *The Sociology of Singapore Religion: Studies in Christianity and Chinese Culture*. Asia Pacific Monograph No. 4. Singapore: Chopman Publishers.

Department of Statistics (1991) *Census of Population, 1990. Advanced Data Release.* Singapore: Government Printing Press.

Department of Statistics (2000) *Census of Population 2000. Advance Data Release.* Singapore: Department of Statistics.

Gibbs, W. Raymond Jr (1999) 'Researching Metaphor', in Lynn Cameron and Graham Low (eds), *Researching and Applying Metaphor*, Cambridge: Cambridge University Press, pp. 29–47.

Kau, Ah Keng et al. (eds) (2004) *Understanding Singaporeans: Values, Lifestyles, Aspirations and Consumption Behaviour*. Singapore: World Scientific.

Kuah-Pearce, Khun Eng (2005) 'Diversities and Unities: Towards a Reformist Buddhism in Singapore'. Paper delivered at IPS workshop on Religious Diversity and Harmony, 1–2 September 2005.

Kovecses, Zoltan (2002) *Metaphor. A Practical Introduction*. Oxford: Oxford University Press.

Lakoff, G. and Johnson, M. (1980) *Metaphors We Live By*. Chicago, Ill.: Chicago University Press.

Leow, Bee Geok (2000) 'Table 18.6. Religion, Educational Attainment and Use of English at Home', *Census of Population. Advanced Data Release No. 2.* Singapore: Dept. of Statistics.

Low, Guat Tin, Ling, Quah May and Leng, Yeap Lay (1991) *Adolescent Loneliness: Schools and Parents to the Rescue*. Singapore: Centre for Applied Research in Education, National Institute of Education.

McMullen, Linda M. and Convey, John B. (1996) 'Conceptualizing the Figurative Expression of Psychotherapy Clients', in J.S. Mio and A.N. Katz (eds), *Metaphor: Implications and Applications*. New Jersey: Lawrence Erlbaum Associates, pp. 59–82.

Mio, J.S. and Katz, A.N. (eds) (1996) *Metaphor: Implications and Applications*. New Jersey: Lawrence Erlbaum Associates, pp. 59–82.

Ortony, A. (1975) 'Why Metaphors Are Necessary and Not Just Nice'. *Educational Theory*, 26, 45–53.

Sinha, Vineeta (2003) 'Scrutinizing the Themes of "Sameness" and "Difference" in the Discourse on Multi-Religiosity and Religious Encounters in Singapore', in Syed Farid Alatas, Lim Teck Ghee and Kazuhiole Kuroda (eds), *Asian Inter-Faith Dialogue: Perspective on Religion, Education and Social Cohesion*, Singapore: Rima Singapore and World Bank, pp. 203–34.

Tamney, J.B. and Hassan, Riaz (1987) *Religious Switching in Singapore. A Study of Religious Mobility*. Singapore: Select Books.

Tamney, J.B. and Hassan, Riaz (n.d.) 'An Analysis of the Decline of Allegiance of Chinese Religions: a Comparison of University Students and Their Parents', in R. Hassan and J.B. Tamney (eds), 'Analysis of an Asian Society', unpublished manuscript.

Tong, C.K. (2002) 'Religion', in C.K Tong and Kwee Fen Lian (eds), *The Making of Singapore Sociology, Society and State*, Singapore: Times Media Pte Ltd.

Wee, Lionel (2005) 'Constructing the Source; Metaphor as Discourse Strategy'. *Discourse Studies*, 7 (3), 363–84.

9
African American Vernacular English, Religion and Ethnicity

Nkonko M. Kamwangamalu

Introduction

African American Vernacular English (AAVE), which is defined by Geneva Smitherman (1977: 32) as 'European-American speech with Afro-American meaning, nuance, tone, and gesture', has been investigated from various perspectives. Some scholars have focused on the status of AAVE, whether it is a(n African) language or a variety of American English (e.g. Baldwin 2002); others have concentrated on its origins, whether AAVE is derived from a prior Creole, as can be inferred from titles such as 'The Creole Origins of African-American Vernacular English: Evidence from Copula Absence' (Rickford 1998), or whether the variety evolved internally from what Poplack and Tagliamonte (2001) call 'Early African American English', which seemingly diverged from mainstream varieties under conditions of community cohesion and segregation from the dominant white society (Kamwangamalu 2003); and still others have been concerned with the issue whether AAVE is suitable or unsuitable for the schooling of African American children (Ramirez et al. 2005).

This chapter explores how African Americans use AAVE to project their ethnic identity in the secular as well as in the sacred arenas of religion. This it does from the perspective of Accommodation Theory (Giles 1977; Giles and Smith 1979) and of 'Ethnicity in the Sociology of Language and Religion Framework' (Fishman 2002, 2006). In his accommodation paradigm, Giles (1977) proposes that people are motivated to adjust their speech style, or *accommodate*, as a means of expressing values, attitudes and intentions towards others. The extent to which individuals shift their speech styles towards (i.e. *convergence*) or away from (i.e. *divergence*) the speech styles of their interlocutors is a mechanism by which social approval or disapproval is communicated. Convergence is a reflection of social integration, whereas divergence is a reflection of social dissociation or distance. Convergence entails *attenuation* of ethnic speech markers especially in inter-ethnic linguistic interactions to accommodate out-group members, while divergence involves *accentuation* of a group's (or an individual's) speech markers to project its ethnic identity (Giles and Smith 1979). I will argue that in the context of predominantly black churches in the United States, preachers tend to accentuate the characteristic features of AAVE and use it as a marker of the congregation's ethnicity. In so doing, they mark themselves off, i.e. diverge, from the mainstream white society.

The exclusive use of AAVE in predominantly black churches does not entail that AAVE is the only variety available in the linguistic repertoire of the church members, and certainly not in that of the pastors. As Fishman (2006: 14) remarks in his '[A] decalogue of basic theoretical perspectives for sociology of language and religion', 'no matter how restricted the role and domain repertoire available in any community may be, the (most-) religious language or variety... always functions within a larger multilingual/multivarietal repertoire'. Against this background, it can be argued that in the context of the sacred arena of the black church in the United States, AAVE has become religiously encumbered, that is, the variety has acquired a certain degree of sanctity of its own which makes it the medium through which church leaders interact with the congregations during the sermons. Along these lines, it would be unimaginable and out of place for a predominantly black church to conduct a sermon through the medium of a variety other than AAVE. The very use of AAVE rather than Standard American English (SAE), whether in the secular or sacred arenas, is of and in itself a form of *othering* intended to mark ethnic boundaries between African Americans and the mainstream white society. It [AAVE use] lends support to the claim in variation studies that a variety of features, whether phonetic, lexical or syntactic – features for which AAVE is both well known and stigmatized – contribute to the construction of speaker identities in terms of particular ethnolects or regional dialects (e.g. Duszak 2002).

The chapter will be organized as follows. The following section discusses briefly the social history of AAVE. The next section overviews the literature on language and ethnicity to provide the theoretical background against which the issue of AAVE and ethnic identity in the black church will be discussed. The subsequent section examines how African Americans use AAVE to project their ethnic identity in the sacred arena of religion. The penultimate section discusses African

Americans' attitudes towards AAVE. The last section addresses briefly how attitudes toward AAVE impact the debates on the role of AAVE in the schooling of African American children.

AAVE: a brief social history

AAVE, also known as *African American English, Black dialect, Black/African American Lingo, Black English, African Negro Non-Standard English, Black English Vernacular, African American Language, African Language Systems, Pan African Communicative Behaviours, Noble Language of the Ghetto* or *Ebonics* (Filmer 2003, Smitherman 1977, 1998, 2002 [1973]), has arguably attracted far more attention from researchers, theorists and the public in general than any other ethnic variety of American English.

Of all the afore-listed terms, Ebonics and AAVE have become more popular in recent years. The conceptual framework of Ebonics, originally proposed in 1973 by Robert Williams, a psychologist, and subsequently endorsed by black scholars, 'represented an avenue for decolonization of the African-American mind, a way to begin repairing the psycholinguistically maimed psyche of Blacks in America' (Smitherman 1998: 30). According to Williams (1975), the term 'Ebonics' means 'black speech sounds'. It is a blend derived from 'ebony', meaning black, and 'phonics', meaning sound. Williams and Rivers (1975: 100–1) define *Ebonics* as

> the linguistic and paralinguistic features which on a concentric continuum represent the communicative competence of West African, Caribbean, and United States slave descendants of African origin. Ebonics includes the various idioms, patois, argots, ideolects [*sic!*] and social dialects of these people. It is thus the culturally appropriate language of black people and is not to be considered deviant.

Williams and Rivers give the following sentence as an example of Ebonics: 'The Hawk definitely ain't jivin' outdoors today', which means 'the air is crisp' or 'the wind of winter is piercing'. It is explained that contrary to popular belief this sentence is neither a slang expression, nor a non-standard English form. Rather, it is stated in [the] culturally appropriate and ingenious language of black people.

The framework of Ebonics gained notoriety in 1996 when the Oakland Unified School District in California adopted a proposal, which black parents, politicians and community leaders opposed, that Ebonics be used as a medium of instruction for the education of African American children to remedy their lacklustre academic performance.

The impermanence of labels identifying the speech patterns of African Americans, says Filmer (2003: 255), is a constant reminder of the ongoing struggle by African Americans to define and identify themselves, rather than to be defined or labelled by others.

Irrespective of the label one uses, scholars are agreed that the variety of English spoken by African Americans, now generally referred to as AAVE, is a by-product of contacts between African and European languages, which led the Africans to adopt Eurocentric patterns without necessarily erasing the traces of their ancestral (African) languages (Smitherman 2002 [1973], Poplack and Tagliamonte 2001, Wolfram and Thomas 2002). AAVE, says Geneva Smitherman (1994: 18, 20), was born from a culture of struggle, a way of talking that has taken surviving African language elements as the base for self-expression in an alien tongue. Smitherman notes that AAVE has its genesis in enslavement, where it was necessary to have a language that would mean one thing to the enslaved Africans but another to the European slave masters. Along these lines, Perry (2004) observes that in order to subvert the power of their masters, the African slaves used linguistic codes that the masters could not understand. Among the slaves the codes served as a means for in-group identification as well as for detachment from the slave masters. Schmid (2002: 341) concurs, noting that an intense process of persecution on the part of the dominant members of a society, as slavery was for the Africans who were brought to America centuries ago, usually leads to a dynamic process of forming a more discrete and clearly defined notion of in-group and out-group identity on the part of the minority group that is undergoing persecution. Thus, not only is AAVE a component of a unifying heritage of an African American community, but it is also, as Morgan (1998: 277) remarks pointedly, '...a bold and elusive instance of the power of human beings to cultivate language in order to ensure that they have cultural and historical memory, control over their identity, and a way to reflect on and make sense of their daily lives as they see them'.

AAVE and ethnicity: a theoretical background

The key argument in this chapter is that AAVE is a marker of ethnic identity or ethnicity for most African Americans. As will be discussed later, African Americans use AAVE to accentuate their ethnicity especially in in-group interactions in various domains of language use, including the secular as well as the sacred domains of religion. Not only is AAVE the principal medium of communication among African Americans, but it is also, as Knight (2002: 369) remarks pointedly, what makes them a separate ethnic group vis-à-vis others in the United States. The review that follows of the literature on language and ethnicity is drawn from Kamwangamalu (2001: 77, 78). Ethnicity, says Nash (1989: 115), entails 'a consciousness of belonging to a group, "large or small, socially dominant or subordinate" (Edwards 1994: 128), with whom one's humanity is inextricably intertwined and has ancestral links'. For Le Page and Tabouret-Keller (1985), ethnicity denotes a sense of common origin and destiny, shared culture and or language, a measure of consensus of the evaluation of others, active self-identification with the in-group, ascription to it by outsiders, and/or some idea of biological kinship and inheritance. Definitional details of ethnicity may vary. However, the central tendency of ethnicity is how people define themselves vis-à-vis others, how distinctions are made between 'we' and 'they' (Newman 1978: 105) or between 'us' and 'them'.

Ethnicity can be expressed through a wide range of media, such as ethnic dress, dance, foods, symbols or language. The latter, however, is generally seen as 'probably the most powerful single symbol of ethnicity because it serves as a shorthand for all that makes a group special and unique (Ross 1979: 9–10). It [language] is, as Fishman (1977) puts it, the most salient symbol of ethnicity because it carries the past and expresses present and future attitudes and aspirations. Along these lines, Saint-Jacques and Giles (1979: ix) note that 'no other factor is as powerful as language in maintaining *by itself* the genuine and lasting distinctiveness of an ethnic group' (italics in the orginal).

Research has shown that language, or a variety of language for that matter, is intimately linked to an individual's or group's social identity (e.g. Gumperz 1982, Tabouret-Keller 1997). The link between language and identity, says Tabouret-Keller (1997: 317), is often so strong that a single feature of language use suffices to identify someone's membership in a given group. Anticipating such a link, Le Page and Tabouret-Keller (1985) argue that linguistic acts are acts of identity. It is explained that 'linguistic items are not just attributes of groups or communities, they are themselves the means by which individuals both identify themselves and identify with others; hence the existential locus of *homo*, be it individuals or groups, is language itself' (1985: 4–5).

For African Americans, AAVE remains, through its distinct structural and discoursal features (for details, see Smitherman 1977, 1994, 1998, 2002 [1973]), the most powerful symbol of their ethnicity. Thus AAVE, or any language system, not only creates identity for its speakers but it also identifies their social group membership (Gumperz 1982: 239).

Concurring with this idea that language creates identities for its speakers, Tabouret-Keller (1997) notes that any identification between A and B, for instance, "is only possible insofar as these two have access to and are part of C', with A and B being individuals or groups, and C defined as 'language in its symbolic function' (1997: 324).

The link between language and a group's or individual's identity cannot be emphasized any further particularly in the American context, where and against the background of slavery and racism, AAVE and SAE coexist in what Sridhar (1996: 54) describes as a state of organic tension, one in which AAVE speakers who do not speak SAE resent the power and the gatekeeping role of the latter variety. As a language system born from a culture of struggle, AAVE is known for its oppositional nature – opposition, in particular, to SAE supremacy and domination. The latent conflict or tension between the speakers of AAVE and of SAE has from time to time surfaced, as was noted earlier with respect to the proposal by the Oakland Unified School District Board to use AAVE as a medium of instruction in the education of black children. This conflict derives from the social meaning, that is the values which AAVE and SAE communicate in the American society. In this society, as will be seen later, AAVE can be described as a variety on the margin, for it does not have the attributes with which SAE is associated, such as prestige, power and upward social mobility. Because of the diglossic situation in which AAVE and SAE coexist in American society, *othering* (via the use of AAVE especially in intra-group linguistic interactions) remains a constant feature of the noted latent conflict between subaltern sensibilities and the white mainstream culture. Therefore, and despite its lack of the attributes that are associated with SAE, AAVE remains the most powerful symbol of ethnic identity for the majority of African Americans. The section that follows explains how African Americans use AAVE to express their ethnic identity in the sacred domain of religion and, in so doing, to distinguish themselves from other ethnic groups in American society.

AAVE in the service of ethnicity in the black church

If we are to understand the complexity and scope of black communication patterns in the United States, says Smitherman (1977: 73), we must have a clear understanding of the oral tradition and the world view that undergirds that tradition. For black America, the oral tradition serves as a vehicle for self and group survival, both culturally and spiritually. The oral tradition is transmitted from one generation to the next via AAVE and its use in genres such as the movies, rap lyrics, hip-hop music, proverbs, myth narratives, comedies and church sermons especially in what Smitherman (1994: 31) calls traditional black churches, that is, a cluster of Protestant denominations (e.g. the Baptists, Methodists, Pentecostals) known for fusing African styles of worship and beliefs with European tenets of Christianity. The traditional black church has been described as 'the cultural womb of the black people in America' (Smitherman 1998: 203), 'a center of social life' and '[a forum] for self-expression and resistance to white dominated-society' (Baer and Singer 1992: x). The church is so valued because of the key role it has played in the spiritual nurturing and the socio-economic advancement of the black people in America.

But why and how does the church use AAVE rather than, say, SAE to achieve this key role it has assigned itself as the guarantor of black culture and oral tradition? With respect to the first part of this question, it seems that a church's language–religion ideology, which Anya Woods (2004) describes as a denomination's actions, attitudes, traditions and official/unofficial policies that pertain to language, determines the language the church uses for the sermons. Ideologies, says van Dijk (1997: 26), 'serve not only to coordinate social practices within the group, but also to coordinate social interaction with members of other groups'. In ethnic churches that attract believers from various ethnic groups, pastors tend to shift between AAVE and SAE to accommodate non-AAVE speakers. In this regard, Woods (2004) remarks that the clergy in multi-ethnic churches walk a religious, cultural and linguistic tightrope in using a variety of means to meet the disparate demands being made of them. However, in the case of a traditional black church, AAVE remains the chief medium through which the clergy delivers the sermons. Indeed, AAVE is not established by dogma as a sacred or religious variety. However, it takes on a sacred value by being used for centuries in the secular as well as in the sacred arena such as the church (Woods 2006: 201). Also, some of the most renowned African American scholars, such as the novelist Toni Morrison, acknowledge that there are certain things that [they] could not say 'without recourse to my language' (Rickford 2002: 331). Rickford observes further that even some of the most accomplished manipulators of SAE, such as the Reverend Jesse Jackson and, before him, the Reverend Martin Luther King Jr, invariably use AAVE in their sermons. Although not all African Americans speak AAVE, the use of the variety in the sermons projects the ethnic identity of the congregation which, in the context of the black church, no other variety of American English can express.

In order to project their ethnic identity via an exclusive use of AAVE in the sermons and, in so doing, ensure the transmission of black culture and oral tradition from generation to generation, black preachers use a sacred style characterized by what Smitherman (2002 [1973]: 315) describes as 'call-and-response'. The sacred style is said to be rural and Southern, emotional and highly charged. The 'call-and-response', which is one of the key characteristics of the sacred style, entails 'the back-and-forth exchange between the preacher and the congregation during the sermon' (Smitherman 1998: 208). It is explained that the speaker's solo voice alternates or is intermingled with the audience response. The minister is urged by the congregation's shouts. These include expressions such as 'Amen', 'That's right, Reverend', 'Preach Reverend', 'Teach Brother', etc. The following extract, in which the preacher exhorts the congregation to take care of themselves and their bodies (Smitherman 1977: 77), is a typical example of the 'call-and-response' as practised in traditional black churches:

Preacher: How many of y'all wanna live to a old age?
Congregation: Hallelujah!
Preacher: Or is y'all ready to die and go to Heaven?
Congregation: (*uncomfortable; some self-conscious laughter*) Well, no Lord, not yet, suh!
Preacher: Y'all wanna stay here awhile?
Congregation: Praise the Lord!
Preacher: Well, y'all better quit all this drankin, smoking, and runnin' round. Cause, see, for me, I got a home in Heaven, but I ain't homesick!

The other characteristic features of the style preachers use for the sermons include *rhythmic pattern* (i.e. cadence, tone, sonorous, musical quality, involving repetition of certain sounds or words), *spontaneity* (i.e. the delivery of the sermon is casual, non-deliberate and uncontrived), *concreteness* (ideas and illustrations used in the sermon are commonplace and grounded in everyday experience), and *signifying* (a deliberate but not offensive way of talking about the audience to hit a point home) (Smitherman 1998, 2002 [1973]). Having established that AAVE is the medium of expression in the sermons especially in traditionally black churches, it would be instructive to determine how AAVE speakers feel about the variety and its use in other domains, such as education, the workplace, etc. The last section of this chapter will be devoted to this issue.

Attitudes towards AAVE

In this section, I argue that African Americans have a love-and-hate relationship with AAVE. For some, AAVE is the glue that binds them together, it is the marker of their identity and of who they are in American society. For others, however, AAVE is an indicator of backwardness, of illiteracy; it is something to be ashamed of and to leave behind once one becomes educated in SAE.

If the discussion in the previous sections is any indication, AAVE has a secure place in the sacred arena of religion, especially in traditional black churches, where it is highly valued and represents, for the majority of black Americans, what the novelist June Jordan calls 'the Spoken Soul' (Rickford 2002: 331). In the public arenas such as the workplace and education, however, AAVE remains arguably one of the most socially stigmatized and stereotyped varieties of American English (Jones 2001: 1068). Although research indicates that many African Americans celebrate AAVE as an emblem of racial pride, other Americans, black as well as white, dismiss it simply as bad, uneducated, English (Perry 2004: 5); as 'improper speech they neither respect nor recognize' (Pandey 2000: 1); as a fancy political cover for abnormal, defective, dysfunctional speech (Todd 1997); as a marker of low social class or lack of intelligence, especially when used in a context where it is not expected (Dyson 2005); as a non-existent distraction to curriculum matters (Scott 2000: 129); and as an anachronism hanging on from the segregated living conditions of plantation life in pre-Civil War days (Jones 2001: 1070).

In a study of black and white adults' attitudes toward AAVE, Koch et al. (2001) found that African American speakers of AAVE were regarded as less likeable and competent than their SAE-speaking counterparts. In a similar study, Jones (2001) found that many participants objected to the use of AAVE in the workplace, insisting that if given a choice, they would hire someone who spoke SAE rather than an AAVE speaker. AAVE has also been viewed negatively by parents and community leaders alike. For instance, many black parents objected strongly when the Oakland School District Board proposed that AAVE be used in Oakland schools as a medium of instruction for black children to remedy their poor academic performance. The issue of the medium of instruction for black children has, unfortunately, always been approached from an 'either (SAE) or (AAVE)' perspective or, put differently, from what Anthony Pinn (2004: 56) calls 'unresolved binary dialectics of slavery and freedom, insider and outsider, black [child] and white [child], struggle and survival'. In this regard, in a keynote speech he gave at a gala event Bill Cosby endorsed SAE rather than AAVE as the medium of instruction for black children, lamenting that the latter had a poor command of SAE. In his speech Cosby not only rebukingly refers to ghetto black children as inanimate objects (see his use of the pronoun 'it'), but he also mockingly mimics the way they speak, as is evident from the following excerpt:

It's standing on da corner. It can't speak English. It doesn't want to speak English. I [i.e. Cosby] can't even talk the way these people talk: 'Why you ain't, where you is go ...'. I don't know who these people are. (Hogan 2006)

The stigmatization of AAVE impacts negatively not only on self and in-group identity construction of the ghetto children, but also on that of their middle-class counterparts, especially those whose parents have made a conscious and deliberate choice not to expose the children to AAVE. For the ghetto children, AAVE remains their only linguistic marker of ethnic identity. They view their middle-class counterparts who do not speak AAVE as outsiders and 'cultural traitors' (Giles 1979). Consequently, middle-class black children (with no proficiency in AAVE) find it difficult to claim membership in the black community. Consider the following story, as recounted by one of my students. The story is about the student's niece, Andrienne, who was raised in a white neighbourhood and hardly had any contacts with peers in the black community. After she was old enough to make her own decisions, Andrienne decided to attend a historically black college in an effort to identify with the members of her race. Unfortunately, she discovered that she was not welcomed because, linguistically, she did not know how to fit in. Andrienne could not fit in because she 'talked white', her accent gave her away as an outsider.

In the Spring of 2004 I received a call for advice from my niece, Andrienne, who grew up in an all white environment. Andrienne's parents had taught her how to make a good impression, how to speak, how to act, and how to follow in their footsteps of success. With all that her parents had to offer, I wondered what could Andrienne possibly need me for. Andrienne needed some advice on how to be black, how to fit in the new environment, a historically black college, she had chosen to attend but where she discovered she was not accepted. She was confused as to why she could easily get along with the few white girls at the college but the members of her own race treated her like an outsider. (Crowley, 2006)

This example illustrates the dilemma that African Americans face in their daily lives. On the one hand, AAVE speakers need SAE in order to succeed in mainstream American society. On the other hand, however, they need AAVE to bond with the members of their own community. African Americans who are competent in one variety, as is the case for Andrienne, are bound to struggle with issues of ethnicity and social mobility. Having a black skin is not enough to qualify as a member of the African American community. Put differently, African American ethnic identity is not essentialist, i.e. it cannot be reduced to a single category such as skin colour. Rather, 'African Americanness' is a mosaic which derives its very identity from a combination of cultural, linguistic, historical, racial and psychological factors. This point is borne out by the fact that, despite the colour of her skin, Andrienne was not welcomed by her black peers. It seems that only competence in both AAVE and SAE, with each used in the appropriate context, would facilitate acceptance in the white as well as in the black communities. It is true that individuals constantly compare their in-groups with other groups and strive for a positive self-image, which is usually associated with the speech patterns of the dominant group, as SAE is in the American society. In so doing, observe Hausendorf and Kesselheim (2002: 267), an individual's goal is to become (or remain) a member of only those groups that make a positive contribution to his or her social identity. It is worth noting, however, that there is always the risk of alienating oneself from one's own group especially if it does not approve of the new identity one has acquired or is aspiring to, as the example given above illustrates.

Conclusion

This chapter has discussed the issue of how African Americans use AAVE to construct or project their ethnic identity, with a focus on the sacred arena of religion. The use of AAVE in the black church indicates what Dubois (1961), quoted in Spears (1998: 248), has termed the 'two-ness' of African American consciousness in the United States. It is explained that 'two-ness' is the dual personality caused by the cohabitation of two consciousness or cultural systems within one mind, the white and the African American, the hegemonic and the subaltern. This 'two-ness' is, as observed earlier, a clear indicator of the latent conflict between AAVE and SAE. This conflict manifests itself in the exclusive use of AAVE in intragroup interactions in virtually all domains of language use, including the secular and the sacred arena such as the black church. Irrespective of the domains, African Americans who are proficient in both AAVE and SAE switch to the latter to accommodate out-group members, as is the case in multi-ethnic churches. In predominantly black churches, however, AAVE remains the unmarked medium through which the sermons are conducted. AAVE is not only a linguistic mechanism of inclusion and exclusion and a marker of ethnic identity for most black Americans, but the variety also illustrates, as Pandey (2000: 24) observes, the extent to which language or a language variety engenders *otherness*. The use of AAVE in the sacred as well as in the secular arenas not only guarantees the survival and maintenance of the variety against social stigmatization, but it also makes AAVE a unique symbol by means of which the African American community distinguishes itself from other communities that make up American society.

References

Baer, Hans A. and Singer, Merrill (1992) *African-American Religion in the 20th Century: Varieties of Protest and Accommodation.* Knoxville, Tennessee: The University of Tennessee Press.

Baldwin, James (2002) 'If Black English isn't a Language, then Tell me what is?' in T. Redd (ed.), *Revelations: an Anthology of Expository Essays by and about Blacks*, Boston, Mass.: Pearson Custom Publishing, pp. 319–23.

Crowley, Dominique (2006) 'Do you Talk Black? An Exploration into Attitudes towards Black English'. Unpublished manuscript, Department of English, Howard University.

Dick, Teun van (1997) 'Discourse as Interaction in Society', in T. van Dick (ed.), *Discourse Studies: a Multidisciplinary Introduction*, vol. 2, London: Sage, pp. 1–37.

Duszak, Anna (ed.) (2002) *US and Others: Social Identities across Languages, Discourses and Cultures.* Amsterdam/Philadelphia: John Benjamins Publishing Company.

Dyson, Michael Eric (2005) *Is Bill Cosby Right? (Or Has the Black Middle Class Lost its Mind?).* New York: Perseus Books Group.

Edwards, John R. (1994) *Multilingualism.* London/New York: Routledge.

Filmer, Alice Ashton (2003) 'African-American Vernacular English: Ethics, Ideology, and Pedagogy in the Conflict between Identity and Power'. *World Englishes*, 22 (3), 253–70.

Fishman, Joshua A. (1977) 'Language and Ethnicity', in Howard Giles (ed.), *Language, Ethnicity and Intergroup Relations*, London: Academic Press, pp. 15–77.

Fishman, Joshua A. (2002) '"Holy Languages" in the Context of Social Bilingualism', in Li Wei, Jean-Marc Dewaele and Alex Housen (eds), *Opportunities and Challenges of Bilingualism*, Berlin: Walter de Gruyter, pp. 15–24.

Fishman, Joshua A. (2006) 'A Decalogue of Basic Theoretical Perspectives for a Sociology of Language and Religion', in Tope Omoniyi and Joshua A. Fishman (eds), *Explorations in the Sociology of Language and Religion*, Amsterdam/Philadelphia: John Benjamins Publishing Company, pp. 13–25.

Giles, Howard (ed.) (1977) *Language, Ethnicity and Intergroup Relations*. London: Academic Press.

Giles, Howard (1979) 'Ethnicity Markers in Speech', in K.R. Scherer and H. Giles (eds), *Social Markers in Speech*, Cambridge: Cambridge University Press, pp. 251–89.

Giles, Howard and Smith, P.M. (1979) 'Accommodation Theory: Optimal Levels of Convergence', in H. Giles and R. St Clair (eds), *Language and Social Psychology*, Oxford: Oxford University Press.

Gumperz, John J. (1982) *Discourse Strategies*. London: Cambridge University Press.

Hausendorf, Heiko and Kesselheim, Wolfgang (2002) 'The Communicative Construction of Group Identities: a Basic Mechanism of Social Categorization', in Anna Duszak (ed.), *Us and Others: Social Identities across Languages, Discourses and Cultures*, Amsterdam/Philadelphia: John Benjamins Publishing Company, pp. 265–89.

Hogan, Alexia (2006) 'Attitudes toward Southern Black English Vernacular'. Unpublished manuscript, Department of English, Howard University.

Jones, Katharine W. (2001) ' "I've Called'em Tom-ah-toes All My Life and I'm not Going to Change!": Maintaining Linguistic Control over English Identity in the US'. *Social Forces*, 79 (3), 1061–94.

Kamwangamalu, Nkonko M. (2001) 'Ethnicity and Language Crossing in Post-Apartheid South Africa'. *International Journal of the Sociology of Language*, 152, 75–95.

Kamwangamalu, Nkonko M. (2003) 'A Review of Shana Poplack and Sali Tagliamonte (2001), *African American English in the Diaspora*. Oxford: Blackwell Publishers'. *World Englishes*, 22 (1), 75–7.

Knight, Kaelie (2002) 'Ebonics: a Racial Profile', in T. Redd (ed.), *Revelations: an Anthology of Expository Essays by and about Blacks*, Boston, Mass.: Pearson Custom Publishing, pp. 369–71.

Koch, Lisa M., Gross, Alan M. and Kolts, Russell (2001) 'Attitudes toward Black English and Codeswitching'. *Journal of Black Psychology*, 27 (1), 29–42.

Le Page, Robert B. and Tabouret-Keller, Andrée (1985) *Acts of Identity: Creole-Based Approaches to Ethnicity and Language*. Cambridge: Cambridge University Press.

Morgan, Marcyliena (1998) 'More than a Mood or an Attitude: Discourse and Verbal Genres in African-American Culture', in Salikoko S. Mufwene, John R. Rickford, Guy Bailey and John Baugh (eds), *African American English: Structure, History and Use*, London/New York: Routledge, pp. 251–81.

Nash, Manning (1989) *The Cauldron of Ethnicity in the Modern World*. Chicago: University of Chicago Press.

Newman, James L. (1978) 'Place and Ethnicity among the Sandawe of Tanzania', in Brian M. du Toit (ed.), *Ethnicity in Modern Africa*, Boulder, Colo.: Westview Press, pp. 105–21.

Pandey, Anita (2000) 'Symposium on the Ebonics Debate and African-American Language: Introduction'. *World Englishes*, 19 (1), 1–4.

Perry, Ronald A. (2004) 'African-American English'. *Revista*, No. 31, 1–10.

Pinn, Anthony B. (2004) 'Black Is, Black Ain't': Victor Anderson, African American Theological Thought, and Identity'. *Dialog: a Journal of Theology*, 43 (1), 54–62.

Poplack, Shana and Tagliamonte, Sali (2001) *African American English in the Diaspora*. Oxford: Blackwell Publishers.

Ramirez, J. David, Wiley, Terence G., de Klerk, Gerda, Lee, Enid and Wright, Wayne E. (eds) (2005) *Ebonics: the Urban Education Debate* (2nd edn). Clevedon: Multilingual Matters.

Rickford, John (1998) 'The Creole Origin of African American English', in Salikoko Mufwene, John R. Rickford, Guy Bailey and John Baugh (eds), *African-American English: Structure, History and Use*, London and New York: Routledge, pp. 154–200.

Rickford, John (2002) 'The Ubiquity of Ebonics', in T. Redd (ed.), *Revelations: an Anthology of Expository Essays by and about Blacks*, Boston, Mass.: Pearson Custom Publishing, pp. 329–33.

Ross, Jeffrey A. (1979). 'Language and the Mobilization of Ethnic Identity', in H. Giles and B. Saint-Jacques (eds), *Language and Ethnic Relations*, Oxford: Pergamon Press, pp. 1–13.

Saint-Jacques, Bernard and Giles, Howard (1979) 'Preface', in B. Saint-Jacques and H. Giles (eds), *Language and Ethnic Relations*, Oxford: Pergamon Press, pp. ix–xii.

Schmid, Monica (2002) 'Persecution and Identity Conflicts. The Case of German Jews', in Anna Duszak (ed.), *Us and Others: Social Identities across Languages, Discourses and Cultures*, Amsterdam/Philadelphia: John Benjamins Publishing Company, pp. 341–55.

Scott, Jerry C. (2000) 'A Review of Salikoko Mufwene, John Rickford, Guy Bailey, and John Baugh (1998, eds), *African American English: Structure, History and Use* (London and New York: Routledge)'. *World Englishes*, 19 (1), 129–32.

Smitherman, Geneva (1977) *Talkin and Testifyin: the Language of Black America*. Boston: Houghton Mifflin Company.

Smitherman, Geneva (1994) *Black Talk: Words and Phrases from the Hood to the Amen Corner*. Boston/New York: Houghton Mifflin Company.

Smitherman, Geneva (1998) 'Word from the Hood: the Lexicon of African-American Vernacular English', in Salikoko S. Mufwene, John R. Rickford, Guy Bailey and John Baugh (eds), *African American English: Structure, History and Use*, London/New York: Routledge, pp. 203–25.

Smitherman, Geneva (2002 [1973]) 'White English in Blackface, or Who Do I Be?' in T. Redd (ed.), *Revelations: an Anthology of Expository Essays by and about Blacks*, Boston, Mass.: Pearson Custom Publishing, pp. 313–18.

Spears, Arthur K. (1998) 'African-American Language Use: Ideology and So-Called Obscenity', in Salikoko S. Mufwene, John R. Rickford, Guy Bailey and John Baugh (eds), *African American English: Structure, History and Use*. London/New York: Routledge, pp. 226–48.

Sridhar, Kamal K. (1996) 'Societal Multilingualism', in Sandra M. Lee McKay and Nancy Hornberger (eds), *Sociolinguistics and Language Teaching*, Cambridge: Cambridge University Press, pp. 47–70.

Tabouret-Keller, Andrée (1997) 'Language and Ethnicity', in Florian Coulmas (ed.), *The Handbook of Sociolinguistics*, Oxford: Blackwell, pp. 315–26.

Todd, Leon W., Jr (1997) 'Ebonics is Defective Speech and a Handicap for Black Children'. *Education*, 118 (2), 177–80. http://www.findarticles.com/p/articles/mi_qa3673/is_199701/ai_n8755161.

Williams, Robert L. (ed.) (1975) *Ebonics: the True Language of Black Folks*. St. Louis: Institute of Black Studies.

Williams, Robert L. and Rivers, L.W. (1975) 'The Effects of Language on the Test Performance of Black Children', in R. L. Williams (ed.), *Ebonics: the True Language of Black Folks*, St. Louis: Institute of Black Studies, pp. 96–109.

Wolfram, Walt and Thomas, Erik R. (2002) *The Development of African American English*. Oxford: Blackwell Publishers.

Woods, Anya (2004) *Medium or Message? Language and Faith in Ethnic Churches*. Clevedon: Multilingual Matters.

Woods, Anya (2006) 'The Role of Language in Some Ethnic Churches in Melbourne', in Tope Omoniyi and Joshua Fishman (eds), *Exploration in the Sociology of Language and Religion*, Amsterdam/Philadelphia: John Benjamins Publishing Company, pp. 197–212.

10
Holy Hip-Hop, Language and Social Change

Tope Omoniyi

Because without music life would be a mistake.

Nietzsche

Introduction

In this chapter, I shall present 'holy hip-hop' as a phenomenon of social change, the transformative and hybridizing processes located in the contact zone between the secular and the sacred. I shall argue that such change conceptualized within the framework of the sociology of language and religion is facilitated both through the secularization of traditional religious language as well as through borrowing and sacralization of secular language and values (cf. Fishman 2006). These exemplify what Pennycook (2007) articulates as transcultural flow which I argue is only possible if there is transcultural accommodation in the zones of contact both in the physical and abstract senses. Stakeholders have expanded religion's remit to include developing strategies for halting decay in the inner cities by taking religion to 'the streets'.

In sociolinguistic scholarship, Alim's (2006) devotion of an entire chapter to Islam and its discursive struggles in mass culture in his book *Roc the Mic Right: the Language of Hip Hop Culture* precedes my current effort. Alim does two significant things in that chapter which resonate with my intentions here. He conceptualizes the artist as a 'verbal mujahidin', and he explores structural and symbolic similarities between hip-hop and Qur'anic texts. These perspectives are significant because of the way they index identity and the politics of language from the standpoint of religion. Both Christianity and Islam have appropriated hip-hop (rap especially) and used it as a rallying tool, a call to the faithful, as an identity-marking vocal bandana. Street Symphony based in South London, described as the 'interdenominational Church [*sic*] response to urban problems', Street Pastors (http://www.streetpastors. co.uk/) and Gospel Gangstaz, aka 'Street Disciples' of Fountain Valley, California, illustrate this expanded role of religion in social healing. The challenge now is to establish the exact language and social correlates of the transformation from traditional religion to popular religion. The core claim is that beyond simply entertaining, hip-hop has the capacity to mediate change, conflict and accommodation in the management of religious identities.

Theoretical underpinnings

In presenting the decalogue of basic principles for the sociology of language and religion as a discipline, Fishman (2006: 19) notes that 'each case of language spread or functional elevation is simultaneously a case of social change, social dislocation and language shift in many sociocultural functions, even before such shift occurs in religious functions per se'. This remark challenges researchers to investigate the character of social change; behaviours, attitudes and practices, the circumstances that shape them, whether and how such changes extend to religion and its practice, the forms they take, and how all of these then are reflected in language. For those of us exploring the new disciplinary interface of the sociology of language and religion, one task that this sets up and which is a fundamental focus of the discussion in this chapter is the re-evaluation both of the source and direction of change in relation to the culture flow that globalization fuels. In other words, is the globalization of religious practice through transnational communities, media and popular culture associated with Pentecostalism, televangelism, television and music ministries as cultural phenomena – influenced by the spread of a variety of language/discourse – or vice versa? The appropriation of hip-hop to make religion attractive will frame my discussion of change, conflict and accommodation.

My discussion is based on narrative data from three religious websites (HolyHipHop.Com, MuslimHipHop.Com, [and] Kingdomandroyalty. com) and an interview with London-based Digital Disc Jockey (DDJ) Kimba aka Klarity of Playvybz.com, as well as the lyrics of songs by religious hip-hop groups Baby Muslims, Blakstone, G-Force, FourKornerz and Jahaziel. The objective is twofold; first to explore the sacralization of secular music and second to examine the discursive processing entailed in such a transformation. The link that I make between

sacred and secular in popular music has been inspired by the long list
of iconic figures in secular R & B and hip-hop whose beginnings are
traceable to early involvement in church choirs including US artistes
Diana Ross, Whitney Houston, MC Hammer, Mary J. Blige among
others.

Unpackin' holy hip-hop

The cultural phenomenon known as 'holy hip-hop' covers the akas
Gospel Hip-Hop, Christian Hip-Hop, Muslim Hip-Hop, Islamic Hip-
Hop. The cohort excludes emcees, deejays and others in the hip-hop
community who use religious tropes and motifs to spice up their lyrics
but are not in the faith ministry per se. For illustration, 'Jesus Walks'
(2005) neither makes Kanye West a holy hip-hopper nor locates him in
the ministry. Kanye raps in the track:

> You know what the Midwest is?
> Young & Restless
> Where restless NIGGAZ! might snatch your necklace
> And next these NIGGAZ! might jack your Lexus
> Somebody tell these NIGGAZ! who Kanye West is
> I walk through the valley of the shadow of death is
> Top floor the view alone will leave you breathless Uhhhh!

He is very clear about his purpose and declares that rapping about Jesus
was simply taking on a challenge:

> We rappers is role models we rap we don't think
> I ain't here to argue about his facial features
> Or here to convert atheists into believers
> I'm just trying to say the way school need teachers
> The way Kathie Lee needed Regis that's the way I need Jesus
> So here go my single dog radio needs this
> They say you can rap about anything except for Jesus
> That means guns, sex, lies, video tapes
> But if I talk about God my record won't get played Huh?

The base remains the hoods that sprung the trope users whereas for
the Ministers and Verbal Mujahidins the earth is a marketplace while
heaven is home. The premodification in 'holy hip-hop' sets it apart
from its unmarked more conventional mainstream secular counterpart simply described as *hip-hop*. It also sets the subgenre up as the

'Other', peripheral and lesser known. That practice extends to subcultural references within Christian hip-hop as in for instance, Gangstaz versus *Gospel Gangstaz*, the Christian double of secular artists involved in the subgenre of 'gangsta rap/hip-hop'. The latter is deemed to celebrate the violence and violent of the hip-hop community in the 1990s. While the metaphor of being 'born again' is used to describe the Christian transformation from an old life of sin, a complete disconnection from the past, Gospel Gangstaz are former members of the Los Angeles street gangs Crips and Bloods who as Christians have been 'taking the gospel message back to their old stompin ground' for over 12 years (http://www.blogcatalog.com/blog/holy-ridaz-blog/ bob668a389ba4ecbcbe1cf2da3a 39266).

The pattern of premodification in the name bears a resemblance to that in the binaries British/black British, and Nigerian/diaspora Nigerian, in which the head referent is the essential core from which the new identity derives its meaning. That would be an uneasy implication for that of Gospel Gangstaz except of course hip-hop's 'cool' factor operates as a departure from established social conventions. Here is another example excerpted from an email announcement:

> Holy Hip Hop Music Awards is a Tri-Alliance Strategic Partner with Christian ministries **RapFest** (Bronx, NY) and **Flavor.Fest** (Tampa, FL) consisting of a combined 20 years of labor towards advancing the mission to proliferate Hip Hop Ministry world-wide, without compromise or delay. James 5: 20. Amen.

What we see here is the emergence of a new arm of the Christian ministry with a specific variety of hip-hop as its arrowhead. That ministry is simply named using 'Hip-Hop' as a premodifier intended as a subdivision of the larger Music Ministry. In other words, holy hip-hop is one of several branches of the ministry. Both the ministry as a whole and the genre are indicative of social and religious change. But are we dealing with a wholesale appropriation of hip-hop? Is there in fact an appropriation? Do some of the elements of hip-hop culture lend themselves more easily than others to appropriation by religion? In earlier research, I identified the following elements of hip-hop culture: MCing (rapping), DJing (spinning records), breakdancing (also known as street dancing,), graffiti art (writing or tagging), knowledge and *overstanding* (going beyond a cursory understanding of something), and the use of pseudonyms or AKAs by hip-hop artists (Omoniyi 2006: 196). We have evidence of appropriation of form including beat poetry/rap, rhythm, intertextuality, dress code and dance style (ibid.) to convey content appropriate to religion. But does holy hip-hop fit into the Global

Hip-Hop Nation (GHHN) as theorized already in the literature (see Alim 2006, Omoniyi 2009)?

Holy hip-hop and HHN-Global

The Hip-Hop Nation (HHN) as articulated in the literature is built around the default American community of hip-hop artists. 'HHN-Global is a multilingual, multiple, and multifarious codes community' (Omoniyi 2009: 121). GHHN, as I shall henceforth refer to HHN-Global, is either the consequence of spread of HHN via globalization or an exemplar of polycentricity in which various independent hoods around the world are connected up into a global union of translocal and transnational kinhoods. In determining how holy hip-hop fits into GHHN, we must bear in mind that it is a cultural phenomenon operating primarily within the realm of one or combinations of Arjun Appadurai's (1996) several 'scapes' which serve as contexts for exploring the disjunctures in the global cultural economy: 'mediascape', 'ethnoscape', 'ideoscape', 'technoscape', 'financescape'. For our purposes here, the first three are probably most relevant, considering the involvement of global media infrastructure such as MTV, Eurovision, Myspace.com and YouTube in interaction with language and religion. If we take the starting point reference grid for GHHN to be essentially spatial thus enabling us to delineate and differentiate between sub-community groups such as HHN-Nigeria, HHN-Japan, HHN-Germany, HHN-China and so on, the flows facilitated by migration and media become the sources of cultural osmoses. Therein lies the legitimacy of engaging with change, conflict and accommodation in contemporary hip-hop research.

Holy hip-hop is unique because it has a certain sense of dualism to it, two separate reference communities. On one hand, reference is to a cultural community (of hip-hoppers) with a characteristic lifestyle that includes performance, and on the other hand, reference is to a discursive tool in religious communities who articulate their terrestrial presence as temporary and a permanent home over on Sugarcandy Mountain (cf. Orwellian paradise). One reason holy hip-hop may not fit squarely in GHHN is that the religious community or *ummah* embraces hip-hop, particularly rap, as a means to an end rather than a way of life, in contrast to secular hip-hoppers. In both Islam and Christianity the Din and Jesus are the way of life respectively, not hip-hop as north-west London-based Baby Muslims' duo of Idris and Troy indicate in their response to media interview questions posed by Muslimhiphop.com:

Extract 1

MUSLIMHIPHOP.COM   What inspired you to do Muslim/Islamic music?

Idris   Hip Hop is huge. A lot of people listen to it, a lot of people are inspired by it, but almost all of it is Haram. So it makes sense to have a Halal alternative. The youth of today insist on listening to music, at least they should have a Halal alternative to encourage them to go back to the din. I heard a talk from Imam Siraj Wahhaj and he said something like, 'for every man selling a Haram magazine, there should be someone selling a Halal magazine'. And also I personally feel the need to correct the misconceptions people have of our beautiful religion (for the time being) the best way I know how, through hip hop.

MUSLIMHIPHOP.COM   What are some of the key issues you are tackling in your songs?

Troy Kamal   For me, it's all about change. The decision to change from materialism to spirituality, from ego to humility, from unruliness to discipline.
[http://www.muslimhiphop.com/index.php?p=Stories/14._Baby_Muslims_Interview]

Idris's response pinpoints the religious end that hip-hop serves such as using it to 'encourage youth to return to the din and to correct misconceptions of Islam'. Troy's response speaks to a reorientation of self in the Foucauldian sense of subjectivation (Foucault 1988) as well as the resulting social transformation from the *ummah* constituted by such selves. While secular hip-hop artists from the provinces or margins do *bridging* (Omoniyi 2009: 132) to authenticate their narrative and art through linkage to a perceived mainstream, holy hip-hop does it to rein in potential converts from religion's margins and recruit and sustain youth faith and loyalty through linkage to God/Allah and Paradise. The authentication sought by the latter is from and by another realm. Baby Muslims' single from 2007 entitled 'Value (currency of the hereafter)' is indexical of that realm. While its articulation may be coloured within local value systems, there are comparable global scales to which the values are subjected such as institutions like the World Congress of Faiths (WCF) and the Organization of Islamic Countries (OIC).

Holy hip-hop texts

Gospel artists substitute the street vernacular texts of conventional hip-hop with sacred texts. Gospel and glory purge negativity out of gangsta and ghetto in Gospel Gangstaz and Ghetto Glory. The announcement 'We at Kingdom And Royalty present Silas Zephania a young Hip Hop Artist whose music is centred on the needs of the people' goes beyond the performative intent of the proposition to assert holy hip-hop's role as a social ministry. These are clear cases of change and accommodation. But the path bifurcates and religious or holy hip-hop breaks into local lects. The conflict and struggle that MC Jeremy Cool Habash, an Israeli rapper of Ethiopian Jewish extraction, addresses in the context of ethnic politics within Israel is a smaller-scale parallel of that which the Verbal Mujahidin confront on a larger more global scale in the seeming clash of religious civilizations between Christianity and Islam. In Extract 2 below, Baby Muslims rap in 'Da'wah' from the album *Life* (the complete first series):

Extract 2

Don't get lost in translation
Riding the train we all read the Metro
Accusing the Muslims always spoiling a job
What happened to freewill
Someone ring the alarm
The revolution will be televised
Bear in mind that large corporations
Own the radio stations
When you see it don't just // leave it
Add a pinch of salt, you know take it or leave it
Islam ain't a secret
But since 9/11 occurred
It's been portrayed as the dirtiest word
If you're wondering what all the fuss is about
Listen to the News on the hour
Da'wah's like medicine and it's good for you
Remove what's negative and you're almost there

I contend that the directive in the opening line is targeted at the *ummah* as a collective, thus underlining its social transformative capacity. Strains of the same sentiments expressed by Baby Muslims above are conveyed in the following account by Blakstone of who they are:

Extract 3

We're just people like you, fed up of being branded criminals for our belief. Tired of the barrage of insults toward our Deen, beloved

Prophet, sisters and brothers. Sickened by the ongoing slaughter of those who carry the banner of La illaha illallah. But admittedly there is a difference here. We do not believe in compromise or violence. We believe that the way out is to concentrate our efforts in re-establishing a home for Islam. A place where Islam comes before race, before colour, before nationality and before language.

In summary, then, the structural concerns about justice, equality and freedom which distil as 'the struggle' that provides a theme for Islamic or Muslim hip-hop are evident in extracts 2 and 3 above. The sisters and brothers receive the message for personal redemption as representatives of the faith. The establishment receives the message as a challenge to its policies and structures and an appeal for change. Parallel Christian hip-hop data may be found in contexts in which small-sized Christian communities exist in a predominantly non-Christian environment, such as, for example, the Orthodox Christian Assyrians of Iraq. While black struggle in the US seems recently to have found a louder voice in Islam than in Christianity, the movements of the mid-twentieth century were born out of biblical teachings; the Reverend Martin Luther King exemplifies that.

The idea that holy hip-hop as a subgenre form has a peripheral status is challenged by two facts. First, gangsta hip-hop, another subgenre form, enjoys a cult following as well as attracting great commercial success, even though its artistic quality continues to raise controversy in some quarters. The second challenge comes from the fact that holy hip-hop is recognized as a category by mainstream institutions such as the Grammy Awards and the MOBO Awards (Music Of Black Origin).

The 'holy' label is a self-ascribed (rather than other-ascribed) identity by stakeholders which clearly suggests purposeful appropriation and a demarcation or, in sociolinguistic thinking, a divergence or difference marker. The London-based gospel hip-hop group, G-Force, in the lyrics of the title song of their award-winning album *Destroy and Rebuild* (2007) provide illustration of the fusion of street and church:

Extract 4

G Force man
UK stand up   invoking the people
Can believe in God
The holy spirit stand up   invoking the Holy Spirit

Takin a word from the streets now	attributing to 'street' – source of hiphop culture
It's about that time, look look	
Eh yo the streets used to do the talking	conscious appropriation, divergence
But now the church is	
our fight is against principalities	link 'fight' to 'movement' – like
we're going in a new direction, (nat nat)	Public Enemy; spiritual war, new dir = appropriating]
and to see the Lord's words on the streets	relocating Lord's words from church
through the words on the beats	to street for specific audience
is the crew's intention (nat nat nat nat)	beats, crew
unbelievers ask me (who's that)	ingroup/outgroup believers/unbel.
now you can't just tell em' about the song	us/them pronominal, identification by contrasting]
without telling em' (who's that)	
the second coming's when he's back	Judeo-Christian return of Christ

Its 'holy' attribute evident in the biblical references especially to the New Testament gospels distinguishes it from unmarked secular hiphop. The questions that arise are: can we talk of difference if holy hiphop is a sacralization of the secular? What are the shared linguistic and other cultural practices, bearing in mind that hybridity points to processes of social change?

'KEEPIN' IT GOSPEL & GANGSTA AT THA' SAME TIME' Gospel Gangstaz, California

In this declared intention on the Gospel Gangstaz website, hybridity and hybridization are admitted as a process of change in religion, a departure from conventional religious practice. One of the core elements of rap as a hip-hop practice is mixing which involves a template or sample on which a remix is based, resulting in a métis(se).

Four Kornerz integrate a paraphrase of 1 Peter 2: 9 into the lyrics of 'Clap Clap':

Extract 5

The bible says I
I am a king a royal priest
Blessed among men (that's right)
That means that I ought to walk like royalty

This exemplifies heavy use of intertextuality and switching and other such language processes that have been reported for contact situations in the sociolinguistic literature. Fishman (2006: 23) remarks that:

> The impact of languages of secular modernization on the languages of religion in the former 'Third World' may never rival that which the Protestant revolution brought about in Europe, particularly if the compartmentalization of religious behavior is better maintained there than it was in Europe, but great changes (both in the direction of greater traditionalization, for some, and in the direction of greater modernization, for others, as the Tamil case reveals) are predictable.

First, if we take Christianity for example, the New Church, which is arguably the fastest growing of all denominations, clearly departs from the practice of separating religious from other aspects of social existence professing that *born-againism* is an identifiable way of life. Jahaziel's lines in 'Ready to Live' *See I've been reborn/Looks like I've been rebuilt/Seems like I've been transformed/Since the truth has been revealed* capture an indexicality that rests squarely on the act of being baptized and the symbolic performative act of accepting Jesus Christ as one's personal Lord and Saviour. In other words, the Christian precepts apply across all compartments of social behaviour. Interestingly, the same new dispensation accounts for liberalization of the Church and creation of single unit churches in contrast to the franchise structure of traditional Christianity. Second, in the sociolinguistics canon, we very often associate religion with the standard forms of languages, particularly written religious literature. Thus the diglossic relationship between the High and Low varieties of Arabic used in the Qur'an and everyday conversations respectively presents us with an idea of normative practice. This is, however, the top–bottom model of missionary activity of the colonial era in which the religious practices of the colonizers were introduced to gradually displace traditional African ones.

Thus we can safely say that contemporary Christianity in some ways has embraced the liberalism of scale in instituting a reversed order of indexicality (cf. Blommaert 2006: 3), a bottom-up model that sanctions the use of non-standard language forms as popular practice, particularly for evangelization in rural Africa. I refer specifically to those Christian sects that are indigenous to, have grown out of and ramified from Africa and which are not associated with a tradition of Western education and structure of religious hierarchization. But the New Church's success derives from its inventiveness, a feature it shares with hip-hop and arguably one that paves the way for the latter's appropriation. The fact that hip-hop is normatively associated with non-standard language varieties, change that entails its appropriation in the religious domain questions such diglossic relationship and at the same time invests non-standard forms with new capital in Bourdieu's (1991) terms, and this needs to be explored.

The principles of contact linguistics and specifically the formation of pidgins and creoles demand that we re-examine observations which indicate that religious rituals were normatively monolingual. Historically, evangelization presupposed contact between missionaries and speakers of languages other than those of the religion they sought to spread. Such contact creates the sorts of phenomena that sociolinguistics has been preoccupied with: bilingualism, code-mixing, code-switching, pidginization, creolization, language choice, language attitudes and in multicultural states, ethnoreligious identity. With religion now digitally packaged and distributed like other cultural products in collaboration with well-established and still expanding music ministries, a new and vibrant dynamism is observable that is clearly dissonant to a perceived need felt by stakeholders to preserve the 'purity' of religion and its rituals, as if these were static phenomena. One of the hallmarks of rap is linguistic inventiveness in the exploitation of the poetic form.

The social processes that transform aspects of secular into sacred culture are as metropolitan as they are provincial. In a sense, it may be argued that they are not completely new since the history of evangelization around the world provides extensive evidence of the borrowing and adaptation of folk songs and music culture in general in the praise and worship of God as the new replacement deity. For instance, among the Yoruba, the same names and songs used to glorify Ogun (god of Iron), Ifa (god of Divination) and other Yoruba traditional deities have been appropriated for glorifying the Christian God-Head, Olorun/

Oluwa/Olodumare. Salami (2006) includes a detailed analysis of Yoruba praise names of God most of which have also been incorporated into popular choruses for praise worship.

Holy hip-hop as métis(se)

Here I am borrowing from the literature on racial identity the concept of hybridity conveyed by the collapsing of two racial identities into one used to describe people of biracial or multiracial heritage (see Ifekwunigwe 1998, Sherzer 1998). The use of this term within anthropology and postcolonial theory is marked by tension, friction and conflict between competing structural locations within a centre–periphery analytical paradigm and the historically hegemonic relationship between the two identities white and black that constitute the mix in métis(se). The analogy works on several levels. First, that often between the sacred and secular, the former is privileged hence the association in sociolinguistic literature on diglossia of the H and L varieties of language with formal religious and informal everyday communicative usage respectively. The second level on which the analogy works is that in which hip-hop as a 'way of life' is regarded as representing 'the street' albeit for different purposes. In the unmarked secular practice, it provided a parallel universe to those shut out by the mainstream and created a different set of values by which they articulated existence. It also doubled as a resistance movement to that mainstream. In contrast, religion is a mainstream institution which then reaches out through missionary activities to the street to shepherd in the flock as it were. In the latter sense then holy hip-hop is not a subculture associated with a parallel universe that is counter-positioned to a non-hip-hop mainstream.

Also, if we treat the spread of religions as following trajectories similar to those we find in globalization literature, we could argue that Christianity and Islam, two religions that have now appropriated hip-hop or at least aspects of its culture, have followed a somewhat North–South trajectory in their spread and have both been closely linked to similar hegemonic structures of colonization that postcolonial studies thematize. For Catholicism, Anglicanism and Islam, the location of power is at the faith centres in Rome, Canterbury and Mecca respectively. However, the Pentecostal Movement with which holy hip-hop is more closely associated is probably the greatest epitome of neo-liberal religious development in late modernity. The movement has multiple centres and in a sense may be construed as a departure from or resistance to the Old Order of religion. I draw a parallel here to Blommaert's (2006) articulation of polycentricity in his analysis of globalization as a sociotheoretical dimension in sociolinguistics. The process of hip-hop's appropriation is, however, not confined to postcolonial contexts except of course in the interesting sense that in most cases postcolonial and/or peripheral subjects are mainly responsible for this postmodern bottom-up 'colonization' of the supposedly free world.

One final level on which the notion of métis(se) may be applicable to holy hip-hop analysis relates to social valuation. Particularly among adolescents, religion is often regarded as 'minus cool'. In other words, social attitudes of being perceived as not modern but traditional, not fashionable, etc. have discouraged youths from embracing religion. However, through the appropriation of hip-hop for religious purposes 'cool' from the street is imported into religion to effect change in valuation to 'religious plus cool'. Now let us examine aspects of hip-hop culture in which we have evidence of mix which as I have suggested is indicative of transcultural accommodation. The spirit of such accommodation is conveyed in Extract 6 below taken from Gospel Gangstaz' virtual home:

Extract 6

We want to make music that represents our people. I think that with God's grace and power, it's gonna create a whole new world of hip-hop. We have a ready defense for what God has called us to do, We are the apostles of today. The message has not changed. The method has changed, and our music is saturated with the word of God. Rap is just a vehicle to transport the gospel of Jesus Christ. As for the 'gangstaz' tag, A [sic] gangsta is someone who's willing to live as well as die for what he believes in. We're laying our lives down for the gospel. We never forget where we came from. But we understand that our weapons are not Tec-9's or 9mm Uzis or Ak-47 rifles, but our weapons are 'mighty through God for the pulling down of strongholds'. We believe that what's from the heart reaches the heart, We speak it how we get it – that's plain, cut and dry. We can't count how many people come up to us and say, 'I relate to your testimony.' SEE U DEALING WITH A 'SAVED-THUG' DO OR DIE (http://profile.myspace.com/index.cfm?fuseaction=user.viewprofile&friendID=91926430)

The message aptly captures the transformation that the artists have gone through in their socioreligious lives as well as giving an indication of the change in language use that is expected to convey a sense of the crew's newfound purpose and objective such as the distinction between 'thug' as used in conventional hip-hop talk and 'saved thug' as used above. It provides the link and context for understanding their stage or perform-ance identity. This leads us next to the social practice of naming.

Names and naming

The contrast above between thug and saved thug underlines the need to explore names and naming practices for further contrasts between secular hip-hop and holy hip-hop based on morphological and semiotic analysis. The former focuses on the shortened forms of given names while the latter focuses on their symbolic content. Both are tied to spe-cific subcultural values in the hoods and streets the artists represent and in the context of which they practise the hip-hop mantra of keep-ing it real. The names usually have a story behind them, some more pro-found than others. It may be an I-story (individual), a We-story (group) or both, depending on the strength of the ideology and agenda being driven. In an interview with Muslim Hip-Hop.Com, UK hip-hop group Blakstone explain the philosophy behind their name:

Extract 7

MUSLIMHIPHOP.COM   Why are you called Blakstone?

BLAKSTONE   The black stone is an obvious reference to our Islamic identity and we knew Muslims would identify with it. But it has yet another meaning for us. The stone represents resistance for the Muslim especially in today's testing times when our armies are only good for parades. We've been stripped of our weaponry and have resorted to masonry. We all aspire to be soldiers, but what does it mean when our kids chuck boulders for this Deen? Regardless of how the odds stack up, if we use what we have, united, we can see this period through to a better time. Stories will be told of those who stood against tanks with nothing but stones to defend them and these stories will inspire generations, Insha Allah.

Mainstream Hip-Hop Nation Language (HHNL) is akin to African American Vernacular English. It mirrors adherence to alternative lex-icographic and literacy conventions evident in the spelling of 'blak-stone', a simplification of blackstone and the font used to give it a graffiti feel. Between the writing convention and the deeper symbol-ism of its religious referent, the Kaaba in Mecca produces a hybrid. What comes across in the explanation above is the religious purpose or assignment that the group had established as their calling. Apart from the religious references, we also notice the construction of hip-hop as the site of production of left-wing radical discourse through the references to, for instance, boulder-chucking protests and soldiers. Similarly, names such as Da Cross Movement, G-Force (God Force), and Street Symphony reflect the social cause that the artists pursue. The names of individual emcees and djs follow the same pattern. Kimba, aka DJ Klarity, explained his name thus:

Extract 8

I started out as K-Psalm because the messages in the Book of Psalms appealed to me then for a while I was Jury for a while. Jury came to me in a whisper during a prayer session leading up to the hearing. I felt for a rap man that was a serious word. I felt that the force behind my message was about judgement but not in the sense of condemning people but more about guidance and love. I was sued by my neighbour for violating the noise ordinance because I had set up a studio when we bought our first home. I had a choice between a Judge or Jury in the determination of the case. My wife convinced me to opt for the Jury. There were twelve jurors. The revelation I got was that God was restoring law and order in the corrupt justice system through men. I won the case. After that incident I began to pray and ask the Lord what I'm about, what He wanted the focus of my message to be. The people I met were from my performances. It was important that what I had to say was clear. There's a belief that people's names have an impact on how they turn out and therefore their identities. I took up the name Klarity and my audiences often said that my message reflected my name.

Both Blakstone and Klarity follow the alternative spelling convention referred to earlier as normative practice in hip-hop culture. At a conceptual level, both names are laden with material and spiritual values so that secular and sacred connotations are assigned to them in context. Mecca2Medina, G-Force, Da T.r.u.t.h and a host of other Christian hip-hop and Muslim hip-hop names show their religious agenda. Yet there are names such as Guvna-B and Muyiwa in which religious agenda is not evident. The latter is an abbreviated form from the original Yoruba name from the original Olumuyiwa (The Lord [Olu] brought this [muyiwa]). This shortening is different from the hip-hop conventional practice that reduces artists' names to initials and forms acronyms out of doctrinal statements. The London-based rapper Guvna-B, who is described in his bebo.com virtual homepage as 'a young motivational recording artiste ... setting the urban music scene alight with Holy Ghost Fire' derives his stage name from an acronym:

Extract 9

Guvna B is setting the urban music scene alight with Holy Ghost Fire. Guvna being an acronym for Gods Unique Vessel Now Assigned, ministers the accounts and teachings of Jesus Christ through music whilst also addressing issues that many youths face nowadays. (http://www.bebo.com/Profile.jsp?MemberId=73695 68600 accessed October 2, 2008) (http://profile.myspace.com/index. cfm?fuseaction=user.viewprofile&friendID=72471785 accessed June 29, 2008)

Guvna B's bebo.com home uses Psalm 27: 1 as a caption: 'The Lord is the strength of my life, of whom shall I be afraid?' and thus reaffirms the religious purpose to which he is addressing his passion for hip-hop. This is a discursive departure from stereotypical hip-hop culture in which beefs and battles, sometimes violent, are resolved on the street. Guvna-B and other gospel hip-hop artists rely on divine assurance. I turn next to the practice of constructing religion as vantage popular culture and how that marks language change.

Language change and popular religion

At a point in history, there was a tradition of one religion, one language, often the language of the founder community. The language of religious practice in the Judaic tradition was Hebrew. But even then the Babelian narrative of the tower of a multitude of tongues alluded to social change and the emergence of multilingualism in a single location. In Roman times, the association between Latin and Christianity also accommodated a narrative of empire which recognized Latinate dominion over non-Latin-speaking people, thus again acknowledging the association of religion with contact, accommodation, multilingualism and change. The translations of the Bible and the Qur'an into other languages tied to the expansion of empire provide further contexts and evidence of contact and métis(se) identity.

Whatever social processes occasion the seeming shift away from the association of the major religions with a specific language, one fact is established and that is that shift is incontrovertible evidence of change. Religion is stereotypically constructed through language as embodying the cultural values of purity, sobriety and reverence. In late modernity, however, globalization and popular culture have had such an immense impact on societal values that religion and its practice has had to transform by reinventing itself and its representations in order to remain relevant and maintain the loyalty of its constituents, especially where youths are concerned.

Music, hip-hop and religion

Music has always had a place in sacred practice as we find documented in several biblical accounts. The most prominent of these perhaps are the 'Songs of David' recorded as the Book of Psalms in the Old Testament in the Bible. Thus music is an obvious site to explore for change in religious practice. This change is evident in the Pentecostal traditions of the various sects of Christendom for instance. Change in mode of practice has engendered a change in the discursive and more general linguistic processes associated with religion. The 'praise and worship' component of Pentecostal church services are absent in the traditional order of service in the older churches. The former showcase contemporary music forms and, in some cases, resident live bands and dances including breakdance. In sharp contrast, the latter have services in which a set of hymns selected from a book of songs are sung at different points during the service.

The notion of change also extends to our understanding of how religious communities are constituted. For instance, the idea of groups of religious practitioners that form a congregation had hitherto been framed in territorial terms either in relation to specific sites of worship with defined locations, such as named churches, mosques or other religious shrines, or a faith group made up of branches associated with the same religious doctrines or modes of worship. This has been altered so that congregations have a much larger, ex-territorial and more inclusive spread in contemporary times. Congregations in late modernity include dispersed collectives or individuals that participate through other forms of social and/or community networks such as on Myspace. com, YouTube-for-gospel-music and Holy Hip-Hop dotcom sites.

The legitimacy of a claim that hip-hop is a vehicle of social change is enhanced by two documented accounts. First, it is being used for rallying youths across the seven Sami nations in the north of Finland, Sweden and Norway for the preservation of their heritage cultures and languages. These languages have been widely researched and described as endangered. Hip-hop is revival [http://virtual.finland.fi/netcomm/news/showarticle.asp?intNWSAID=55407]. My second example is drawn from Israel. The following entry on Loolwa Khazzoom's Jewish Multicultural Project website is an incisive commentary on hip-hop's capacity to manage intra-faith conflicts and diversity:

Extract 10

Between the Zionist pride of Subliminal, the bisexual boldness of MC Shorti, the cultural angst of MC Jeremy Cool Habash, and the feminist mission of Arapiot, students come to recognize how diverse struggles for social justice propel Israeli hip hop today.

In Hebrew, Arabic, French, and English, hip hop has swept the nation of Israel, providing youth a platform for self-expression. Utilizing music, video clips, photographs, and song translations, this program offers students a comprehensive overview of Israel's thriving new music scene. (http://www.loolwa.com/archive/multiculturalism/programs. html#hiphop)

While unlike biblical verses, the incorporation of Qur'anic texts into rap lyrics is considered blasphemous and therefore forbidden, hip-hop's evangelization and jihad agendas remain evident [http://www.msnbc.msn. com/id/11219692/]. Hip-hop is the vehicle for taking religion outside of and beyond its traditional locus in the churches and mosques, thus extending the traditional sites of reverence to include previously unfathomable spaces. Open-air crusades are already quite well established, drawing huge crowds and causing heightened frenzy similar to those of Glastonbury, the Reading Rock Festival, Premier League and FA Cup matches and any other arenas of cultural expression. On 6 May 2007 I attended Gospel Aid Nigeria, a popular religious programme held at ClubNTyce in Woolwich (38 Wellington Street, London SE18), which was sponsored by a cooperative to raise money and awareness for Aids treatment in Nigeria. My attraction to the event was the inclusion of a comedian (Julius Agwa) as well as two gospel rap groups (G-Force and FourKornerz) on the bill for the evening. The event formed the nucleus for my subsequent decision to add the groups to my research subjects list.

In order to further illustrate these processes of change, let us look at data elicited from the subject of my case study, DJ Klarity. 'Top Gun' as a phrase entered the discourse of popular culture as the title of a film (1986). It starred Tom Cruise as Maverick, a fighter pilot who trains at the top pilot academy in the country and falls in love with Charlie (Kelly McGillis), one of his instructors. On a track of the same title in the album *Rare Jewelz,* Klarity's freestyling is marked by an intertextual flow that marries that secular world experience to the reality of Pentecost. The métis(se) is constructed from free-flowing juxtapositions and contrasts evident in the following extracts taken from the rap lyrics for Top Gun (2008):

Extract 11

Some pen killer raps
But me, I kill tracks

I'm stiff as erections, when time to produce,
I make love to the track, you can hear me get loose,
I promise you that I'm the truth, And you can start believing
Hot as candle wax, and plus I love Jesus,
Never carried gats, but still I got heaters,
Count Blackula, tooth in the track like Dracula
Blood from the groove be making me spit emaculant,

Tackling wall headed cats, then spackling,
Remodeled hip hop, till it's attractive again,
A stallion with blends, a talent without end,
They say *the end* coming soon,
Well it's bout to begin,
Here it comes

In the extract above we have references to the secular Dracula narrative mythology, erections and making love, loving Jesus, redemptive blood which enables him to 'spit emaculant' which I presume to be immaculate. Count Blackula is a pun that references the rapper's racial blackness. Klarity tackles his supposedly unintelligent ('wall headed', i.e. thick) secular counterparts through divine wisdom in order to remodel 'hip-hop till it's attractive again'. The track ends with an invocation of the Revelation and Rapture in its reference to 'the end coming soon'.

On a different track titled 'With you all the way' we encounter a dialogue/duet between Kasha and Klarity the rap of which is more obviously laid on biblical samples. In Kasha's chorus we find an allusion to one of Jesus' famous final statements on the cross 'Lord forgive them for they know not what they do' and in Klarity's chorus which includes an allusion to Old Testament scripture from Psalm 23: 4.

Extract 12

Yea though I walk through the valley of the shadow of death,
I stay composed, no fear complex,
Though amongst gritty streets, lost souls and petty beef,

I ready heat from my pen on a blank sheet,
My rap feat is a track meet, taking batons from the crippled and
    weak
So my definition of a real emcee,
Is Christ in tan skin, resembling me,
The reflection of reality,
Hope is living in Klarity

In these excerpts, Klarity mixes the psalmic reference to the valley of
the shadow of death with the traditional hip-hop idea of gritty streets,
petty beefs and track meets (athletics) as he takes the batons from the
'crippled and weak'. Thus the text is neither wholly secular nor wholly
sacred but somewhere in between, a kind of third space (cf. Bhabha
1994, Bhatt 2008). Nevertheless the secular references help to reveal
a sense of keeping it real in terms of the real Christian injunction to
save lost souls by preaching the Word. Klarity's entry for the 100K
Battleshow in the summer of 2008 was 'The City is Ours'. The rap is laid
on 9th Wonder Beat 1. Klarity's declaration in the opening,

Extract 13

Intro. It's the 100K Battle

It's your boy Klarity,
Kimba aka Paradise Skillz
Listen I don't rap, I revelate
Cos wordplay is for artists
But I was told Prophets produce the artists
(http://ursession.com/wakeupshow/100kbattleshow/a91f4a65-
    THE%20CITY%20IS%20OURS)

This use of bridging establishes a link between Klarity the holy hip-
hopper and the community of rappers through his participation in
the 100K Battleshow, the street setting of the battle in the video clip.
However, in line with subgenre practice in holy hip-hop, Klarity articulates a divergent identity away from the secular to the sacred through
invoking Paradise, the revelation and prophet. This is a reaffirmation
of the distinction between the hip-hoppers and those who explore hip-
hop for a religious end.

Dress and other signifyin' codes

The political controversy over the hijab and the principle of covering as
much flesh as possible, which is obviously a religious issue, is in conflict

with mainstream hip-hop's liberal fashion. Or perhaps there is not a 'hip-hop fashion' per se and it's anything goes? Omoniyi (2009: 123) argues for instance that one of the ways in which HHN-Nigeria acquires a local identity is through divergence in couture. The baggy hip pants, female midriff-showing tops and male oversize jerseys which are quintessential signifyin' paraphernalia of hip-hop couture in some contexts are not 'anti-religious' or 'areligious'. We may argue that the same fundamental principle of change behind an acceptance that religion and music may now be mixed extends to clothing which is another signifying code of being young, hip and religious. One seeming difference however is in the nature of the accompanying bling. Religious blings have faith markings. Christian and Muslim hip-hoppers are adorned with extra-large pendants of crucifixes and crescents respectively. Jewish MCs and DJs like MC Subliminal wear the Star of David as a Judaic symbol (aka Shield of David). But these symbols are not exclusively worn by the named groups. Some secular artists subscribe to bling crossing in the same way that they do language crossing. In other words, bling cannot serve as an exclusive identity marker, so there again is the métis(se).

Extract 14

From: Holy Hip Hop Ministry [http://www.holyhiphop.com/]

Welcome to HolyHipHop.com. Our Mission, since 1997, is to Take the Gospel to the Streets through the global proliferation of Spiritually-Enlightening Holy Hip Hop Ministry, Music & Entertainment Glorifying Christ. We appreciate you visiting us. Thank you for your, Prayers, Support and GOD Bless. (Psalm 146: 10)

Christianity and Islam both employ hip-hop as a means to an end. It is a classic case of transformation of secular materialism to an idealist end. If we go by the narratives of origin accounts, both the Western mainstream claim that hip-hop came from the Bronx in New York City in the 1970s and the more recent Boomerang Hypothesis (Omoniyi 2009: 116) that locates hip-hop's roots in the lifestyle of the African griots are secular accounts. That account suggests that hip-hop journeyed through the Middle Passage to experience reformation in America, at which point it had little or no link to either Christianity or Islam. There may have been a link between traditional narrative poetry and ancient African ritual practice though. In borrowing hip-hop's form for the conveyance of religious content, a purposeful attempt is made to appeal to a generation of areligious youths. Alim (2005, 2006) refers to the existence of a 'the transglobal hip-hop ummah'. The emergence of Islamic hip-hop as a subgenre or indeed of 'hip-hop Islam' as a sect is thus interpretable as an indication of social change that accommodates or negotiates the appropriation of hip-hop for religious purposes. It has been used as a tool for stemming the activities of radical Islamists through its appeal to youths to whom they preach 'suicide bombing is not the way'. Blakstone, the UK rap crew I referred to earlier, claim on their website:

Extract 15

Hip Hop is not Dawah, but when it is used as a rally [sic] cry it touches the youth, our youth, from places the Imams can't reach or fear to tread. Our message is spreading far and wide and in the alleyways of munkar we have seen the yearning faces of our brothers who have found that their love for this Deen can be expressed in new and exciting ways. We have seen many turn away from the habits of jahaliyah and embrace Islam, not because their parents are Muslim, but because they themselves believe. Blakstone is not a person or a group, it's a struggle. The irony is that we want this struggle to end, so those who join us do so, in the hope that they won't have to.

A blog entry from [Feb 24 2007 11:18P] on the Baby Muslims myspace. com website demonstrates that hybridity or the appropriation of one form for the transmission of content that it is not traditionally associated with may be a diasporic social practice and instantiates culture-crossing as a consequence of urban osmotic experience. What is even more significant is the indication that the religious hip-hoppers see themselves as post-modern-imams complementing the activities of the institutional imams. As a matter of fact, they represent themselves as more effective in being able to take their message to places that 'Imams can't reach or fear to tread' giving opportunity to the youth to express their love for this Deen 'in new and exciting ways'. That is change.

Conclusion

I have attempted in this final chapter to explore ways in which holy hip-hop as a cultural phenomenon provides us with a context for looking at change, conflict and accommodation in the sociology of language and religion. I have attempted to show how holy hip-hop is both an appropriation of secular culture for a sacred objective. In its context, beat poetry is no longer mere entertainment but a means to winning souls and negotiating successful investment in the afterlife. What is evident in the discussions and data presented above is that the genre (if regarded as entertainment) is a marked change on several fronts. First, its inclusion as an award category in institutions such as the Grammys and MOBO indicates a widening of scope in what qualifies as entertainment. The preparedness of the artists themselves to participate in these secular events, albeit under the caption 'Best Gospel Act', also indicates liberalization in how religion is perceived and articulated. Second, the contemplation by religious stakeholders of free market economic principles as an acceptable strategy for stemming growing faith attrition is definitely indicative also of change in values and norms within the two major faith groups. Third, the verbal mujahidin that Alim wrote of and represented in my discussion by Baby Muslims, Blakstone and Mecca2Medina, explore religious resources to solve sociopolitical problems and thus engage with conflict and accommodation. However, they have to appeal to the conservative base of their religious groups who see (hip-hop) music and Islam as strange bedfellows. What I have not included in my discussion but which is definitely worth investigating is how holy hip-hop artists relate to some of the other cultural practices associated with hip-hop such as battling. My reference to Klarity's 100K Battleshow above is both preliminary and insufficient. What or how does holy hip-hop do, for instance, with 'Yo Mama' and 'You Yourself'?

Appendix

Top Gun
(Lyrics by Kimba aka Klarity taken from Rare Jewelz)
Some pen killer raps
But me, I kill tracks
Acid breath, breathe and exhale a heart attack,
My artefacts, new format to an old movement
Pat Ewing with ball skills, and spit fluid
These new sucka emcees,
Thinking I'mma be misfortunate, please
I'mma get a fortune ease,
My steaze, wit out greed, superhead's or weed,
Believe Klarity is harder than most of these dweeds
Imagine Kimba at the top of the game,
Probably living in the North Pole,
On top of the plains
As smooth as ice capades, so the tongue is a flame,

Melting polar caps, I condescend when I reign,
Torrential thoughts explain,
My pedigree and pain, integrity to stain these critics with yes
    yaw's
Smacking fish skills with the size of bear claws,
I bare thoughts, a grizzly whenever the snares talk,
With rare thoughts, and probably throb hearts,
Rob charts, eat up chicken cats with hot sauce,
They knock offs,
I'm on the block, knocking they block off,
Blocking all of they shots, calling they shots cause,
I'm interesting, cat's skills is in question,
I'm stiff as erections, when time to produce,
I make love to the track, you can hear me get loose,
I promise you that I'm the truth, And you can start believing
Hot as candle wax, and plus I love Jesus,
Never carried gats, but still I got heaters,
Count Blackula, tooth in the track like Dracula
Blood from the groove be making me spit emaculant,
Tackling wall headed cats, then spackling,
Remodeled hip hop, till it's attractive again,
A stallion with blends, a talent without end,
They say the end coming soon,
Well it's bout to begin,
Here it comes

With You All The Way
(Lyrics by Kasha of Vivid Imagery & Kimba aka Klarity of Rare
    Jewelz)

1st Verse by Kasha

A yo she cried in the street, after watching her pain,
Couldn't believe what I'd seen, her soul tortured by flames,
Obviously she made screams, each cutting my love,
She said, somebody help me to find help, yo
So I approached her, asked her if she needed my coat,
Cause it was raining, and life had her shivering cold,
Said here's a fag if you smoke, I see you looking a hero,
Well me I find it in the mirror, when I look real close,
She turned to me, eyes held stories and songs,
She said what if you look and find that your reflection is gone,
Must admit it had me shook hearing pain that strong,

Cause when you spoke it's like compassion was a slave to her
    tongue
I said talk to me, tell me where it all stems from,
She said walk with me, where do I start, Huh?
She wished her heart would stop beating,
Like that of her sons, and she had drunk herself sober,
Wishing sanity'd come, she said she held him
As his last breath left from his lungs,
But didn't know he was involved with the road and the guns
She blamed herself for not keeping him away from the slums,
And wished his father would have helped,
But he was always a bum,
She knows now why he selled, he was tired of crumbs
Wished she could have gave him everything that he'd
    ever want
What could I say, my heart bled with every thumb
She said if I was on the roof now I surely would jump
She said his name, I dare not say it again, I saw the pain,
Life had written it on her face, she said the day,
The day took my sunshine away, the night sky came,
And every since then it stayed, memories leave a stain,
Faces tried to be brave, I can't even touch his room
Or his jacket the same, I fade and I fade, as each hour passes,
It plays and it plays, the scene just won't leave me alone,
I held my breath, had to think about my words when I spoke
I said do you feel his soul, when you feel the wind blow,
She replied, I see him in my dreams at night, He and I flied,
And I awaked to reality's lie, watching her speak,
I realize to die to the beef of nines, it's coming like sin sells,
The sound of a mother crying, streets is cold, I hear em spitting
    firey rhymes
Giving sight to blind, as vivid as every line, I read the signs,
That life throws up, these are the times of no love, spraying and
    for the dough cuz,
The road is full of doughnuts,
Niggaz from prison smoking roll ups,
Didn't learn they lesson back in jail, before they could get they
    fro cut
Maybe we dumb, maybe we stupid,
This love for the money surely ain't the work of cupid,
We all just trying to clock the rubix cube of life,

Some are tried for ruthless, others still strive though it seems
    useless,
So after talking to my mystery lady, I get's to thinking,
Will it change, or forever stay crazy,
So as I walk through the valley of the shadow of death,
May peace be with you all, Kasha signing off

Kasha Chorus (repeat 2×)

Stay with em, listen please *Lord forgive em,*
For they sinning, cause they know not what was written
How we living I believe that there will be a change,
So speak through me, I'm with you all the way,

Klarity – 2nd Verse

Yea though I walk through the valley of the shadow of
    death,
I stay composed, no fear complex,
Though amongst gritty streets, lost souls and petty beef,
I ready heat from my pen on a blank sheet,
My rap feat is a track meet, taking batons from the crippled and
    weak,
That's overworked to eat, they struggling on the grind,
To find time to sleep, or find it hard to dream, or spend they
    money in peace,
My premonition, spit life, crush competition,
My origins originate from them dark quarters,
So I spew fresh water for the dark horses,
The race is for the faithful, not the swift porsches,
But for the ones that be looking for the orphans,
These fatherless times and sons bucking with nines,
Before they got hair or puberty's even defined,
So my definition of a real emcee,
Is Christ in tan skin, resembling me,
The reflection of reality, hope is living in Klarity
I'm with em Lord, Be with us Lord,
I'm with em Lord, Cause you with em Lord,

The anguish of villains, put hatred in children,
And train em as killers, til they nature is cold as the winter
It's chilling, it' Grisham with pillows, suffocating they lungs and
    they feelings,
Mother's will miss em, puppets in prison, cussing and dealing,

Destructive resilience, knuckles and niggaz, punching they figures,
It's figures they swallowing liquors, and pouring for kindred,
Ignored by the system, so bored in the school that they hardly
    listen,
It's hard to dismiss it as just youngins lack of attention,
Something is missing, depicting puzzling pictures,
We fumble with sickness, and only use all the medicine for the
    symptoms
Its pedestals for the pimping, perpetual hellish positions,
I speculate when I spit this, will they ever take interest,

Klarity Chorus – repeat 2×

Yea though I walk through the valley of the shadow of death
I stay composed, Cause you guide my steps
Regardless of what I face, none of it is a threat
For worst or better, all of my trials, are just a test,

Kasha Chorus

Stay with em, listen *please Lord forgive em,*
For they sinning, cause they know not what was written
How we living I believe that there will be a change,
So speak through me, I'm with you all the way.

Imagine
(Lyrics by Klarity & Praverb the Wise – featuring Ama Oliver on
    Singing Vocals)

Verse 1 – Klarity

A picture's worth a thousand words, and mirrors speak in
    images,
Nature tries to talk with many deaf listeners, ears clogged from
    hurt feelings
Deferred dreams,
Memories from shortcomings from efforts to achieve,
Blood, sweat, and tears left on many stained sleeves,
But when you close your eyes, is everything that you see,
Something that you wanna become, but have yet to be,
Well God's an artist, at a canvas or blank sheet,
And when He breathes life, He defines what you need,
His brush strokes are light, starts with a sketch,
Begins with a thought, puts spirit in flesh,
Knows it's limitations, it's height, it's depth,
The capacity it can hold, or snap from stress,

The details of it's character, uniqueness from the rest,
The minor details to resize or stretch,
No matter how long it takes, til it's perfectly correct,
They say an artist with a target can get lost in his
workmanship,
Cause he knows that his end goal, would have so much
permanence,
And make such a beautiful statement, for all to behold, in
glorious amazement
Just imagine, be patient, imagine, be patient,

Verse 2 – PraVerb

Imagine if I wasn't rapper, would I be on the street corner, trying
to be a star,
Living a lil lavish, with more cabbage, expensive taste and
probably fast cars,
That's not my life, I don't do crime,
But I'm judged by these criminal cats,
You're a hater, might as well stand in line,
Cause I'll keep progressing with these spiritual raps,
I'll watch my words, cause the tongue spews life or death,
So I pace toward the light, with righteous steps,
I know that my path is bleek, And sometimes I feel that no one's
backing me,
But God said hold up, you're attached to me,
I gave you freedom, and didn't even attach the lease,
Don't worry about the bling or ice,
Just give me your soul, and call me majesty, Yahweh, or
Christ,

(Singing vocals – Sung by Ama Oliver)

He said I was created, In His image and His likeness,
I may not yet be finished, But I will be just like Him,
(Repeat 2×)

I will be just like Him, unique and so exciting,
Surrounded by His highness, and all His other finest
(Repeat 2×)

I am so excited, I imagine I am
I am so excited, I imagine I am

I Imagine ... ... I Imagine ... ...
I Imagine ... . I Imagine ... ...

References

Alim, H. Samy (2005) 'Hip-Hop Islam', feature in *Al-hram Weekly on-line*, Issue No. 750, 7–13 July.

Alim, H. Samy (2006) *Roc the Mic Right: the Language of Hip-Hop Culture*. London: Routledge.

Appadurai, Arjun (1996) *Modernity at Large: Cultural Dimensions of Globalization*. Minneapolis: University of Minnesota Press.

Bhabha, H. (1994) *The Location of Culture*. London: Routledge.

Bhatt, R. (2008) 'In Other Words: Language Mixing, Identity Representations, and Third Space'. *Journal of Sociolinguistics*, 12(2), 177–200.

Blommaert, J. (2006) 'Sociolinguistic Scales'. Paper 37, Working Papers in Urban Language and Literacies, King's College London.

Bourdieu, P. (1991) *Language and Symbolic Power*. Cambridge, UK: Polity Press.

Fishman, J. (2006) 'A Decalogue of Basic Theoretical Perspectives for a Sociology of Language and Religion', in T. Omoniyi and J. A. Fishman (eds), *Explorations in the Sociology of Language and Religion*, Amsterdam: John Benjamins, pp. 13–25.

Foucault, M. (1988) 'Technologies of the Self', in L. H. Martin, H. Gutman and P. H. Hutton (eds), *Technologies of the Self*, Amherst: University of Massachusetts Press, pp. 16–49.

Ifekwunigwe, Jayne (1998) 'Re-invoking the Griotte Tradition as a Feminist Textual Strategy'. http://www.arts.uwa.edu.au/MotsPluriels/MP898jol.html, accessed 26 June 2008.

Omoniyi, T. (2006) 'Societal Multilingualism and Multifaithism: a Sociology of Language and Religion Perspective', in T. Omoniyi and J. A. Fishman (eds), *Explorations in the Sociology of Language and Religion*, Amsterdam: John Benjamins, pp. 121–40.

Omoniyi, T. (2009) 'So I Choose to Do am Naija Style: Hip-Hop and Postcolonial Identities', in H. S. Alim, A. Ibrahim and A. Pennycook (eds), *Global Linguistic Flows: Hip-Hop Cultures, Youth Identities, and the Politics of Language*, New York/London: Routledge, pp. 113–35.

Pennycook, A. (2007) *Global Englishes and Transcultural Flows*. London: Routledge.

Salami, O. (2006) 'Creating God in Our Image: the attributes of God in the Yoruba Sociocultural Eenvironment', in T. Omoniyi and J. A. Fishman (eds), *Explorations in the Sociology of Language and Religion*, Amsterdam: John Benjamins, pp. 97–118.

Sherzer, Dina (1998) 'French Colonial and Post-Colonial Hybridity: Condition Metisse'. *Journal of European Studies*, 28.

Index

Chapter 7

Chapter 9

Chapter 10